SHE DARED

Abhishek Dubey is India's foremost sports journalist who has covered international sports for over fifteen years now. A topper in MA, History, from Hansraj College, he fancied himself as a right arm fast bowler and a hard-hitting lower order batsman. Instead, he plunged headlong into sports journalism, at a very young age, and ended up leading cross-functional teams in organizations like NDTV and IBN7 (Network18), to name a few. A regular columnist with leading dailies and news magazines, his earlier works include the critically acclaimed *Dressing Room: The Inside Story* and *The IPL Story: Cricket, Glamour and Big Money*. He is currently the National Advisor at Prasar Bharati Sports, India's state broadcaster.

Sanjeeb Mukherjea is an award-winning journalist and anchor who has covered sports for well over a decade now. Formerly the cricket editor at CNN-IBN, he has now struck out on his own as a broadcaster, currently as one of the lead anchor-commentators on the Star Sports network. Prior to this, he has also anchored live shows on Doordarshan and ESPN Cricinfo. He has also dabbled in print and advertising, as well as in radio journalism.

Praise for the book

Great sports books are not about the game, statistics and figures but about the characters involved. The book *She Dared: Women in Indian Sports* deals with strong characters who dared to script history and laid a strong foundation for future generations to build a beautiful structure of Indian sports on it. P.T. Usha, Anju Bobby George, Karnam Malleswari, M.C. Mary Kom, Sania Mirza, Saina Nehwal and P.V. Sindhu are the living legends of our times, and to showcase their journey in a comprehensive manner in a refreshingly different direction is a unique initiative. I hope that this book inspires millions to take up sports in our young country. The book, full of substance, is on the life and times of the women of substance in Indian sports.

—Mahesh Bhupathi

SHE
DARED
WOMEN
IN INDIAN SPORTS

ABHISHEK DUBEY | SANJEEB MUKHERJEA

RUPA

Published by
Rupa Publications India Pvt. Ltd 2019
7/16, Ansari Road, Daryaganj
New Delhi 110002

Sales centres:
Allahabad Bengaluru Chennai
Hyderabad Jaipur Kathmandu
Kolkata Mumbai

ISBN: 978-93-5333-708-7

First impression 2019

10 9 8 7 6 5 4 3 2 1

The moral right of the author has been asserted.

Printed at Parksons Graphics Pvt. Ltd, Mumbai

Contents

Introduction   *vii*

1. 'Hiranya': The Golden Girls   1

2. P.T. Usha: Get, Set, Go!   15

3. Ashwini Nachappa: India's Flo Jo   48

4. Karnam Malleswari: The Iron Lady   66

5. Anju Bobby George: A Leap of Faith   84

6. M.C. Mary Kom: A Fistful of Glory   101

7. Sania Mirza: Changing the Game   122

8. Saina Nehwal: The Promise of a Bountiful Summer   142

9. P.V. Sindhu: The Toast of a Nation   160

10. Ashwini Ponnappa: A Blithe Spirit   180

11. Sakshi Malik: It's Not Just a Man's Sport   196

12. Deepa Malik: Born Again   211

13. Santhi Soundarajan and Dutee Chand: 225
    'I Am A Woman'

14. Dipa Karmakar and Deepika Kumari: Pivot Point   247

15. The Show Must Go On: The Promise   270
    of Eternal Sunshine

Acknowledgements   283

Introduction

There is a fair bit of literature on Indian athletes. With the emergence of a new bunch of athletes who are challenging the established names in sports, India has much to be hopeful about regarding its prospects at international sporting events. During a discussion over tea on a sultry evening, about the literature on sportspersons who have shone and stood shoulder to shoulder with the best in the world, we realized how remarkable the emergence of Indian women athletes has been. It turned out that more often than not, success was achieved despite the system, rather than because of it. Indian women athletes have challenged societal norms as well as unsurmountable obstacles to carve a place for themselves in the pantheon of India's sporting history. And having been sports journalists and colleagues for a long time, we realized that we knew a fair bit about them. From how it all started, to how these remarkable women shook off taboos, apathy and ignorance to perch themselves atop the highest branch of their respective sports, we realized it was time we found out more about them and shared the knowledge.

To borrow from an eloquent cricket enthusiast who doubles up as a fine writer, along with straddling the world of Indian politics, a farrago of news stories emerge whenever these athletes perform exceptionally, or as the media refrain has been for ages, 'crash out' of the competition.

This book, a journey we undertook with cold feet at the prospect of not being able to do justice to the task at hand, is not meant to be a chronology, which is something our great historians and scholars of sports in India are best at.

Rather this is our search for the defining moments of the protagonists who have shaped the history of women's sports in

India and have helped craft the great Indian sporting dream, starting with the peerless P.T. Usha to the scintillating Sindhu who now commands as much attention and respect as any superstar cricketer.

This book is as much a journey through the sporting landscape that more often than not was a difficult terrain for women wanting to excel in their respective fields, as it is about the changing mindset of a country that now celebrates its women fervently for their sporting success.

The history of women in Indian sports still remains a rather sketchy account, with records and reportage being few and far between. Nearly a hundred years ago, India (still under British rule) sent its first woman participant to the Olympics. Nora Polley would forever be known for the 1924 Paris Games, as she featured in the women's singles tennis competition. There are unsubstantiated reports about another lady, a certain M. Tata having taken part in the mixed doubles event in Paris, but not much is known of either Polley or Tata, especially post the Games.

So is the case with most other sports that women took to in India, with mostly inaccurate and unsubstantiated accounts that do not do justice to them. But as we must reiterate, ours is no attempt to document a definite construct of all those women who have played some sport in India. This book is neither a pedagogic investigation, nor a detailed history. This is the story of those intrepid women who dared to challenge a pervasive patriarchal society and its norms and a complete lack of support from the sporting ecosystem in most cases, to chart their own course and inspire future generations.

Our focus has been to flesh out the real narrative of their way of life (sport), their many struggles and their strong sense of belief that they could achieve what they had set out to. Mary D'Souza, who won the first two medals by an Indian woman at the 1951 Asian Games, received only an autographed picture of India's first Prime Minister Jawaharlal Nehru, with no reception accorded to her, or the others who had performed creditably.

Karnam Malleswari, the first Indian woman to win an Olympic medal (Sydney 2000) was soon forgotten after her heroic feat at the Games. These are some instances of how women who have taken to sports and performed well for the country, have been treated over decades. The felicitation that is given to women sportspersons today wasn't fashioned in a day, a year, or for that matter, in decades. Recognition and respect have been hard to come by for most of these extraordinary fighters who have given their life to sports.

To put together a framework for our subject was a tough task, as we realized; More so as we had to decide about the ones we would write about prominently in this book. We didn't want an exhaustive list based on sheer athletic merit. We have tried to put forward the stories of those women who stand out for being pioneers in their sport, and bringing greater meaning and dimension to their sport through their journey.

This book, while scripting the life and times of a dozen and more extraordinary women, is also a salute to others who have made the country proud with their sporting feats over the years, but have not been included in this volume. Ami Ghia, Shanta Rangaswamy, Zenia Ayrton, Madhumita Bisht, Diana Edulji, Indu Puri, Bula Choudhury, Reeth Abraham, Bachendri Pal, Jyotirmoyee Sikdar, Jasmine Arethna, Suma Shirur, Koneru Humpy, Anjali Bhagwat, Nisha Millet, Aparna Popat, Laishram Sarita Devi or Jhulan Goswami...the list of women who redefined their sport, while sacrificing everything else, is endless and each person deserves a book of their own, and is way beyond the scope of this one.

We hope that as you read this book, you get a sense of what it really takes to be a woman sportsperson in India, and we truly wish you relive their special journeys.

ONE

'Hiranya': The Golden Girls

God's own country: Kerala. The state owes this title to several reasons, the primary one being its timeless traditions. People like Meenakshi Amma have been the torchbearers for keeping the ancient tradition of Kalaripayattu, an Indian version of the martial arts, alive. There have been many Meenakshi Ammas across generations who have played a pivotal role in keeping dance forms, sports, ayurveda, herbal spas and many more timeless traditions alive.

Gradually, one more tradition with huge potential has started building up—a pantheon of athletics goddesses in God's own country. Angel Mary John won the silver for India at the Bangkok Asian Games in 1978. Subsequently, M.D. Valsamma, P.T. Usha, Shiny Wilson, Mercy Kuttan, Rosa Kutty, Padmini Thomas, Philomina Thomas, Saramma, Tessymol, K.M. Beenamol, Anju Bobby George, Chitra Soman, Sinimol Paulose and Preeja Sreedharan came one after another, further strengthening and enriching the tradition.

This low-cost assembly-line of raw talent has saved the face of the country many a time at the highest of the global sporting platforms. If we see the list of Arjuna awardees from the state, this becomes all the more striking. Most of these athletes come from modest or poor migrant Christian families and live in the pollution-free environment of the hilly villages on the eastern belt of the state.

Coincidentally, this belt has also produced the bulk of the state's nuns, farmers and nurses. Is there a discernible pattern in this? Is it the by-product of the socio-economic circumstances?

Or just sheer desperation to succeed? If we delve deep, the trend points to the fact that their success is a by-product of the existing socio-economic conditions. And if we go deeper, we will see that sheer desperation translates into an innate hunger for success throughout their respective careers.

The tough terrain that most of them come from makes them physically fit and naturally inclined towards endurance sports. They turn the lack of opportunities and their tough way of life into an advantage. The stars that strode before them showed the way, and they ran and jumped: first in school meets which are the veritable nurseries for the state's athletes and then in inter-state and national events, before ending up in state-run sports schools.

These schools are ill-equipped and players face many challenges training here. However, their endurance skills see them through. Though they start with sports, they do well even after they retire and get into other professions, proving to hundreds of waiting aspirants that sports indeed is a great career option. Their families work as a team and they are able to strike a perfect balance between work and home. Records show an influx of girl athletes in Kerala's school meets, beginning in the Eighties.

If becoming a nurse was the most commonly-cherished dream of the girls in the hilly villages, running and jumping became a better career option for some, thanks to the Valsamma-Usha-Shiny trio.

P.T. Usha heralded the new dawn. M.D. Valsamma was the one who had fuelled this dawn. Shiny Wilson sustained this with gusto.

Valsamma was born on 21 October 1960 in Ottathai in Kannur district. She was interested in athletics since her school days and participated in various school sports. However, athletics became her prime goal when she moved to Mercy College, Palakkad, for further studies.

She won her first medal for Kerala in the 100 m hurdles and pentathlon in the inter-university championships at Pune in

1979. Then she moved on to Southern Railway, where Mr A.K. Kutty became her coach. Things started changing fast from here. Mr Kutty, who passed away in 2013, had served in the Indian Air Force, where he had left a mark as an athlete. On retirement from service, he became the trainer in the Kerala Sports Council. Mr Kutty had splendid skills in spotting talent and training them in a systematic manner to extract the best from them. Once Mr Kutty started mentoring her, Valsamma's career started paying rich dividends.

Valsamma came into the spotlight after the inter-state meet at Bangalore in 1981 by winning five gold medals. This catapulted her into the railway and national teams. In the year 1982, she became the national champion in the 400 m hurdles, with a new record. This record of hers was considered better than the Asian record. In the same year, she won the gold medal in the 400 m hurdles in what was a record time in both Indian and Asian hurdles—58.47 sec in front of a home crowd at the Jawaharlal Nehru Stadium in the Asian Games.

Two years later, for the first time in history, the Indian women's team entered the finals in the Los Angeles Olympics and finished in the seventh position. The moment and its significance in the given circumstances could best be understood by the article published in the name of M.D. Valsamma in *The Hindu*. The article reads:

> I was not in the best frame of mind when I went to Los Angeles for the 1984 Olympics. I was the Asian Games champion in the 400 m hurdles which came with an Asian record in 1982 but I did not get any international exposure before the Olympics.
>
> We were five girls and we went to LA a month before the games but my coach, A.K. Kutty, was cleared late, which meant that I did not get proper practice, and my mental preparations were not good. It was cold too.
>
> Since we had gone early, we stayed at the University of California hostel, which was very far away from the Games stadium. There was a lot of drama back home before the

Olympics, and my rivalry with P.T. Usha in the 400 m hurdles was getting bitter.

When we got on the track, there was a lot of bitterness, the rivalry was intense, of course that is professional rivalry but off the track we were friends. I went out in the first round but we were very excited when Usha qualified for the 400 m hurdles final.

And we were very, very sad when she narrowly missed a medal. I felt Usha ran a very bad race... She was too fast in the first 300 m and messed it up. She should have maintained a steady pace throughout, which she did not. She ran the first 300 like she would run the 400 flat. The 400 m hurdle is supposed to be the toughest event in athletics and needs careful planning.

Later, we finished seventh in the 4x400 m relay. We were a strong side, all of us were good 400 m runners and there were three girls from Kerala in that team—Shiny and Usha, apart from me...(Vandana Rao was the other girl). It was good that day, I did the first leg and Usha ran the last and we came up with an Asian record. We did not get much time in LA after the Olympics. There was a bomb threat and we had to leave the place soon after the Games. We had to virtually rush from our rooms to the airport.[1]

This can be further understood when one goes through the statements of Shiny Wilson (Shiny Abraham then), the third female protagonist from God's own country. In an interview with rediff.com she says:

Of course, how can I forget my first Olympics? The ultimate dream of any athlete is to participate in an Olympic Games. So you can imagine how excited I was when I was selected to go to Los Angeles when I was just eighteen. It was my performance of 2 min 49 sec in the 800 m at the national

---

[1] M.D. Valsamma, 'When bitterness, sadness came together', *The Hindu*, 5 July 2016

meet which was better than the Asian Games record that got me a ticket to Los Angeles. When the news about my selection came, I didn't know how to react—I was that elated. Myself, Usha, M.D. Valsamma and Vandana Rao started our journey together. Geeta Zutshi, who was the Asian Games gold medallist, was training in the United States itself.

We went by an Indian Airlines flight via Dubai, stayed in New York for a day and then proceeded to Los Angeles. I was awestruck when I saw the Olympic Village for the first time. Till then I had not seen a village where even the track to practise was inside.

We used to practise daily there under the guidance of Joginder Saini sir. I still remember the kind of food they served there: chicken and ice creams of all varieties and lots and lots of fruits. In those days, in none of the camps were we served such good food, and I ate as if I had not seen chicken or ice cream or fruits before!

I was also very young! Whenever Saini sir caught me eating lots of chicken, he would tease me, 'Only Shiny has no problem with the food.' Though we carried lots of pickles with us, I was not much bothered about that because I simply loved what was available there.[2]

When asked about that famous 800 m race that made her the first Indian woman athlete to qualify for the semi-finals in the Olympics, she said:

I was so nervous and tense the previous night that I could not even close my eyes. I did not eat anything that night. I don't know how many times I read the Bible and prayed to the image of Jesus Christ that I carried with me.

I was tense even when I was doing the warm-up and jogging. Only when I stood there waiting for the gun to go was I no more tense. I ran and the result was my best timing—

---

[2]'If luck is with Anju she can win a medal', rediff.com, 18 August 2004

2 min 46 sec! I was selected for the semi-finals. I didn't know what had happened. All the Malayali journalists ran to me and congratulated me. It was they who told me that I was the first Indian woman athlete to qualify for the semi-finals in the Olympics. I can only say I was very, very happy.

The semi-finals were on the very next day, and I did not have the experience to run on two consecutive days. My legs were paining badly when I started running. I was not sad at all when I lost in the semi-finals. Qualifying for the semi-finals itself was good enough for me because I was not expecting such a result.

About that epochal 'so near yet so far' moment in Indian sports where Usha narrowly missed the medal, she said in the interview with rediff.com:

We were all there to cheer her, and, actually, we all thought she had won the bronze. When we came to know that she lost in the photo-finish, we were terribly sad; Usha was also inconsolable. That was the first time the 400 m hurdle was introduced in the Olympics.[3]

And to the specific question on the 4x400 m relay, in which the women's brigade created history, she said:

It was one of the last events, and all of us were very fresh. Much to our pleasant surprise we reached the final with a timing of 3.32 sec, which was the Asian record and one of the best timings in those days. Imagine, till then we had not won any Asian medal, and there we were, clocking the best Asian timing!

Myself and Usha ran excellent races. It was just great! Of course, in the 1986 Asian Games we won the gold medal.

Some French newspaper wrote about me running the 800 m and 400 m relays quite well. It was such a shock for

---

[3]'If luck is with Anju she can win a medal', rediff.com, 18 August 2004

everyone there in the US to see Indian girls in athletics final. Just before that Usha had narrowly missed the medal. Anyway, it was a great Olympics for all of us girls.[4]

The athletics goddesses from God's own country became the sporting stars overnight. And the feeling started sinking in when they returned to the country.

Shiny Wilson said in one of her interviews with Doordarshan, the public broadcaster:

> When we landed in Delhi there were many people to receive us. I booked a train ticket to go back home. When I was about to leave, I was told that Prime Minister Indira Gandhi wanted to meet all of us. Since I had to catch the train I didn't go. There was nobody to tell me that I should go and meet her. Like Usha and Valsamma met the prime minister.
>
> I still remember what happened at the Trivandrum airport later. The Kerala government wanted to give us a reception at the airport after Usha and Valsamma reached. So I was also asked to reach there and be with them. The chief minister and the sports minister also were there and there was a very huge crowd waiting. In a midi skirt and t-shirt I might have looked like a school girl!
>
> As I was walking towards Usha and Valsamma, a police officer pushed me away, asking, 'What are you doing here?' I got so upset that I ran away, crying. Soon the minister came to console me. It became such a big issue that the next day's papers carried it as headlines on the front page. Today, when I think about all that, I feel like laughing.

As it often happens in the life of an active sportsperson, life changed overnight for the teenager.[5] She was a clerk in the Food Corporation of India, just before she went to participate in the Olympics. After a few months, she was offered the post of an

---

[4]'If luck is with Anju she can win a medal', rediff.com, 18 August 2004
[5]'Barcelona was my best, Atlanta the worst', *DNA*, 15 May 2008

officer. As the news of her selection came, she was made the officer. And when she qualified for the semi-finals, her managing director gave her three increments in one go.

Sports is the image of the society and the time we live in. India in the 1980s was slowly and gradually starting to get the hang of things in the world. As in other fields, the exposure to the competitive sporting universe was slowly increasing, but it was truly limited. In this overall scenario, the triumvirate of Usha-Valsamma-Shiny started exploring and navigating the sporting world to find out a route on which the future generation could tread with confidence.

They came out as torchbearers, following which the coming waves of sportswomen in the country could actualize their potential. They helped in giving an adage to their home state: before the women of the state rock babies in their cradles, they rock the sports stadiums.

The three shining female stars of Indian athletics studied at the same sports division, though in different parts of the state. All the three were coached by NIS coach P.J. Devesla. Valsamma came into the spotlight a tad earlier than Usha, and Shiny Abraham's athletics career ran alongside that of Usha.

The tales around each of the four racers in the 4x400 m race in the Los Angeles Olympics started being narrated at homes and schools. It had become the stuff of legends.

Valsamma, after the 1984 Los Angeles Olympics, began concentrating more on 100 m hurdles. She made a national record in the first National Games in 1985, winning gold in the 100 m hurdles. She also appeared in the 1983 Spartakiad in Moscow and the South Asian Federation (SAF) Games in Islamabad which fetched her a bronze in the 100 m, a silver in the quarter-mile and gold in the 4x400 m relay.

In a career spanning nearly fifteen years, M.D. Valsamma took part in the World Cup meets in Haryana, Tokyo, London and the Asian Games editions of 1982, 1986, 1990 and 1994. Besides this, she participated in all the Asian Track and Field meets and

SAF Games in this period, leaving her mark in each and every competition. Like Valsamma, Shiny Wilson too continued shinying after the 1984 Los Angeles Olympics.

Shiny took a firm and determined start with the 1985 Asian Track and Athletics Meet. In the 800 m, she clocked 2:03.16 to take gold, finishing ahead of the athletes from Thailand and China. In the 400 m event, she finished behind P.T. Usha to take silver. She was also part of the 4x400 m team that came first in 3:34:10 sec.

Shiny had sweet 'n' sour times in the Seoul Asiad in 1986. She participated in the 400 m event and came second to P.T. Usha. She was part of the 4x400 m team that took the gold, defeating defending champions Japan. And then came the anticlimax. Wilson, who was touted to be the winner in the 800 m event, was disqualified for shifting tracks before finishing the first 200 m. In the 1987 Singapore Asian Athletics, she failed to even make her presence felt.

However, soon she bounced back with vigour. In the New Delhi Asian Track and Athletics Meet, she took silver in the 400 m, behind Usha who won the gold medal. The 800 m saw an unusual drama, with Chinese athlete Sun Sunei, who had come in first, failing a drug test. Shiny Wilson, who had finished after Sunei, thus took gold.

She also participated in the 1988 Summer Olympics in Seoul, coming in sixth in the 800 m heat and was part of the 4x400 m relay team that came seventh in the heats. In the 1991 Asian Athletics event, she took gold in the 400 m and silver in the 800 m races. In the 1994 Hiroshima Asian Games, Shiny clinched the bronze medal and also teamed up with Usha, Kutty Saramma and G.V. Dhanalakshmi to take silver in the 4x400 m relay.

In the 1995 South Asian Games in Chennai, Wilson set a national record of 1:59:85 sec. The record stood for fifteen long years, before it was bettered by P.T. Usha's protégé, Tintu Luka, in the 2010 Continental Cup. She was conferred with the Arjuna Award in 1984 and the Padma Shri award in 1998. The girl who shone like a beacon in the sporting landscape of the country for more than two decades, will have many fond memories to share. However, the moments she still cherishes the most are all majorly related to the Olympics.

Shiny Wilson, in her conversation with DD Sports, said:

I was fortunate enough to represent the country for four consecutive games. Usha was also there for four Olympics but there was a break in between, and then she didn't participate in the Atlanta Olympics, although she was there. She was injured. In the 1992 Barcelona Olympics only two people were selected to the athletics team: Bahdur Prasad (5000 m) and myself (800 m). I still cherish the Barcelona Olympics because I was selected as the captain of the Indian contingent. Everybody was surprised to see an Indian lady in a sari leading the team and carrying the flag. It was one of the best moments in my entire career as an athlete.

As I entered the stadium with the flag in my hand, and when they announced 'India', I cannot explain what I felt; I still get goosebumps when I think of that moment. It is a great, great feeling to hear your country's name when you are carrying the flag. I cannot express the feeling in words.

I broke the national record, clocking 2:19 sec, but that was not good enough to reach the semis. About the Atlanta Olympics, I would like to say that I was in great form when I started from India. I was hopeful of reaching the final. In the South Asian games I even clocked less than two minutes. But when we reached Atlanta I started getting a slight pain in my legs. So I was asked not to run the 800 m. Atlanta was the most disappointing experience of my life.

The Olympics, as an experience for her, was full of crests and troughs, making her mentally tougher further on in her life.

These athletes competed with several limitations. They had too many hurdles. Under these circumstances, whatever shortfalls remained in their performances in their sporting careers were more than made up when they retired from the track.

For the triumvirate, their second life began at forty and they have been triumphant role models there as well. After hanging up their boots, all the three have been successful career women. Usha worked as senior officer with Southern Railways before getting involved full time with her Usha School of Athletics. M.D. Valsamma was a commercial manager with the Southern Railways. Shiny Wilson was a general manager with the Food Corporation of India.

There are a few clear inferences that could be drawn from their lives.

Firstly, one common thread in their success stories is their dedication, sincerity and hard work. They were honest in their approach and their athletic journey entailed supreme sacrifices in the early stages of their life.

Secondly, behind each of these successful women are the men who proved to be their constant pillars of strength. V. Srinivasan, the husband of P.T. Usha, encouraged her to make a comeback after her first retirement. Shiny got married to the ace swimmer Cherian Wilson and the couple have three children. She became Asian Champion in the 400 m after attaining motherhood—which speaks volumes about her dedication and resolve. As per the star athlete, this would not have been possible without the support of her husband. In one of her interviews with Doordarshan, Shiny says, 'He provided constant encouragement and motivated me to achieve things. I consider myself very lucky.'

Thirdly, sports gave them the confidence to excel in their respective chosen fields in the later stages of life. But what exemplifies the confidence that sports gives to an individual is clear from their fourth partner in the 1984 Los Angeles Games, Vandana Rao. Unlike the three, Vandana is from Karnataka.

Vandana travelled around the world as an athlete and performed credibly in the Los Angeles and Seoul Olympics and in the Rome and Canberra World Athletics Championships. But more importantly, when she changed track from athletics to tourism, she proved to be highly successful there too.

Globetrotting became the full-time job for the track athlete as she became a tour manager with SOTC Holidays. She used to chaperone groups of tourists through European cities, and Rome topped her 'favourites' list. Talking about her experience and responsibilities, she said in an interview with the English daily, *The Hindu*, 'Dealing with Italian bus drivers is tough. They will do things their own way; it takes great effort to convince them to adjust to the tourists' desire to see places they paid for.'

Vandana Rao earlier toured Rome as a competitor in the World Athletics Championships. She says, 'I passed the Stadio Olimpico on one of my trips, but did not get time to step inside the athletics venue.' Vandana used to take care to conceal her sporting identity on such tours. 'As tour manager, my focus is to see that my group gets value for money. Tourists from Karnataka, my home state, sometimes recognize me,' she further said.

But how did she come into the travel business? Vandana was a banker—a branch manager with Corporation Bank before deciding to follow a career close to her heart. 'Bank work was monotonous and I always enjoyed travelling and meeting new people. I took leave from bank work to do a tour manager's course in 2007 at Thomas Cook and switched to travel full-time from 2010 with Vacation Exotica as a tour manager.'

Vandana Rao further elaborates on how travelling as a sportsperson helped her to make a career in tourism. She says, 'My role is similar to that of an athletics squad manager. Every sportsperson is different and needs to be handled differently. The manager is expected to ensure they are ready for their event in time, as per the day's schedule. Sportspersons used to get curious when I told them about the work I do, but then they felt my job is glamorous and I have the opportunity to see places. I don't know about any other sportsperson getting into tourism. It's tough and I am away from home for long stretches.'

The state boundary may separate Vandana from the triumvirate, but she shares one commonality with them. Her husband Joaqium Carvalho, a hockey player, and son, Akshay, manage their Vakola home in her absence. Success in a lot of sports is about team performance and the families of the golden girls worked as a team to meet the challenges in their life.

Sports teaches you to accept both victory and defeat with grace and come out of it. In real life, this is akin to accepting both accolades and adversities with the same gusto. Mercy Kuttan is a former track and field athlete from Kerala. She was India's first long jumper to cross 6 m. Her first international success came in the 1981 Asian Championships in athletics when she won the double bronze in long jump and the 4x400 m relay.

In the next year in the 1982 Asian Games, she won a silver medal in long jump. She represented India in long jump at the 1983 World Championships in athletics, but did not qualify for the final round. In a later stage in her career she switched to sprint. She competed in the 400 m in the 1988 Seoul Olympics and managed to reach the second round.

In the selection camp for the 1980 Moscow Olympics, she met Murali Kuttan. Murali was an Indian track and field athlete who represented India as a sprinter on several occasions. The two fell in love and got married within two years. They were the first Indian athletic couple to emerge as national champions and win Asian medals. Murali took the role of her coach and influenced Mercy to shift from long jump to 400 m.

Both Murali and Mercy worked for Tata Steel at Jamshedpur. They set up the Mercy Kuttan Athletics Academy in Kochi—a non-profit organization to train promising youth for major international competitions. However, a far tougher test, beyond the sporting arena, awaited her later in life.

Sujith Kuttan, their son, was running in the State School Athletics Meet in the senior boys' 100 m category. The showdown between Sujith, the younger son of the former international athletes and Binish K. Shaji, silver medallist at the World School Athletics Meet in Estonia, was the most awaited event of the meet. Murali's last wish was that Sujith should run the race as he was being rushed to the hospital, after complaining of breathlessness in the early hours of the morning.

Twenty minutes after hospitalization, Murali Kuttan passed away. And Mercy Kuttan, despite being overcome with grief, was insistent that the news of the death of her husband and 400 m medallist in the 1978 Bangkok Asian Games should not be broken to Sujith until the 100 m final was over. The media, told in friendly terms not to flash the bad news, complied in full measure. And the air was pregnant with poignancy as Sujith took to the blocks.

There was little joy among the friends of Murali and Mercy as the eighteen-year-old came through easily to emerge the winner. They stood in silence before escorting Sujith to the nearby hospital. Once told, the young boy naturally broke down in the arms of the mother and was inconsolable. As the sports world paid its last respects to one of its finest athletes, a heartbroken Sujith stayed back in the rear of a waiting car outside, sharing space with his mother and elder brother, deep anguish and incomprehension writ large on his face. Like the car left the mortuary and moved on, so did their lives.

Mercy started focusing on her athletics academy. There were irritants and roadblocks on the way, but like a true hurdle racer, she started crossing them one by one and inching towards the finishing line. She got engrossed in training her protégés like P.R. Aleesha, Linet George and Gowri Nandana.

Broadly, the attitude of working hard and fighting back is the special trait of the athletes from God's own country. The attitude of the women athletes of Kerala is best summarized in the painting that adorned the living room of their greatest ambassador of all times, P.T. Usha. It says, 'Attitude: Things turn out best for people who make the best of the way things turn out.'

TWO

P.T. Usha: Get, Set, Go!

The road to success is always under construction. The success stories of Indian sportswomen of substance are still works in progress. They are in the midst of a marathon race in which they have to cover miles before they can sleep. It is important to keep in mind that a marathon is not only about the start and finishing line. The preparations leading to the marathon in terms of training, exercises and warm-up sessions start well before the start line and continue beyond the finishing line.

Even before a frail-looking, shy and reticent girl coming from the backwaters of Kerala and representing the middle class took off on the marathon journey of Indian sportswomen, the ground for the same was prepared by athletes who came before her. Indian women participated for the first time in the Helsinki Olympic Games in 1952.

Though Mary D'Souza (sprint) and Nilima Ghose (100 m hurdles) were inexperienced, they were eager contestants. They came out as silver linings, and made us believe that this marathon journey was indeed possible. Mary Leela Rao, sprint athlete, was the proud leader of India's march past at the 1956 Melbourne Olympic Games. She gave all Indians a ray of hope. Stephie D'Souza née Sequeira, who represented India in athletics and women's hockey, Meena Shah, who represented the country in badminton, Arati Saha, who was the first Indian woman to cross the English Channel, and Kamaljeet Sandhu, who won a gold medal at the 1970 Bangkok Asian Games in the 400 m race, were some of the early protagonists who prepared the ground for the formal 'Get, set, go.'

A marathon journey that is a mirror image of life is not only about winning and losing. It's more than that. There are 'so near yet so far' moments in this journey that are more significant than the victories and defeats. There have been two 'so near yet so far' moments in India's Olympics history that have brought about seminal changes in the mindsets of aspiring athletes for generations to come.

For the first time, the 'so near yet so far' moment came way back in the 1960 Rome Olympics. The young nation was trying to find its feet in the global order. Thirteen summers back, the country, with one of the most ancient civilizational roots, had become independent, embraced democracy and boldly decided for universal adult franchise in one go. All these landmark decisions were taken amidst the prophets of doom predicting the disintegration of the country within a decade of its birth.

The solemn occasion of Independence was interspersed with the sadness of Partition. Milkha Singh was the by-product of this post-partition legacy. In him emerged a hero and a symbol that would give the young nation the much-required recognition on the highest global sporting platforms where the most talented lot of athletes from across the world compete.

Milkha Singh entered the 400 m race as the favourite in the 1960 Rome Olympics. He led the race till the 200 m mark before easing off, allowing others to pass him. This was the race in which various records were broken. The hearts of millions of Indians were also broken. The race required a photo finish and saw American Otis Davis being declared the winner by one-hundredth of a second over German Carl Kaufmann. Milkha finished fourth, clocking 45.73 sec which stayed as the country's national record for 40 long years.

Some say that the country's sporting landscape would have been different had Milkha Singh won the medal. But the sporting evolution of the nation, like history, doesn't give us the leeway for ifs and buts. The impact of the moment could best be assessed by these lines published by *The Independent* as recently as

July 2012—'India's most revered Olympian is a gallant loser'—and it noted the paucity of success at that time—20 medals won by Indian competitors in the Olympic Games despite the country having a population in excess of one billion.

Oh no, not again! Another 'so near and yet so far' moment... Then came India's performance in 1984 and this time it was the Los Angeles Summer Olympics.

India, by this time, had proved its credentials as a lively and functioning democracy with all its inherent sensibilities, despite the Emergency in 1975. In fact, the voice of resistance against the Emergency proved how much the country loves democracy. The country had established its identity as a non-aligned force in the Cold War-driven bi-polar world. However, the image of the country as one still steeped in poverty, illiteracy and inflation was refusing to fade away, and the entrepreneurial energy of the masses was chained by an archaic system and the License-Quota-Permit Raj.

In the sporting field, the frustration was mounting, as other nations were running away with a bagful of medals and Indians were returning empty-handed. The golden era of Indian hockey had long ended and the country's sporting horizon needed a new dawn. Usha, meaning 'dawn' in Sanskrit, raised the hope for this new dawn in the 1984 Los Angeles Olympics.

We often say, our destiny lies in our own hands. But here was a girl from Kerala who started guiding the sporting destiny of the nation with the strength of her two legs. P.T. Usha had a string of good results in the run-up to the Games. In the 1982 Asian Games in New Delhi, she finished second in both 100 m and 200 m. Of course, her performance in the World Championships in Moscow wasn't flattering. In a field of seven, she finished sixth in the 100 m race. In the 200 m race, she finished 31st out of 39 competitors.

But a year later, she claimed the 400 m gold at the Asian Track and Field Meet in Kuwait. That prompted Usha to concentrate on the 400 m hurdles, a race that would be introduced for the first time for women at the Olympics. She clocked a world-class

55.7 sec at the Olympics trials. Usha had qualified for the Games. She finished her heats in 56.81 sec. Now she was in the semi-finals. The semi-finals turned out to be a historic affair. She clocked a time of 55.54 sec. Not only was it a Commonwealth record, but it was also the first instance of an Indian athlete winning in an Olympic semi-final.

In the finals, Usha started superbly, but one of her competitors made a false start. Perhaps this broke her rhythm and she got off the block a bit slow at the restart. The flow was missing, but by the eighth hurdle, she had caught up with the leaders. Finally, it was a photo finish. The announcer declared that P.T. Usha had finished fourth. The finish was replayed again and again on the giant screen at the Los Angeles Memorial Coliseum before the results were declared. Another 'so near and yet so far' moment... 'Oh no, not again!' the nation cried in unison.

Usha was beaten by a last desperate lunge by Romania's Cristina Cojocaru who was credited with the time of 55.41 sec for the third place. Usha's run was officially clocked at 55.42 sec. In fact, to make sure that nothing was left to chance, India lodged a formal protest, claiming third place for Usha. The medal ceremony was delayed to make sure that every doubt had been cleared. After the event, Usha retreated to her room in the Olympic Village without speaking a word to anyone. Her silence said it all.

The significance of Usha's Los Angeles Olympics moment of loss on the psyche of India in those times could best be understood through these lines spoken by the legendary athlete. Usha says in her autobiography, 'In those days, the postman arrived with the day's mail. Although it was difficult to reply to all the letters, I made it a point to read all of them when at home. One of the letters read: "I always offer prayers at a mosque a day before you run in an international meet. Somehow, I forgot to do so just before the Los Angeles Olympics 400 m hurdles final. I shall not repeat this mistake ever again in my life".'[1]

Her full name, Pilavullakandi Thekkeparambil Usha, is a tongue-twister for people who are not native to her place and don't speak her language, but she was the first female sportswoman to be a household name in the country.

Three decades have passed since that day at the Los Angeles Olympics. From player to coach and now to an elder stateswoman of Indian sports, P.T. Usha has traversed a long and arduous way. The shy and reticent girl of those days is now identified for her bold and decisive demeanour in the power corridors of India's sporting fraternity. She looks more mature now, but the innocence of the yesteryears returns to her face the moment she is reminded of the 1984 Los Angeles Olympics.

On the lawns of The Ashok Hotel in Delhi, when pointedly asked, if given an opportunity, what would be the one thing that she would like to change in her life, Usha says, 'If I could come back, if I could roll back the years, I would like to relive my most cherished moment, the Los Angeles Olympics. I would like to compete with the same fellow runners, but this time with a podium finish.'[2]

A brief pause is followed by a look to the heavens before she regains her composure. And, once again, the moment being fresh in her memories, becomes a trip down memory lane—as if it was three days and not three decades back.

'See, when I left for the Los Angeles Olympics, I was only twenty years old. Before this big event, I had participated only twice in the 400 m hurdles. In these two runs in the country, I had romped home with as huge a lead as 40 m—there was hardly any tough competition within the country.' Elaborating on this, she further says, 'My own state, Kerala, had objected to my entry when I wished to try my hand at the event in the interstate meet. The

---

[1] P.T. Usha and Lokesh Sharma, *Golden Girl: The Autobiography of P.T. Usha*, Penguin, pg 97

[2] 'The Proust Questionnaire—"I always want to be happy": P.T. Usha', *The Hindu*, 24 July 2016

only reason my name was entered for the federation was because the interstate meet is the selection trials for the Olympics. But when I went for the race, other coaches and athletes did not want me to compete. So the competition was further delayed. Finally, I had to come back from the track saying I didn't want to participate that time and maybe I would try the next time. So that chance was gone for me, the first competition.

'The second one was the Open Nationals and this was in Bombay. This was the second trial for the Olympics. I had to face problems here as well. When the Inter Railway competition was held, I could not participate as I had not learnt hurdles by then. The railways however helped me as they had entered my name for the first round. So finally, I participated for the Open Nationals. In the first race itself, I won, breaking the Asian Games record. See, these were the only two races that I could get before the Olympics. When you go for a big meet like the Olympics, you should have the opportunity to run at least 10–15 races, that too at different venues in Europe.

'My third race before the Olympics was when my coach entered my name for the race in Angel Woods, before the Olympics. In this I won the race, competing along with Judi Brown-King of America. After the Angel Woods performance, I was determined enough to do well. Eventually, I lost because of the lack of exposure. If you go back to the video you will see that my leg is in the front, but I could not dip my chest. Actually, I did hurdles in 6.2 sec in my first attempt, but that day I could do only 6.8 sec. If I could have done 6.2 or 6.3, I could have won silver, if I could have dipped my chest, I could have won bronze, and if I could have got exposure outside the country, I could have won gold. This was the reason why I lost the historic opportunity to win a medal there.'

These are her on-field memories. Off the field, she carries one strong memory, still very close to her heart. 'While I was sitting alone in my room that evening, I got a message from the then Prime Minister Indira Gandhi. I had always admired her. "Don't worry, you may not have won a medal, but you have won the hearts of your countrymen," the message read.' Usha says this with a certain pride.

A marathon, in many ways, is a reflection of real life. Most of us sitting outside fail to appreciate the efforts of all the others who fail to achieve a podium finish. But this is not the case with the runners—for they realize the smallest of differences between the winners and those who just failed to be on the top. The importance of this 'so near yet so far' moment in Indian sports can best be understood when seen through the lens of the gold medallist of the event, Nawal El Moutawakel. She was the first Muslim-born woman from Africa to clinch an Olympic gold in athletics by finishing on top in the 400 m hurdles. And she was the one who appreciated the importance of Usha's contribution in the race, despite failing to get the medal.

Her medal had such an impact at that time that the king of Morocco declared that girls born on the day she won the Olympic gold would be named in her honour. Moutawakel says in one of her interviews, 'That day, as much as I was happy for myself, I was sad for her (P.T. Usha), because we come from countries where athletics is not that big. When she came fourth, I cried so hard. I really wanted her to be on the podium. I wanted to win but I also wanted her to win along with me.'[3]

There is a saying that the value of water can best be understood in a dry and parched land and not in the flood plains. With a glint in her eyes, P.T. Usha puts this in perspective when she says, 'When I won the semi-finals in Los Angeles, Judi Brown, who eventually won the silver medal, told me that she was wondering how it was that though from India no man was doing well, one woman was forcing the world to pause and notice the entire contingent. This was reported in the press also. When she came to know from others that I was competing in the 100 m and 200 m races as well, she wondered as to how anyone could manage such a heavy workload and compete in five different events at the highest

---

[3]Moutawakel said this during the Laureus World Sports Awards 2011.

global sporting stage. Even the world record holder of that time Edwin Moses congratulated me.'

One cannot recall an athlete at the highest level who could tackle six different events, including two relays, so consistently and with that rate of success. Usha did that repeatedly for the sake of the country, most of the time willingly. Those were the times when the Indian contingent used to participate in the Olympics largely to just be a part of the ceremonial parade. Not any more. Usha inspired many girls to take up sports with the hope that they could compete with the best and win. Usha thus pioneered a new dawn in the Indian sporting horizon.

Usha, in the preface to her autobiography, *Golden Girl: The Autobiography of P.T. Usha,* says, 'Mr C.M. Pythal, my headmaster in the sports division, reminded me of the day when I was called in front of the school assembly for my first triumph in an inter-school competition. During the assembly he called out my name and made me stand next to him under a gulmohar tree. Just as I got under the tree a breeze blew across the compound and some flowers fell on me. Mr Pythal says that even God was with me right from the beginning.'

Mr Pythal's words may have sentimental overtones, however, there is no denying the fact that Usha's arrival was like a breath of fresh air in Indian sports. As to why the shy girl from Kerala, who refused to stand in the front row for a class photograph session, was considered to be at the forefront of the women's wave in Indian sports, can best be understood if we go back and reflect on the sporting landscape in those years.

Till she arrived as a precocious sixteen-year-old talent in 1979, Indian sportswomen were few and far between. The women's hockey team, some swimmers and the occasional shot-putter aside, there were hardly any women athletes competing at the global level. Until the eighth Asian Games at Bangkok, in 1978, Indian women athletes were mere token participants. Sports historians consider the 1978 performance to be one-of-a-kind because in the first seven Asian games, women's contribution to the overall tally had been meagre—2 gold, 4 silver and 10 bronze medals. In the two peak years of her career,1985 and 1986, P.T. Usha surpassed this tally by a good margin. Secondly, apart from Manjit Walia's 80 m hurdles medal in 1966 and Kamaljit Sandhu's 400 m gold in 1970, all the remaining medals were won in the early years of the Asian Games. This was the period when women's athletics in Asia was in its formative stage. Thirdly, all these victories were confined to the one Parsee and eight Anglo-Indian girls from Bombay, namely Roshan Mistry, Christie Brown, Mary D'Souza, Violet Peters, S. Gauntlet, Marie Simoes, Barbara Webster and Elizabeth Davenport.

Jal D. Pardiwala, renowned coach and veteran sports administrator, further elaborates on this in the autobiography of P.T. Usha, 'There was no organized athletics in the country till the late sixties. The success of these Bombay girls in the first few Asian Games was largely due to their family backgrounds. As a community, the Parsees and Anglo-Indians were far more progressive than the other Indian communities, which formed the majority.'[4]

Importantly, the true potential of the sporting talent of any nation can only be realized when it covers its vast majority base and not its microscopic minority. With P.T. Usha, Indian women's sports became more inclusive and encouraged mass participation. Women's empowerment in India in the 1970s and 1980s was a lofty dream confined to the elite class. Women comprised a small portion of the office space. And amongst them also, almost all were placed in slotted roles.

Seen in this overall context, even for elites, pursuing athletics was wishful thinking. P.T. Usha says, 'The very fact that we practised and competed in half pants made many people curious. People certainly did not have a proactive approach for women's participation in athletics. In those days, facilities for women

---

[4]P.T. Usha and Lokesh Sharma, *Golden Girl: The Autobiography of P.T. Usha*, Penguin, pg 72

athletes in a major part of the country left a lot to be desired.'

Olympian Ranjit Bhatia, who was a national selector in the mid-seventies, says in *Golden Girl: The Autobiography of P.T. Usha*, 'Usha's greatest contribution is that she made some sense out of women's athletics. Till a few years ago, women's athletics was of secondary importance. She gave it a stature that has, I am sure, encouraged many others to excel. Today our women are much closer to world standards than men.'

Though there were talented Indian women athletes before P.T. Usha as well, but with her they started coming in with regularity and were not few and far between any longer.[5]

There are players who perform and there are players who perform and transform. In the words of India's greatest opening batsman, Sunil Gavaskar, Haryana hurricane Kapil Dev had that transformative impact on Indian cricket. He says, 'Kapil, by sheer example, led others by the way he played and the flair he brought into the game. He showed other Indian fast bowlers the way ahead... It was because of him that we showed that we too could have fast bowlers, because prior to him we never really had a tradition of good fast bowlers. So, thanks to him, we have developed this pool of fast bowlers today.'[6]

Similarly, if we talk of one female athlete who performed and transformed the Indian women's sporting scenario forever, it has to be P.T. Usha. Numerous women athletes who have been part of the incredible group of women sportspersons in the country owe it to P.T. Usha. Most of them admit this in so many words.

The fraction of a second by which Usha lost in the Olympics, which made all the difference between hope and despair, will remain unforgettable in India's sporting history. However, this momentous occasion spearheaded by this incredible woman of Indian sports has inspired generations to come and more than

[5]P.T. Usha and Lokesh Sharma, *Golden Girl: The Autobiography of P.T. Usha*, Penguin, pg 163

[6]'Kapil Dev is India's greatest match-winner, says Sunil Gavaskar', Cricket Country, 23 February 2017

made up for that fateful fraction of a second. Inspired by Usha and her Los Angeles feat, the likes of Anju Bobby George, Karnam Malleswari, M.C. Mary Kom, Saina Nehwal, Sania Mirza and many more have subsequently done the country proud.

As Usha says, 'In those days, women in serious sports were a rarity. We didn't have many women icons in sports to look up to. Now it's different. It's really great to see the likes of Saina Nehwal, P.V. Sindhu, M.C. Mary Kom, Sania Mirza and the others doing so well on an international stage. The subsequent generations will have many more icons to look up to.'

India's reigning badminton queen Saina Nehwal could not agree more. She says, 'My mother used to often say, when I took to serious badminton, P.T. Usha narrowly missed a medal in the Olympics. You will have to win an Olympic medal for the country.' Thus, the message, 'If I can, so can you...' that originated thirty years back in Los Angeles has now become 'If we can, so can you...'

This signature tune of 'If we can, so can you...' that emanated from the Payyoli district of Kerala has now gathered a pan-India momentum. The legend of P.T. Usha was, however, not born in Los Angeles. It was born much before. And it did not die after the Los Angeles Olympics. It gathered momentum from there to reach its brightest phase subsequently. Sports journalist K.P. Mohan, in one of his articles for *The Hindu*, says, 'It was born in Moscow in the 1980 Olympics, at the tender age of sixteen, though without any notable achievement, evolved through the Asian Games at home in 1982, reached its first bright phase at the 1984 Olympics and then passed through the most productive segment at Jakarta and Seoul in 1985 and 1986 respectively.'

Usha was the chosen one who transformed women's sports in the country. But why do we often find in history that the one who looks the most unlikely is often the chosen one for such roles? Melady happens to be one of the smallest villages in the Payyoli panchayat. This is the place where she was born and spent her early childhood. The place still, on the face of it, doesn't look like the birthplace of one of India's tallest sporting legends. As a child, she was like any other normal girl, and athletics never crossed her mind. So was the case with her parents. No one in Usha's immediate family ever excelled in sports. Neither their physique nor the nature of their work conveyed any latent sporting talent or possibility.

Her father, E.P.M. Paithal, was a slightly-built man, who spent a lifetime behind the counter of his cloth shop. He was not into any formal physical activities as he didn't have any time for the same. His only informal physical exercise, if it may be so called, was his 2 km daily to and fro walk from his home to the family shop near Payyoli station. It was the same with Usha's tiny and frail mother, T.V. Lakshmi. Drawing water from the well, washing clothes and tending to the house, Lakshmi, from morning to evening, had to do a lot of physical work. But none of these even remotely resembled any athletic activities.

Remembering those days, Usha says, 'Both my father and my mother were very hardworking; they slogged from dawn till dusk and had no time left for anything else. My father left home at 7 in the morning and returned home around 9 in the evening. Morning and late evening were peak hours in the shop. As far as my mother was concerned, she was so engrossed in her work throughout the day that I and my sisters did not even dare to disturb her. So, from the family's perspective, if you will see, serious sport was not even the last thing on our minds.'

Then, why was P.T. Usha sent to the sports division in the first place?

Usha's father E.P.M. Paithal says in her autobiography, 'We sent her to sports division hoping that she would eventually become a physical education teacher. A job always helps in marriage.' This was very common in Kerala, especially in those days. The state has got a commendable literacy record and a sizeable expatriate population and a good CV always helps in marriages.

How the hesitant feet of P.T. Usha made an entry into the sports division and changed the course of her life becomes clear when she says, 'Sreedharan, my maternal uncle, was only ten years elder to me. We were very close to each other. I still remember that when we were kids, he helped us in our homework, teaching us the fundamentals of English and other subjects. People say that "Usha" would not have been "Usha" if she had not stepped into the sports division. There were many in our village who were of the opinion that a girl should not be sent to such a faraway school in Cannanore, when Payyoli High School was there in the village itself. They used to instil all sorts of fears in my mother's mind. To be frank, I was also indecisive. Again, it was Sreedharan uncle who motivated my parents and me to enroll in the sports division school.' Usha then says with pride, 'I started taking myself as an athlete seriously only once I joined the sports division. If I was able to win so many medals for the country in important international events, the foundation for the same was laid in the sports division. And one of the persons who played a crucial role in my entry to the sports division was Sreedharan uncle.'

Joining the sports division was the first major milestone in her journey of becoming a sporting legend. However, her limitation was that she was far away from the elitist background from which most of the handful of medals in women's sports had come till then.

Usha's family was not very poor, but they were not rich either. The family was somehow able to make ends meet. Usha says, 'The family did not enjoy even the simplest of luxuries in life. We had a well in our house, but no suction pump. My mother had to draw water from there. We had steady electricity supply, but lacked even the basic electrical appliances. Our only form of recreation was the visit to our maternal uncle's place. I, in particular, enjoyed the hilly terrains of Koothali, which gave me the liberty to run up and down, and a feel of adventure.'

To add to this, Usha, right from her birth, was very weak and prone to illness. Her mother Lakshmi is quoted in her autobiography as saying, 'She was very weak, weighing no more than 2 kg. Of all my children she was the smallest. From birth, she had frequent bouts of illness.'[7]

The game of hide and seek between Usha and her illness which started early in her life continued throughout her career. If Usha's coach Mr Nambiar could count her major records in a single breath, her mother Lakshmi could narrate all her illnesses with their respective durations extempore. And it was not a small and simple list to memorize. Usha, clearly, was least positioned to be the pioneer of the women's athletics movement in the country. But then, what made her tick as a sportsperson?

Ima Market in Imphal, Manipur, is the world's only all-women-run market. And amongst many things that attract our attention in this market is the beautiful clay art. When a woman potter was asked the reason for the beauty of the pottery, she said, 'Listen, this is not about me, it's about the clay. In my years of gathered experience about the art, I often wondered as to why the best pottery comes out of the clay that is brutally raw and authentically original—the clay that is willing to shape up as we want rather than be rigid about the shape that it wants to take.'[8]

In hindsight, it seems that P.T. Usha from Payyoli was the clay that the potter in Ima Market desired every time. Unfettered by any chain of sporting expectations from herself and her immediate family, she set off on the course which gave her one sporting laurel after another in her career. The rest is history. This authentic and original clay was fortunate to be shaped by the right people and circumstances at the right time, so that eventually a beautiful piece of pottery could emerge.

Usha's parents may not have had athletic physiques, but they certainly taught her the virtues of hard work and sacrifice. They could not afford to spend time with their children, but perhaps their absence taught the lessons of sincerity and perseverance to her. Usha's childhood was devoid of the basic luxuries of life.

---

[7]P.T. Usha and Lokesh Sharma, *Golden Girl: The Autobiography of P.T. Usha*, Penguin, pg 27

[8]This was said to author Abhishek Dubey by one of the potters when he went to Ima Market to film a documentary.

Perhaps the hunger for the same egged her on to consistently keep going in life. This gave her the mindset and temperament of an ascetic focused on her target.

As Usha says, 'An athlete's life entails lots of sacrifice in the prime of her youth. If we went for any late night events or parties, it would disturb the morning practice session, which is so critical for any athlete. When we went outside for events, I preferred sticking to my regimen and gave my shopping list to my coach. Even when I went shopping, it was only when our events were over. This strict regimen is often killing, but this is what separates a champion from others. This is something I imbibed right from my childhood.'

Usha may have been weak in her childhood and consistently ill. However, psychologically it is a proven fact that the strongest of human characters are forged in the furnace of relative deprivation; both physical and circumstantial. One of the things depravity teaches us is the optimum understanding and utilization of the time that is in our hands, which is so crucial for success in professional sports. One specific episode from the earlier days in her career clearly indicates this.

The 1979 National Games at Nagpur was scheduled one month before her class X board examinations. Usha had already missed lots of classes due to athletics and she took all her books along with her when she went to participate in the Games. All through the competition she was running a fever. However, when everybody was fooling around after the competition, she locked herself in a room with her books. On the field she won four gold medals. Off the field she completed her lessons for the board examinations. Usha says, 'I had learnt to live with illness. Perhaps I got this training straight from my childhood. I had learnt to balance my life between sports and academics and diligently carried on both till the time came when I had to choose between them.'

Usha can be seen as the raw material that is truly original and authentic. She moulded herself into a proper shape and form at the right time in her life. When one is destined for big things in life, one comes across the right people at the right time who come up with the right answers to questions from time to time. Usha's case was no different. The finest of artefacts we hold in our hands are shaped by the best of the artists, at the right time, like the beautiful pottery of the Ima Market in Imphal.

Kerala is beautiful: God's own country is believed to be a gift of the Arabian Sea. Gorgeous and exotic beaches, breathtaking hill stations, enchanting waterfalls, beautiful lagoons, meandering rivers and amazing natural scenery are some of the defining features of this mindboggling beauty. High mountains, gorges, deep-cut valleys, lush evergreen rainforests and coconut trees are some of its prominent attractions.

Kerala loves its women. There is a high aggregate female literacy rate in the state. The female-to-male ratio is commendable.

Kerala loves sports as well. Kerala and soccer are intrinsically linked with one another. Apart from football, the state's love affair with basketball, volleyball, athletics, kabaddi, hockey, badminton and, of late, cricket, continue. Symbols of this love affair are scattered all across the state. Trivandrum International Stadium, Jimmy George Indoor Stadium, University Stadium and Chandrasekharan Nair Stadium in Trivandrum, Jawaharlal Nehru Stadium and Rajiv Gandhi Indoor Stadium in Kochi, an international astro-turf hockey stadium at Kollam city, EMS Stadium in Kozhikode, Lal Bahadur Shastri Stadium in Kollam and Kannur Indoor Stadium in Kannur are all structures of the state standing tall, epitomizing the boundless love between Kerala and sports. This love affair has its own indigenous beauty as well. And the one that connects with the soul the most is Kalaripayattu.

The relation between this martial art and the Kerala dance form is symbiotic. One of the brand ambassadors of the art who helps to connect with this symbol of soulful relationship is Meenakshi amma or Meenakshi Gurukkal. She is one of the oldest Kalaripayattu gurus... Hailing from the picturesque small town of Vadakara, about 45 km away from Kannur in Kerala, her Kadathanadan Kalari Sangam centre represents the pristine beauty inherent in our age-old 'Guru-Shishya parampara'.

The Guru-Shishya parampara thrived and flourished for a thousand years in India. In this culture, when there was the need to convey a subtle and powerful knowledge, it was always done in the atmosphere of utter trust, dedication and intimacy between the Guru and the Shishya. 'Parampara' is literally defined as 'an uninterrupted tradition'—in other words, it denotes an unbroken lineage of imparted knowledge.[9]

Meenakshi amma perfectly fits into the 'unsung hero' category that has been introduced in the Padma awards by PM Narendra Modi's government in 2017. Like Meenakshi amma, P.T. Usha too has donned the mantle of a Guru today. She is passing on the recipe of the making of the champions to the future generation through her Usha School of Athletics. There are other similarities between Meenakshi amma and Usha—their sport helped them rediscover themselves and carve out their respective identities. They are the symbols of the Guru-Shishya parampara, which is unique to Indian culture.

There is an inherent dichotomy in Kalaripayattu, represented by Meenakshi amma. The low crouching stance, unwavering stare, forbidding expression and the shining long, sharp steel sword in the right hand and a brass shield in the other would scare the daylights out of any opponent or attacker. The first thought that comes to mind while reading this description is of an angry tiger ready to pounce. Once you meet Meenakshi amma, you definitely get to meet the tiger. When in the ring, she looks ferocious. When out of the ring, the lady in her mid-70s has the most beautiful, warm and affectionate nature.

Streaks of this inherent dichotomy are palpable in P.T. Usha too. She was a shy, frail-looking, reticent girl when she was in her village town. But the moment she became interested in sports in Kannur, she entered the ring for the battle of her life. And

---

[9]'Classical Yoga: The Guru-Shishya Paramparya', isha.sadhguru.org, 30 March 2013

this started transforming her personality forever, guided by the unwillingness to even concede an inch of space to her opponents.

The Padma Shri award winner says, 'Learning Kalari not only arms a person against adversaries but also boosts the confidence of the learner.'

When she started training in Kannur, P.T. Usha started arming herself against her adversaries. And with Mr O.M. Nambiar coming into her life as a coach, there was a boost in her confidence.

Athletics, unlike Kalaripayattu, is not combat sports. Here you don't knock down your adversaries. Rather, you sail past them. After going to Kannur—with O.M. Nambiar as company—she started sailing past her adversaries in every race and every walk of life. Her batch in the Kannur school still remembers this. Usha was accompanied by her father, and maternal uncle Sreedharan when she went to Kannur for the first time. Initially there were economic and time constraints, and training there didn't seem like a sustainable long-term option. This is when her coach-cum-mentor, Mr O.M. Nambiar, entered her life.

Mr Nambiar, who was among the staff faculty in the sports division of Cannanore, was from the same panchayat area as Usha. As O.M. Nambiar said in an interview with NDTV, 'Initially I didn't know that Usha was the daughter of E.P.M. Paithal, but Mr Paithal was known to me. Once her father introduced her to me, she started travelling with me from her home to the sports division.'

Perhaps, theirs was the meeting waiting to happen. O.M. Nambiar, when in college, was a champion sprinter. But there was no one to encourage him. Nambiar joined the Indian Air Force in 1955 and made his mark as a decathlon champion. Here also he found himself crippled on account of the lack of any encouragement. Eventually he joined Kerala Sports Council as an athletics coach.

At this point of time in his life, Nambiar had a choice between two routes to follow. The first was the road of pessimism and negativity which would have made him a recluse. The second one was of optimism and positivity which would see the fulfilment of the unaccomplished aspirations and dreams of others. Mr Nambiar chose the second route. But then, why not train dozens of budding athletes rather than focus on one athlete? As he says in Usha's autobiography, 'Some people will be curious to know why I have confined myself to training just one athlete. This is because as a nation we are woefully short of champions. In that context, I think it's of far greater service to produce one champion than a hundred losers.'[10]

Meenakshi amma and her protégés, Usha and her protégés and before that Usha and Nambiar—the incredible Guru-Shishya parampara touches the lives of all the leading protagonists in the marathon journey of women's sports in India.

Sadhguru says, 'A guru is not a teacher. The Guru-Shishya relationship is on an energy basis. He touches you in a dimension where no one else can. There is a space where nobody else—your husband, your wife, your child, your parent—can touch you. They can only touch you in your emotion, your mind or your body. If you want to reach the very peak of your consciousness, you need a lot of energy—all the energy you have, and more. A Guru-Shishya relationship has become so sacred and important because when the crisis moment comes in a disciple's growth, he needs a little push on the energy level. Without that push, he doesn't have the necessary energy to reach the peak. Only someone who is on a higher plane than yourself can give that little push to you. Nobody else.'[11]

In the case of P.T. Usha, it was O.M. Nambiar. For Dipa Karmakar it's Bisweswar Nandi, for Saina Nehwal and P.V. Sindhu it's P. Gopichand, for Anju Bobby George it's Bobby George and for the Phogat sisters it's Mahavir Singh Phogat. The spirit of this parampara may or may not exist in our modern sports academies, but it's critical for success in professional journeys.

---

[10]P.T. Usha and Lokesh Sharma, *Golden Girl: The Autobiography of P.T. Usha*, Penguin, pg 77

[11]'Classical Yoga: The Guru-Shishya Paramparya', isha.sadhguru.org, 30 March 2013

As Sanjay Bangar, a former India cricketer and now an accomplished coach, puts it nicely, 'If we go through the list of the Dronacharya Award winners, we notice that most of these coaches may not have played at a very high level; they were able to develop champions because of their passion and dedication towards them. They were there for their students at all times. They made immense sacrifices on personal and family levels to ensure that the progress of the students is not hindered.'[12]

An elder statesman of Indian sports and one of the country's most successful coaches by far, Gopichand, says, 'As a player, you primarily focus on your own game. As a coach, you need to plan for different individuals, mapping their talent and temperament, planning for them and often mentoring the growth process of their entire personality, and not only the skill set required for the particular game.' In the case of Indian women in sports, the trust factor in this relationship should be unmatched and uncompromising. We hear about sexual harassment and exploitation of women players in academies and schools. These incidents act as a major deterrent for many potential champions joining this incredible marathon journey of women in sports. This is critical for the journey getting a fresh impetus, the possibilities of which were shown by P.T. Usha years ago.

Usha and Nambiar had a partnership that seemed to be ill at ease when looked at initially. As Usha's autobiography says, 'They make an odd twosome. One, five foot seven inches of lean muscle, the other, short, and running to fat. When they came together, the athlete found it difficult to keep up with the coach. Now, with a great deal of patience, she tolerates his tortoise-like pace. With long, measured strides, she darts ahead, never more than 50 m, and then jogs easily back to Nambiar, and exchanges a few words with him before pacing forward again.'[13]

---

[12]Sanjay Bangar said this to the author, Abhishek Dubey, in one of his interviews while he was at Network18.

[13]P.T. Usha and Lokesh Sharma, *Golden Girl: The Autobiography of P.T. Usha*, Penguin, pg 34

However, these two extreme personalities forged an indomitable partnership as they went along. This was the partnership that entailed huge sacrifices. P.T. Usha's training never had a break, and to be with her, Nambiar had to follow her to Mercy College and from Palghat to Providence College, Calicut. This meant being away from his children and wife K.V. Leena for months altogether. Often people were amazed at what Nambiar was doing, being away from his family for years altogether, leaving everything to his wife.

Usha recollects one meet in Pakistan, when her coach was not around. Though she managed to win medals there, she attributes this to the fact that there was hardly any competition there. 'Often as I approached the starting line, my eyes searched for sir, who used to be always there standing somewhere in the stands. This time, as I approached the starting line, I realized that he was not there and I was alone... It was difficult, but I somehow managed to romp home. If the opposition would have been of quality, it would have been tougher,' Usha says.

Like most talented athletes, Usha was temperamental. Sometimes she got irritated before an important race. Again it was the jovial nature of Nambiar that worked as a soothing balm to her increasing anxiety level. For instance, once, disappointed with her performance, Usha was on the verge of quitting a race hours before its start. Nambiar patiently and on time, brought her back to the track. He realized that the same rigorous training day in and day out was becoming monotonous for her. This was making her irritable.

Nambiar always introduced an element of play and fun to break the monotony of the rigid regimen. This is also clear from the way Nambiar conducted regular assessments, planning and execution at the right stages. He timed these decisions well, sometimes taking Usha into his confidence and sometimes waiting for the right moment to confide in her about the future course of action.

For instance, after the Helsinki World Championships in August

1983, it was clear to him that as far as timing was concerned, there was literally no chance of reaching the sprint final in the world level meet. The only possibility was the 400 m hurdles.

Usha says, 'We went to Czechoslovakia, I think in 1985, for the World Railways Meet. I am a compulsive rice eater, but where do I get rice in a country of bread and beef eaters? Sir sensed my irritation. After scouring for hours, he turned up with rice. He arranged for a heater and we would cook rice for ourselves and eat it with tomato.' Her mood changed overnight and henceforth she could focus on her preparations. There are numerous such small instances related to their unique partnership.

Though the Usha and Nambiar partnership clicked right from the word go, there are many who argue that if after the 1984 Los Angeles Olympics she would have got training under a reputed coach overseas, her career would have been different. But the response to this can be better understood in context of the times she lived in and the system she was operating within. In those days, getting into serious sports itself was a luxury and even the thought of getting trained abroad by a reputed foreign coach was unthinkable. We need to delve deep to understand how difficult it would have been for her to adjust to the climate, food and language in an alien setting, under an alien coach. More than a coach, Nambiar was like a father figure to her, who understood the hopes and aspirations of a shy and simple girl quite well. It would have been far better for her if, instead of getting a foreign coach, she would have been allowed planned training programmes abroad with her personal coach O.M. Nambiar accompanying her.

P.T. Usha summarizes this beautifully when she says, 'Right from the age of thirteen, Nambiar sir was always with me. In all, I won 103 prestigious medals for the country. Of these 103 medals and a near-medal in the Olympics, Nambiar sir has had a huge contribution. This would not have been possible without him. I myself don't know what my life would have been without Nambiar sir. I may have become a physical education teacher and got married. I would have completed my intermediate and got married. I would not have been either and still got married. In fact, through a major part of my career, I left dreaming partly to him; I just executed whatever he dreamt for me.'

Nambiar too felt the same. In one of his interviews with George Lype, the coach befittingly answered, 'By the time I stopped being her trainer, I had made a star in 100 m, 200 m and 400 m hurdles. People say that I parted company with her in dissatisfaction. But that is not true. I left her when she was at the peak of her athletic career. We continue to be great friends even today. If I am well known today, if I received awards, it is all because of Usha. Therefore I am indebted to her as she is indebted to me.'[14]

Though there were anxious moments leading to both of them parting with each other, it never became dirty.

As Nambiar started fading out of her life, Sreenivasan entered it.

Usha says, 'I was enjoying my athletics, but I had also started realizing that there was more to life than running races. There has to be a time when one settles down. In 1991, I got married to Sreenivasan, a CISF inspector and athletics buff. Subsequently, I also took a break from athletics. Mine has been a happy marriage and I was blessed with a son, Ujjwal. However, subsequently my husband inspired me to make a comeback in 1994. He wanted to see me fulfilling the unfulfilled desire of winning an Olympic medal. I may have not accomplished that, but I have no regrets about my comeback.' This more than summarises the reasons behind her leaving athletics and then making a comeback.

Some of the sports writers over the years have been critical of Usha's decision of making a comeback. But then, ask any sportsperson—the most difficult thing for them is to convince themselves that one could not get something one has so badly desired. And P.T. Usha was one of the great sportspersons. Usha

---

[14]P.T. Usha and Lokesh Sharma, *Golden Girl: The Autobiography of P.T. Usha,* Penguin, pg 96

says, 'In 1998, with 30-odd Asian medals behind me, I participated in the Asian Track and Field Championships in Japan and won bronze medals in the 200 m and 400 m, plus two medals in a relay. I also set a new national record for the 200 m, bettering my 1989 record. People ridiculed me about my comeback. But I knew from the core of my heart that there was something more to contribute left in me.'

From her parents and sisters to her uncle Sreedharan and from her coach Nambiar to her husband Sreenivasan, Usha was fortunate to come across the right people at the right time in her life. Besides the right people coming in at the right time in her life, Usha was born at the right place at the right time too.

The Kerala state government had by then initiated a pioneering effort in the field of sports by establishing sports schools and providing hostel facilities for aspiring athletes. Parents took these hostels as homes away from home, in the safe environment of which their daughters could hone their athletic skills. Attributing her success to the school, P.T. Usha says, 'When I passed class VII, the Kerala government started sports schools. I was a student in the first batch of the Connor Sports Division. At the school level, the state was taking a lot of interest. In comparison to the other states in the country, the schools in Kerala had better facilities. This can be attributed to the fact that the Kerala State Schools Athletics Meet is far tougher and more competitive than the National Schools Athletics Meet. All these, perhaps, played a critical role in my initial development as an athlete.'

She further adds, 'The very year I joined the sports school, I started participating in the heats for the state meet. In the first year I could not proceed beyond it. But I won the district meet. In the second year, I started winning every event like the 100 m, 200 m, long jump, high jump, shot-put and the 60 m hurdle. When I was under fourteen, I used to compete and win in the under-16 level. This was the time when I started taking sports seriously.'

Usha trained with her coach and support staff and this

collaboration worked like a well-oiled machine. The faculty comprised of O.M. Nambiar, Michael Francis (basketball) and Mukundan Nambiar (volleyball) and the group, besides sharing a flat, also shared brilliant camaraderie and a close relationship. They shared their inputs with the dream of making the Cannanore Sports Division scheme a roaring success. Importantly, they directed their efforts in producing rounded and balanced individuals and not merely book and field robots.

Beaches are a familiar sight in Kerala, and Usha considered them her favourite training spot. Usha says, 'It's my favourite training spot. The vastness gives me a sense of freedom which I don't experience anywhere else. On the track you can keep running in circles. But here there is no limit. I can run anywhere, till the end of my energy. I can run on the soft sand or the slightly firm wet sand or sometimes even in water. It's my own little temple. There is serenity and peace. I get my strength here.'

Sand training has enhanced the performance of many great athletes. Some of the best middle-distance men like Herb Elliott and Peter Snell have trained on sand. Even the legendary Edwin Moses, two-time Olympic champion, used to train on the beach, using hurdles. Top Indian athletes like Milkha Singh and Sriram Singh have also done some of their most useful training on the sandbanks of the river Yamuna in New Delhi. In her autobiography, Usha says, 'I have to take just twenty steps from my bed before I have sand beneath my feet. When I ran to the school, it was on sand. If I ran a household errand it was on sand. Every step I took was on sand. Unknowingly, I went through some very effective and rigorous training. Even the upper primary school, just a stone's throw from my house, had only a sandy playground. After this training on sand, running on tracks seems so simple. I literally float, as unlike sand, it offers no resistance.'

Running on sand before she took to serious running clearly gave Usha the competitive edge.

Usha set a national record at the State Athletics Meet at Kottayam in 1977. She garnered attention as a junior athlete in the National Inter State Meet at Kollam in 1978. She became the youngest Indian sprinter to enter the Olympics foray at the time. Usha was sixteen when she made her debut at the 1980 Moscow Olympic Games. Though she was eliminated at the heats, it was a landmark moment for India.

The same year, she made a mark by winning 4 gold medals in the 1980 Pakistan Open National Meet at Karachi. In 1982 she won a gold medal in the 200 m race and a bronze medal in the 100 m race in the World Junior Invitation Meet, currently known as the World Junior Athletics Championships, at Seoul. As a national appreciation towards her exemplary performance, she was awarded the Arjuna Award in 1983. And then, that epochal 'so near yet so far' moment of Indian sports came in the Los Angeles Olympics in 1984. She was awarded the Padma Shri in 1985. From here, the Payyoli Express was truly on the warpath—particularly at the Asian level.

As renowned sports journalist, K.P. Mohan, writes,

> On a stroll at the Jawaharlal Nehru Stadium in Delhi, back in 1984, coach O.M. Nambiar said rather prophetically, 'Now we can tackle anybody in Asia. Lydia (de Vega) will be no great challenge either. You will see what Usha can do in Jakarta.' They were back from the Los Angeles Olympics where P.T. Usha had written a new chapter in the country's athletics history...[15]

The confidence that Usha gained in finishing fourth in the Los Angeles Olympics contributed to her coach's optimism and prediction.

The reference was to the Asian Athletics Championships in Jakarta in 1985 and Lydia de Vega of the Philippines, the sprint champion of Asia then. The Filipino, popular throughout Asia, was the 100 m champion in the 1982 Asian Games in

---

[15]K.P. Mohan, 'P.T. Usha's tryst with the Asian Championships, the event that shaped her legacy', scroll.in, 4 July 2017

New Delhi, beating Usha and retaining her hold at the Asian Athletics Championships in Kuwait next year, without Usha in the fray. Jakarta provided Usha with the opportunity to parade her undisputed talent over a mix of events, not all of them pure sprints that she was specializing in since making her Olympic debut in Moscow at the age of sixteen.

A year before Los Angeles, in Kuwait, at the Asian Championships, Usha had added the 400 m to her repertoire, winning it on her first attempt, beating Lydia de Vega among others. Usha was literally the golden girl in the Indonesian capital. Four gold medals came in the individual event and the fifth one in the 4x400 m relay. Team India and Usha narrowly missed the sixth gold in the shorter relay—the team finishing with the bronze. Usha says, 'We were at Crystal Palace, London, for about three months during the preparatory phase. Shiny was with us in a batch of Indian athletes in London. We competed in meets in Europe and I went for the World Railways Meet in Czechoslovakia also. I won in four of the six meets that I competed in in Europe.'

Clearly, learning her lessons from the Los Angeles Olympics well, she had approached Jakarta with a strong base. She ran eleven races including the heats in the four individual events—100 m, 200 m, 400 m and 400 m hurdles, three days after the two relays in the Jakarta Meet. What startled Usha's adversaries was the variety of events she would participate in at the international meet.

P.T. Usha says, 'Normally, 100 m and 200 m are my events; these are the events I ran in during the 1982 Delhi Asian Games too. Slowly, 400 m was brought into my schedule as Nambiar sir wanted me to run the 400 m hurdles at the 1984 Olympics. Hurdles weren't completely new to me—I had run hurdles during my school days. I used to be fascinated by the beauty of hurdling— there was this athlete called Mercy who was a good hurdler, and I used to watch her and try out the event. Nambiar sir taught me hurdling, though we did not perfect my technique then. You might be aware that I had a solid base, having competed in different events in my formative years. Besides running and hurdling, I had also done long jump, high jump and shot-put.'

She further adds, 'As I moved up in my career, we started specializing in certain events. By the time the Asian Meet came along, I was good in all four individual events—100 m, 200 m, 400 m and 400 m hurdles. I was setting records in each of these events and did not want to drop any. I was physically fit and my willpower was never in question. I had trained hard and was very confident. Thanks to my fourth-place finish at the Los Angeles Olympics, I got the opportunity to run a few races in Europe—in Hungary, Czech Republic and Austria. Competing against the Europeans also made me bolder. So we decided to go for it at Jakarta; four individual events and two relay races.'

This again has to do with the grooming she received at the sports division and her athletic growth process in the formative years. Whether it was the district school championships or the national games, Usha always ended up competing in four or five events. She believed that competing in so many events benefitted her immensely.

She says in her autobiography, 'In a way, I have benefitted considerably by competing in a wide range of events. It developed my all-round ability. For hurdles and jumps, you need a lot of strength and flexibility, and I have worked for these in school.'[16]

The media often packages and markets sporting events building on rivalries. More often than not, this rivalry positioning turns out to be misplaced. The same was the case in Jakarta. It was not Lydia de Vega who finished second to Usha (11.64 sec after having set a national record of 11.39 sec in the semis) but Thai sprinter Ratjai Sripet (11.95 sec), with the Filipino third at 11.96 sec. Usha won the 200 m comfortably, and Lydia was beaten to the fifth place. Such a commendable performance sometimes raises doubts in people who have no faith. Adolf Hitler had closely scrutinized Dhyan Chand's stick to check whether he had applied

---

[16]P.T. Usha and Lokesh Sharma, *Golden Girl: The Autobiography of P.T. Usha*, Penguin, pg 91

glue to it after the latter had scored three goals to help India defeat Germany 8-1 and win gold in Berlin in 1936. Similarly, Usha had to go through a series of dope tests in Jakarta. She says, 'They were probably unconvinced that someone could win so many races. Each of the tests led to a delay of two to two and a half hours.'

With a wry smile on her face, the Indian queen of track and field, who created a sensation in Jakarta, says, 'Lydia was friendly with me, but in Jakarta, after every race, she and her father went to the authorities and appealed for my drug test. I was tested literally after each run.' And after Jakarta, it was time for the Seoul Asian Games in 1986. This was the epochal point in Indian sporting history—women sportspersons of the country surging ahead of their male counterparts.

Sprint queen P.T. Usha set the Seoul track blazing, winning an unprecedented 4 gold and 1 silver medal in the Games. She shattered the existing Games records in all of the events she took part in. For the first time, women athletes performed better than their male counterparts. For the first time, male athletes returned home without a gold. Indian athletes failed miserably in coping with the intense heat of the competition. They bagged just nine medals in the Games and were far behind the New Delhi Games tally. Women athletes won 7 of the 9 medals while the men could win only 2 bronze medals. This trend has continued ever since.

P.T. Usha says, 'Actually, one month before the Asian Games, I went and participated in the Moscow Goodwill Games. I struggled at the Goodwill Games due to the weather as well as the lack of preparation, and finished eighth. I came under fire from all quarters and people even wrote me off. I knew where I stood and I was determined to prove them wrong. That inspired me. I kept those criticisms in mind. I wanted to show the world that I had not gone anywhere. I was still there. I wanted to prove them wrong.

'We had a 475-member-strong contingent (for the Seoul Asian Games) and I was quite optimistic that we would do well this time. As you know, for athletic events, medals are awarded almost at the fag end of the Games. Shoulders began drooping as the gold column in our medal tally remained blank. It was then that my medals started coming in. I was happy in Seoul as I could lift the morale of my contingent. When I reached home, it gradually started sinking in...how my performance had contributed to lift the morale of the nation,' she says.

The twenty-two-year-old Usha was at the peak of her career during this edition of the Asian Games. Her gold medals came in the 200 m, 400 m, 400 m hurdles and the 4x400 m relay, while she had to settle for silver behind Lydia de Vega of Philippines in the 100 m, losing the race by a wafer-thin margin. She became a massive star in Korea with the crowds chanting her name every time she stepped out to compete. She became the sporting legend of the country forever.

Usha has 23 medals, including 14 gold, from the Asian Championships, from 1983 to 1998, the maximum for any athlete, male or female.

A heel injury meant Usha was unable to accomplish her cherished dream of winning an Olympic medal in 1988. She did continue to be the force at the Asian Games though, clinching 2 silver medals in the Beijing Asian Games in 1990. Post Beijing, she took a break from athletics. After giving birth to son Ujjwal in 1992, Usha staged a comeback to the track. She won a silver at the 1994 Asian Games in Hiroshima as part of the 4x400 m relay team.

After bidding adieu to the track, she is focusing her energies on shaping the career of budding athletes in her Usha School of Athletics. Usha decided to start her school to help Indian athletes overcome the shortcomings of the Indian sporting system and to help them succeed internationally. But she didn't realize then that even for someone with her credentials, between an idea and its execution lay a huge chasm.

There was little government assistance and no private sponsorship, even in a state like Kerala, having a proven track record in athletics. A leading Mumbai-based corporate house showed their interest, only to back out. She eventually managed to get the school off the ground in 2001, on cramped rented premises.

Slowly, things got better. In 2006, the Kerala government donated land for a new campus. Then Shobha Developers sponsored the construction of a new school building and the families of three Infosys founders—N.R. Narayana Murthy, Kris Gopalakrishnan and S.D. Shibulal—adopted athletes, committing themselves to bear their expenses. Finally, the central government sanctioned funds for the much-needed synthetic track. The journey continues. As she loved running on the beaches endlessly, she takes her trainees from the Usha School of Athletics to the Payyoli beach even today, to the beach that was witness to a legend taking shape.

'Look, the fact that people like you and your team still do come to interview me like this means a lot to me. It means that I must have done something great. About sports, yes, I am fortunate to pursue the occupation I love. There is nothing like experiencing victory and defeat on the track. And now, as a Guru, I am enjoying an extension of my favourite occupation—which I hope to continue for long,' Usha says.

Usha had no hero to look up to when she started. Has she got a hero now?

'Myself. Right through, I have been battling and competing with myself. And that self has been ahead always. If there's another hero, it must be Edwin Moses, whom I met for the first time in 1984 at Los Angeles,' she says. She has been, and is, a firm believer in hard work. When asked what is the one thing that she would like to change about her family, she says, 'More faith in hard work.'

Perseverance and hard work, being sincere in her approach and honest in her efforts has been the mantra of her life. Usha believes in the philosophy of karma, and when asked about her favourite author and book, she says, 'I cannot think of anyone beyond Ved Vyas. For me, the *Mahabharata* is the greatest literary work ever written. The *Ramayana* is another work that has influenced me. One of my favourite characters is Hanuman. It's because he symbolizes speed and loyalty. I have always believed that loyalty is a quality that should exist in human beings.'

Where does she see herself going from where she stands

today? What is her message to aspiring women sportspersons? And how can India emerge as a sporting nation?

About India's aspiration to become a sporting nation, Usha says, 'Firstly, see, when you go to European countries and other places, everyone likes athletics there. In our case, even when we have competitions, it's very difficult to invite people and fill up space. To do well in sports, we need to bring more and more awareness to people. Moreover, sports should be getting support from every quarter. If the media backs athletics and helps people understand the intricacies of the sport, a lot of sponsorships will come to the game. Right now, getting sponsorships is extremely difficult.

'Secondly, the system should not be such that first an athlete has to reach the senior level and then we will provide coaching. We have to catch them young, when they are thirteen years old, and then train them in the academies. Every state should have at least one state-of-the-art academy. We should ensure that the athletes get the best of the facilities. Food and kit are important, and their living conditions should be perfect. Every month their blood should be tested and health profile details checked. A proper record should thus be maintained, and accordingly, their group for participation decided, and exposure given. So, a proper system should be put in place right from the grassroots level.

'Thirdly, if someone is working sincerely to bring about a change and get results, they should be backed to the hilt. Unfortunately, despite showing that with a proper system in place a girl can win 11 medals (referring to Tintu Luka), enough help has not been forthcoming in my case. In our case and in our times, we lacked even basic facilities. Just because of the hard work, I could reach this level. I strongly feel that in our country we have lots of talent. If we start at a young age and if we do little things scientifically and systematically, we will be able to do well and bring an Olympic medal.'

Usha's message to the budding women athletes is loud and clear. 'Our country has loads and loads of talent. If you feel that you have quality, come forward, express yourself and do well in whatever you choose. Don't expect big things and every facility; do your work with sincerity. I am 100 per cent sure that you will achieve your target. Always remember, while you go through the peaks, everyone will be with you, but when you are in the trough, you will be a loner. You might raise the level of expectations, and when people will naturally start expecting more, a time will come when your performance will fail to meet their expectations. You may become vulnerable to negativity then, but you have to remain more and more positive in these times.

'However talented you may be, there is no substitute for hard work. In each of my practice sessions, I was ever willing for a few more rounds of the field or a few more exercises, even when my coach felt that it was enough for me for that session. Athletes have a rigid lifestyle and sometimes it gets on your nerves. It's your urge and craving that will help you to keep going in such times.'

When asked how she prepared to compete with the best in the world when she had no serious competition at home, she says, 'Winning made me more and more interested in athletics. Slowly, running became a part of my life. My only aim was to better my timing...my aim was never to defeat anybody. I only worked to improve my timing.'

It is with Usha that the 'Ready, Steady, Go' moment for Indian women in sports really started.

THREE

Ashwini Nachappa: India's Flo Jo

She ran like the wind, gazelle-like strides carrying her far away from hustling opponents as she beat the clock with ridiculous ease.

Silken strides hit the turf in a beautiful rhythm, the perfect motion synchronized with the rhythm with effortless ease as she sauntered down, leaving legends in her wake.

With copious amounts of good press, and the added incentive of out-running a legend of the sport and was Indian athletics' first and foremost giant-killer.

Athlete. Media darling. Social activist. Actor. Educator.

Ashwini Nachappa's story is like no other's.

If Kerala is God's own country, Karnataka is not far behind. Rapid industrial development, scenic natural beauty marked by abundant wildlife and exquisite beaches, pilgrimage destinations and renowned shopping malls—the state has enviable variety, all succinctly juxtaposed on the same topography. The state is a tourist's paradise on account of its hospitable natives, pleasant weather, lip-smacking cuisine and a well-connected transport system. Amongst the various must-visit places in the state is Coorg—referred to as the Kashmir of the south. Breathtaking hill stations, replete with picturesque natural beauty and cool weather, are the defining features of the place.

The widespread greenery, in sharp contrast with the clear blue sky and water, makes Coorg one of the most-visited hill stations of the country—especially during the scorching summer months.

Coorg is an excellent trekking destination due to the abundance of adventurous trails that go deep into the hills. There is something for everyone here. People from faraway places come here to get a reprieve from the lack of greenery synonymous with metropolitan cities—the lush green forests here bring in a breath of fresh air. Nature enthusiasts specifically visit this place to get a glimpse of the expansive teakwood forests and coffee plantations.

That its men are brave and the women beautiful is a blanket statement about Coorg.[1] More importantly, women's empowerment and love for sports are the defining hallmarks of the beauty of Coorgi society. As Pattamada Sundar Muthanna writes in a coffee-table book on Coorg tourism, the Kodavas or Coorgis are ethnic minorities who are largely privileged. A pleasant colonial hangover stays with the people, who enjoy a good life with evening drinks, golf and hockey.[2] 'Easily one of the most martial cultures in the country, these are a people who ritually worship their guns and swords. Interestingly, till a few decades ago, the birth of a male child was marked with a gunshot, announcing to the world the arrival of a warrior.'[3]

The people's right to carry arms was originally granted by the Kodagu kings, who did not maintain a standing army, but called on the people to fight when an invasion threatened. The right was formalized by the British when they exempted the Coorgis from the Arms Act. Today the Coorgis and a few other communities have the right to own guns without having to go through the process of getting a license.'[4]

If the birth of a male child is marked with gunshots, it is evident how women are respected deeply in Coorg's liberal society, known for its egalitarian attitude towards the former. Here the birth of a girl child is a cause for celebration and the loud ringing of a bell announces her arrival into the world. In

---

[1]'Kodavas of Coorg: Bold, beautiful and brainy', *DNA*, 13 November 2011
[2]Ibid.
[3]Ibid.
[4]Ibid.

household matters, women's decisions hold sway. The highly educated women of Coorg are a respected horde in the social mosaic of the place.

During important events such as weddings and other ceremonies, women play a crucial role. At weddings, for instance, women bless couples along with men, in lieu of the conventional blessings of couples by Brahmin priests. Kodavatakk, the Coorgi language, has no word for dowry or prostitution—both of which are absent among the Coorgis. The general level of culture and education among the women of Coorg has always been higher when compared to the other communities in other parts of the state. Women know their rights and are treated well in the family. A widow may remarry, which is quite common and has always been acceptable in Coorgi culture, and can participate in important social occasions such as marriages and naming ceremonies. A Kodava woman's rights are well protected. Clearly, the hand that rocks the cradles rules the world in Coorg.

Kodavas' love for sports has got a strong history and legacy. They have a long history of association with the game of field hockey. More than fifty Kodavas have represented India in international hockey tournaments. M.P. Ganesh, M.M. Somaiah, B.K. Subramani, A.B. Subbaiah, K.K. Poonacha, amongst others, belong to this illustrious list. The Coorgis' contribution to the sporting landscape of the country other than in hockey has also been seminal. Ashwini Nachappa in athletics, Rohan Bopanna in lawn tennis, Joshna Chinappa in squash, Jagat and Anita Nanjappa in motorcycling, C.C. Machaiah in boxing and P.G. Chengappa and M.R. Poovamma in badminton, to name a few, have made the country proud. However, to understand the Kodavas' passion for sports, one has to attend an annual Kodava hockey festival.

In 1997, Pandanda Kuttappa, a prominent Kodagu, decided to organize a hockey tournament for the different clans. From sixty clans that participated then, the number has swelled to more than two hundred at present. In a combined team, women are equal participants and married women play for the clans they have married into. Each year, families of one clan pool their resources to organize and host the tournament, which is played out over a month, with elimination matches held daily. One has to be there to soak in the festive and vibrant atmosphere during these matches. There are food stalls and other pavilions; the men come dressed in traditional robes and the women in sarees draped in the special Coorgi style.

When our crew went to cover the tournament, it was held at an elegant bamboo stadium in Ponnampet, erected by the Maneyapanda clan. The stadium could accommodate 25,000 spectators. Almost everyone from the hills turned up for the inauguration, all in ceremonial clothing. Entry was free, and the fun gathering of the disciplined people was an amazing sight. Apart from the Kodavas' love for women and sports, some of their customs and lifestyles are truly remarkable. We know of their folklore that celebrates the involvement of women in cultivating the land and reaping the harvest; of their confident initiatives in love affairs and their bravery in dealing with clan enemies, and most importantly, eking out a living in inhospitable terrain inhabited by wild animals.

The ballad, 'Polladevira Aiyappa', tells of Chiyavva of the Kelappanda Okka clan who encounters a tigress when she goes to the jungle to fetch wood. She kills the tigress and captures her cubs. Then, referring to the social practice of honouring a man who kills a tiger, she demands to be similarly honoured by her community. We get a glimpse of the woman as we see the portrait in the gallery leading up to the beautiful house of one of the beautiful Coorgi sportswomen, Ashwini Nachappa. In this portrait, both her legs are hanging in the air—with the lovely face sporting a determined look of the tigress in action.

As we come to know her further in our subsequent conversations, we find a metaphor, similar to the women in the ballad, who, after defeating P.T. Usha twice, staked her claim for her rightful place within the sporting fraternity. Her fight for honour, athletics and clean sports has continued thereafter. As an Olympic athlete, a Tollywood actress, a social worker and an educationist, the transitions for Ashwini Nachappa have been seamless. The Coorgi girl played the game on the field and beyond the field, in actual life, with great versatility.

We, as journalists, are trained to do as much research as possible on the subject and the personality we are focusing on. Before her warm and infectious smile greeted us, our eyes got fixed on a portrait akin to the ballad, 'Polladevira Aiyappa'. The portrait encapsulated the beauty of short-distance running and the beauty of a tigress in her full glory, cutting the air with her gentle and determined posture and expressing her intention to break free. While our eyes were glued to the portrait, Ashwini appeared in person, informing us that it had been gifted to her by a close photographer friend. As my (Abhishek Dubey's) eyes made a seamless transition from the portrait to her physical self, there certainly was a fast forward of more than a decade, but the transition seemed to be seamless.

She certainly looked older than the girl in the photograph, but that grace, that determination, that confidence, that attitude— all were intact. There was an attitude in her stride. There was confidence in the way she carried herself. 'Please have these refreshments; you will like them. I will be back in a few minutes,' saying this, she started moving up the stairs.

As we got ready for the interview, she came back, elegantly dressed. Though things are changing fast, in our experience of sports journalism, we have come across many talented sportspersons who are brilliant on the field of action but shy before the camera. They do take their own time to open up. In India, this holds true for sports other than cricket. Cricket in India dawned with the television age—which emphasized on lights, camera and action in terms of appearance in the post-presentation ceremony, sponsorship and advertisement shoot, public appearances and then gyaan as experts during matches.

Though the scenario is changing fast in sports other than cricket, a lot of catching up has to be done. Based on this assumption, I started with a cliché. I told her, 'Relax, you can take your own time for the answers; you can have retakes if you are not satisfied with your answer. This is not a live show, but a recorded one.'

Cutting me short, she politely but firmly replied, 'Even while I acted in films, while delivering my dialogues, I hated retakes. I don't believe in retakes, both in real and reel life.' She was indeed different; we understood instantly, and the tone was set for the session.

'How did things start?'

'Actually, when I look back at things, I realize that my name, Ashwini, means a mare, and a mare is primarily meant to run. Way back when we were small, my dad used to work for the Birlas in Kolkata. We used to live there, my sister, my mom, my dad and myself. In 1975, we moved down to Bangalore, now Bengaluru, basically to pursue education, because at that point of time there were a number of factory lockouts in Kolkata, which was then Calcutta. Though we are from Coorg, many of our relatives, including most of our cousins, lived in Bangalore as it was closer home. It so happened that our house was situated near a continuous stretch of estates in Bangalore, and as we were very small, my mother would not allow us to play in the streets.

'So we used to go to the stadium in the evening and play with our friends there. And this is how my love for the game began. When we were seven-eight years old, after school we used to go to the Sree Kanteerava Stadium, which was nearby, where we regularly played. There used to be a coach named Mohinder Singh Gill and he used to bribe six-seven kids who used to come from the schools, with Nutrine sweets. Basically, it was the lure of every extra sweet that prodded Pushpa and me. And this is how the journey began. I ran for sweets and then for medals and then certificates and awards. And so there was really no looking back after that,' says Ashwini.

Ashwini's growth process as an outstanding athlete had a solid initial foundation. In her supportive parents, she got encouragement to give wings to her sporting desires.

'I feel that for any child in any sport or in any field, for that matter, to be successful requires encouragement from home. Be it sports, music, art, you name it. I think both my sister and I were very very fortunate that we had very encouraging parents. Though my dad worked very hard in Kolkata, earning and living for the three of us who were in Bangalore, my mother took the onus of seeing to it that we got the best of parenthood. This type of encouragement really became a motivating force for us to actually go ahead and do well in life.'

Her foundation was solid and her parents left no stone unturned in providing her the right atmosphere to succeed. Ashwini was born on 21 October 1967. At the age of six she moved to Bangalore. Since the age of six or seven, Ashwini started beating boys of her class in 50 m races. Since then, she had an intense desire to race like the wind. Her mother was her motivator and so was her PT teacher, who encouraged her a lot.

Professional athletes who make their names in the sporting landscape have got one thing in common. They start early and start moving up the age-group ladder with breathtaking speed and style. Ashwini was no different. In the 1982 Asian Games, she was the youngest member of the Indian camp in Patiala. She was studying in class VIII then. She has been in this field since then.

What is the thing that has helped her enjoy the journey most since she was young?

'Personally, if on hindsight I sit down to analyse why I did not take anything up, other than athletics, I see only one reason. I was personally the athlete who started winning at a young age. Be it school sports in Bangalore or the Karnataka State Meet, I always won as a young child. I think the first time I took part in the nationals, representing Karnataka, was when I was barely twelve years old. In the All India Nationals, I won the first medal for Karnataka in 100 m. I remember, the then chief minister R. Gundu Rao came and gave me ₹1000, which, at that point of time, was a good amount. In the Mangalore Nationals, Anand Shetty and I emerged as the 'fastest man and woman', and I ran the 400 m for the very first time, finishing behind P.T. Usha, Shiny Wilson, Vandana Shanbagh and M.D. Valsamma. You know, these things were such an encouragement that I did not look at any other option, and one thing followed another.'

This spirited woman of Indian athletics, with her attractive personality, backed by tremendous and impactful performances in varied fields, is today the role model for many.

As American novelist Stephen Chbosky said, 'We are who we are for a lot of reasons. And maybe we will never know most of them.'[5] Despite this, we remain in the eternal quest of getting behind those reasons. And one of the things we try to figure out are the men or women who inspired, motivated, shaped and backed the journey of those who are successful. We call them role models.

Did she have a role model when she started? If yes, who was it?

When asked this question, Ashwini says, 'As a young child, when I started at the age of eight or nine years, my role models were the people who were the best at that point of time, and those who were training at the stadium where I used to play. Mr Saldanha and Mr A.P. Ramaswamy were two of them. When I was eight years old, we had no exposure, there was no television and we didn't talk about role models. In fact, we didn't know what role models were all about. But as I started evolving as a person and athlete, at every step there was a role model. First and foremost, my mother was the greatest role model for her determination and sacrifice. Then there was Florence Griffith Joyner and Erin Ashford; I think both these sprinters really made an impact in my life. Having said that, I don't think and believe that we should emulate them, as each one of us is a separate individual. But I wanted to achieve success in my field as Griffith

---

[5]Quoted from goodreads.com

Joyner had achieved in her field. And that driving force clearly enhances your performance. If you have that drive at that point of time in your life, it helps you to move in your goal to excellence. This is, I think, how my role models came about.'

As Stephen Chobsky says in *The Perks of Being a Wallflower*, 'We cannot choose where we come from, but we can choose where we go from there.'[6] Ashwini clearly was fortunate to get a good environment to take off into the athletics universe. Many of us are not that fortunate. Most of the women athletes who came from Kerala before her, and to an extent even today, were certainly not as fortunate. But what Ashwini Nachappa's journey teaches us is that we certainly do have a say in and control over where we go in our life's journey. She had made a seamless transition from being an international athlete to moving to the silver screen and from philanthropy and education to coaching and activism.

Ashwini Nachappa's serious athletics journey started when she was being trained by veteran coach N. Lingappa. In one of the many glaring ironies connected with recognition in Indian sports, Lingappa received the Dronacharya Award at the age of ninety-one, in 2014. It took us so many years to recognize the contribution of one of the towering stalwarts of Indian sports. Lingappa was an athlete himself and represented the erstwhile Mysore state for seven consecutive years in the National Games. A 10,000 m walker, he was also part of the contingent for the 1954 Manila Asian Games.

As he said in an interview after receiving the Dronacharya Award, 'I won the silver medal in the 10,000 m walk during the first National Games in Delhi in 1954. I was also selected for the Asian Games in Manila the same year, but sadly my event was cancelled.'[7]

Lingappa then cleared the coaching exam conducted by the Athletics Federation of India in 1956. This was followed by

---

[6]Quoted from goodreads.com
[7]N. Lingappa said this in an interview with Doordarshan.

three stints as an assistant coach for three Olympic Games from 1956–1964. He said that the stint with the Indian team at the Olympics helped him hone his skills as a coach. 'I learnt a lot in my stint. It helped me understand the needs of my wards and helped harness their talents.'[8] However, life was not easy for the nonagenarian. He waged a long and arduous battle, first with the Karnataka government, over his pension, which he got much later. This was followed by his countless written applications to the Centre for the Dronacharya Award. When finally he was conferred the award, some of the journalists had a query for his son, L. Nagaraj.

Would he have shot off another letter to the centre if he was ignored that year?

'After years of being snubbed, I asked my father to stop writing to the Centre. But he insisted that he would do so until his death.'

The coaching honour he received was unlikely to change Lingappa's daily pilgrimage. This became apparent when he said, 'Despite the Dronacharya, life will go on... I will be travelling on my TVS Scooty every morning to the Kanteerava Stadium to train my students.'[9]

The seniormost athletics coach in the country had wards such as Ashwini Nachappa, D.Y. Biradhar, Satish Pillay and Uday K. Prabhu, to name a few. His wards revere him for his discipline, dedication and passion—the virtues that helped Ashwini Nachappa take rapid strides in the initial phases of her career.

Ashwini Nachappa represented India in three South Asian Federation Games. She won 2 silver medals in 1984, 2 silver medals in 1986 and 3 gold medals in 1988. In the 1986 Asian Games in South Africa, Ashwini stood sixth in long jump. In the 1990 Asian Games held in China, she was part of the Indian team that won a silver medal in the 4x400 m relay race. She represented the country at the IAAF World Championships as a part of the relay team in Rome in 1987 and in Tokyo in 1991. In

---

[8]N. Lingappa said this in an interview with Doordarshan.
[9]'Better late than never: 91-year-old athletics coach N. Lingappa finally receives Dronacharya Award', *Indian Express*, 30 August 2014

her chequered career, she took part in four Asian Track and Field Championships. In Indonesia (1985), she won the bronze medal in relay and in Singapore (1987), she earned a silver for the same event. She bagged 2 silver medals in New Delhi (1989), and in yet another event held in Malaysia (1991), she was part of the relay team which won gold for India. Irrespective of these medals, Ashwini is most remembered for two races in her career.

Ashwini rose to fame when she outran the legendary P.T. Usha, not once but twice in the 1980s. This is the best acknowledged feat of her career as an Indian athlete. She outran champion P.T. Usha during the 1991 Open Nationals at New Delhi. Within the span of two weeks, her dominance over P.T. Usha hit the headlines again, when she beat Usha at the international event permit meet in New Delhi.

'With regard to beating P.T. Usha, there was a process involved. Right from 1984–85, when we ran and whenever Usha ran with me, it was given that she would get gold and I would land up getting silver. So, for me, it was more of doing a mind training and working, working more mentally than physically to be able to achieve that. I was very fortunate to come across Rupen Das who was a sports psychologist and who had come back from the US at that point of time. He saw me running in the stadium and he said, "Ashwini, can I offer you this (some tips) and would you just give it a try?"

'I am known for taking risks. I jumped at this opportunity and said, "Yes, why not?" And then I realized that no amount of camp training and being under coaches tells you that it's all about mind being over matter and how we strengthen ourselves mentally. Mental training is as important as physical training, setting targets and goals at every step and at every phase. And so I actually did mind training, visualizing the race. I did not visualize Usha as my competitor, but I competed against the time I set for myself. And so, running against time and trying to achieve the target really helped me in beating P.T. Usha.

'The first time when I beat her, everyone took this as a fluke, but when this happened the second time, they accepted this fact. Two weeks later, in an international permit meet, also in New Delhi, when I finished behind a Russian, pushing Usha to the third spot, the critics were silenced for good,' she says with an assured look and confidence today.

However, Ashwini feels that beating Usha then was not the only achievement in her athletics career. The selection in the 1988 Olympics trials in Bangalore and being part of the team to Seoul for the mega event was Ashwini's biggest moment.

'It's any sportsperson's dream to be part of the nation's Olympics team,' says Ashwini.

However, the experience was a sour one for her. Kept as reserve for the 4x400 m relay, she did not get a chance to participate in the Games.

The Indian relay team failed to get past the first round. Reflecting on this, Ashwini says in one of her interviews, 'There is nothing to beat the one that came at the relay trials during the Seoul Olympics. We were five of us—Shiny, the two Vandanas, Rao and Shanbagh, Mercy Kuttan and myself—competing. There were many pushing Usha's case, and on the day before the event, we were called for one last trial. But neither Usha nor her coach O.M. Nambiar turned up, which only resulted in the bigwigs calling for another trial in the evening. Vandana Rao, Shanbagh and myself skipped the trial and went to watch our hockey team in action. Subsequently, Mercy Kuttan and I were relegated to the reserves, and Usha was brought in. Our relay team was out in the very first round.'[10]

Ashwini was unable to participate in the Barcelona Olympics in 1992 as an injury kept her out of the selection process.

Professional competitive sports is tough, and there are times in an athlete's life when they think of giving up. Did the thought of giving up her career cross her mind?

Ashwini stares into vacuum in an introspective mood and says,

---

[10]Ashwini Nachappa said this in an interview with Doordarshan.

'Not really, I never thought of giving up. Every hurdle and every failure has been challenging. To bounce back from there, I have looked at every hurdle and failure from that aspect. Nobody has taught me that, but I always thought that for me it's a challenge personally to rise up, dust myself and get back into the business. As far as giving up sports is concerned, I was contemplating it just before the Barcelona Olympics—whether to go ahead or continue in sports, or whether to focus on films. At that time, when I was not at the peak of my career, yes, I really had doubts whether I should pursue sports or not. I think I took a good call at that point of time, to move away from sports, which has given me everything, to look for opportunities and avenues in other areas that I wanted to pursue.'

Ashwini decided to hang up her boots at the right time. Not many athletes are able to do this, as they are unable to reconcile with the fact that their time is up. Perhaps sports is the only thing they have dreamt of and done since childhood, and the very thought of 'what after sports' makes them procrastinate to call it quits. Financial security, along with the ability and confidence to think of life beyond the sports grounds, are the two essential requirements for any athlete to call it a day at the right time. Ashwini possessed both these virtues in abundance.

As Ashwini made forays into other avenues after leaving the athletics track, the challenges were many. But she never shied away from taking up new challenges. 'I think that without challenges life is meaningless, and all of us who have achieved any success in any profession have faced challenges and hurdles. I was no exception. Challenges were many, financial, emotional and professional. But I think they help you evolve as a person because those experiences are something that you carry everywhere you go. You cannot acquire experiences within the four walls of the classroom. This has been my experience and this has made me what I am today. I owe it to sports. Because it is a unique experience,' says Ashwini.

What separates Ashwini from the athletes of her previous

generation is the way she explored diverse fields.

Ashwini Nachappa set the tracks ablaze not just with her performances but also her impeccable fashion sense. She was dubbed the glamour girl of Indian athletics by the media. She tried her luck in films. She had a reasonably successful career there. She acted in five films, *Ashwini, Miss 420, Inspector Ashwini, Andaroo Andare* and *Aadarsham*, with the same director. Her biographical film titled *Ashwini* gave her the Andhra Pradesh Nandi Award for best debut actress. She played the role of a sportswoman in this film but tried out other characters in her later films.

'Though I did just five films, it was a wonderful experience. I even played a cop in *Inspector Ashwini*. The award for the best newcomer from the Andhra Pradesh government and the Tamil Cine Film Critics Award were very encouraging for me,' says Ashwini.

She has also been involved in social work and education. She is the trustee of an NGO, Parikrama, which works to improve the lot of slum children as well as orphans in Bangalore. Her desire to take education and sports forward prompted Ashwini to start her own school, Karaumbiah's Academy for Learning and Sports, in Coorg.

'I wanted to do something positive for Kodagu, my hometown. With the mission to instil a strong sporting culture in the rural areas of the country, we launched Karaumbiah's Academy for Learning and Sports at Gonikoppal, a small town in Kodagu.' Ashwini's Sports Foundation in the school provides training in various sporting disciplines such as athletics, hockey and swimming. 'I am of the firm belief that encouraging community sports and building a following outside cities is important to attract youngsters to sports.' The best sportspersons from her school are being offered college seats by reputed institutions. The academy is named after her husband, Datta Karaumbiah, a former junior India hockey player, now engrossed in his business and institution.

How has the woman from Coorg been able to do all this?

'Though sports is what I have always been associated with, education is also necessary. I have been able to have a successful career outside sports because I was fortunate enough to have a college education. Many of the people I competed with and against have not been so fortunate. That's why I decided to start a combined school and sports academy.'

Ashwini has shaped herself as the 'woman with a cause'. In recent years she has turned her attention to promoting clean sport. She is the founding member of Clean Sports India, that aims to facilitate better management of Olympic sports in India and discourage drug use among athletes. She joined hands with Mercy Kuttan and Vandana Rao to uphold the integrity of sports in the country. The glamour girl of Indian athletics has successfully lived through many roles.

Why did people draw comparisons between the great Florence Griffith Joyner and her?

'Well, being compared to Flo Jo was great, as she was one of my role models at that point of time. But this was the name given by the press. I always felt that I need to be different both on and off the field, and that is why I feel my media friends called me by this name,' says Ashwini.

The ESPN Classics Sports Century series introduces Florence Griffith Joyner with the following words, 'With her outrageous looks and lightning speed, Florence Griffith Joyner mesmerized the world. Her racing attire consisted of a variety of outfits— some lace, some fluorescent, some bearing one leg. Her nails, sometimes longer than four inches, became a trademark.' In the words of Phil Hersh of the *Chicago Tribune*, 'Flo Jo was someone who wanted to make a fashion statement, as well as do it while running so fast you could barely see the fashion.'[11]

Comparing Ashwini Nachappa to one of the all-time legends who still holds the world record in the 100 m and 200 m events is certainly a tall order. But for the way Ashwini added beauty

---

[11]*Kris Schwartz*, 'Flo Jo Made Speed Fashionable', ESPN, accessed 2 September 2019

and romance to running, and shifted gears with élan, accepting new challenges in life, she has been the Flo Jo for thousands of aspiring Indian women athletes over the years.

Where does the Indian Flo Jo stand in the Indian athletics firmament?

Historically, the 1980s symbolized the major decisive upheavals in Indian sports. Kapil Dev's daredevils had stunned the cricketing world by winning the World Cup in England. That this was not a fluke became clear when almost the same team, albeit under a different captain, won the Benson and Hedges Cup and became the Champion of Champions in Australia. That the trend was there to stay became palpably clear when the Indian subcontinent, propelled by India, hosted the first-ever World Cup outside England.

In 1982, India hosted the Asian Games and the birth of the colour television coincided with this. Starting with 1982, the Indian women athletics brigade started catching the attention of the world with surprising regularity. M.D. Valsamma was one of the stars who won gold in the 400 m hurdles. The Indian women's hockey team also made up for the ignominy suffered by the men's team that was trounced 7-1 in the finals by Pakistan. The phenomenon of the Indian women athletes starting to make their mark got a decisive boost with the Los Angeles Olympics in 1984. Then, the Indian contingent left for Seoul.

An *India Today* cover story on the event further indicates the direction the wind was blowing in. The cover story read,

> For the Indian contingent, there will be pressure on two counts. For one, there is the medal tally of 1982 to live up to—57—the highest ever by India. Further, TV and the interest stirred by the Delhi Asiad means that the public expectations from the Indian squad will be greater than before. And the question that will be most frequently asked until 5 October, when the Games end, is: Where does India figure on the medal chart? In 1982, India acquired 21 of its medals from track and field events: this time too, athletics—with 42 golds

for the taking—is certain to provide the largest contribution. But there will be one major difference. The last time around, men accounted for 13 medals, 3 of them gold, out of 21. In this Asiad, however, the hopes are largely pinned on the women who dominated the Indian contingent's performance late last year at the Asian Athletics Meet in Jakarta.[12]

The dawn of the women's era in the Indian sporting horizon was loud and clear. The fact that it was not a mere flash in the pan became all the more clear with the Jakarta Asian Athletics Meet and subsequently, the 1986 Seoul Asian Games. Angel Mary Joseph, Valsamma, Usha and Shiny Abraham were at the forefront of the Kerala surge, while Karnataka produced the first glamour girls of Indian sports in Ashwini Nachappa, Reeth Abraham and Vandana Rao.

This trio could not match the medal-winning feats of the Kerala counterparts, but were daring in their performance and captured the media glare with their looks and outfits. Indian sportswomen had started making the right noises, both on and off the field. The present generation of women superstars and budding sportswomen owe their present success, both on and off the field, to them.

Like the impeccable journey of Indian women in sports, the journey of Ashwini Nachappa continues. However, the time to wrap up our interview and discussion session was nearing. But before signing off, she had a message for all those who have been a part of her incredible journey, 'I want to attribute my success to all my coaches, right from the day I started as an eight-year-old child, from Mohinder Singh Gill, to Purushottam Ray, to Lingappa and Abraham sir. Each one of them taught me, which helped me improve in sports and life.'

Ashwini Nachappa indeed is the living example of the beauty of women in sports. A beauty from the perspective of Eleanor

---

[12]Sreekant Khandekar, '10th Asian Games in Seoul: How well will India perform?', *India Today*, 13 February 2014

Roosevelt when he said, 'No matter how plain a woman may be, if truth and honesty are written across her face, she will be beautiful.' A beauty from the canvas of Kahlil Gibran who said, 'Beauty is not in the face; beauty is a light in the heart.' A beauty from the angle of a reality check provided by Marilyn Monroe when she said, 'Boys think that girls are like books. If the cover doesn't catch their eye, they don't bother to read what is inside.'

The portrait that attracted us while entering her house was the beautiful cover. But, more beautiful were her achievements, her demeanour and her versatility—the intent to explore and excel.

FOUR

Karnam Malleswari:
The Iron Lady

Grip. Bend. Inhale. Lift!

Lifting twice her bodyweight. Would you try lifting a panda? Or a reindeer?

Every day. Morning. Noon. Evening. With a break of only thirty days every year, for a decade.

World champion. Yet, ignored and uncared-for in a country mired in sporting obscurity.

Critics and disbelievers sniping forever, with rumours of doping.

An Indian woman climbed Everest. Another took the prime minister's chair.

But will *she* be able to do it? An Olympic medal for a country used to sporting mediocrity?

No lipstick, no fancy outfits. No make-up either, to conceal the scars the iron left on her throat.

No accolades, or acknowledgement. No respect.

Detractors pushing in for the kill, with reports of her having beer and fried food before the Games!

The national media contingent flocks to the hockey match while she steps forward for the lift of her life.

Ten years of toil. Joints. Muscles. Sinews. Pain. Pain. Pain.

Walks to the bar. Looks at it, stares at it. Sniff or grunt? Somewhere in between...

Exhales. Rubs palms firmly. Shuts eyes...

Adjusts grip. Bends.

Breathes in. Breathes out...

137.5 kg. More than double her weight... Think about it.

And lift she does...the bar landing on her neck... She is dizzy...

Uncoiled muscles push for the final assault. It is over her head...

And she does it. Blue ribbon coiling down to a bronzed sphere that she clutches in her hand...

Karnam Malleswari honoured her nation. What did the nation give her back?

Indian women have excelled in fields as diverse as agriculture, nursing, hospitality, law, administration, politics, social service, business administration, entrepreneurship and even prison reforms.

There's hardly a field where a woman's worth hasn't been proven. But no one in a hundred years has arduously toiled to win an Olympic medal like this woman from an obscure village in north Andhra Pradesh. The first Indian woman on an Olympic podium. The first to shimmy away from multitudes of detractors and naysayers, fight a non-existent, recalcitrant system, and bring glory to India. She is Karnam Malleswari.

Malleswari was within sniffing distance of the ultimate Olympic dream—India's first individual gold, at the Sydney Olympics. Sixteen grams of that glittering metal that would perhaps elevate the worth of sports in India, a sporting nation that had rejoiced each time the men's hockey team dazzled one and all to become Olympic champions. Hockey had acquired a place of pride in independent India's sporting legacy. But even those triumphs had since dried up, and the wait for a sporting miracle seemed eternal. Till Malleswari came along.

While the gold medal slipped through her grasp, she would emerge as the first-ever Indian woman to win an Olympic medal.

Malleswari was a supremely confident performer. But the ecosystem surrounding her did not share her conviction. The trend continued. Her Olympic glory could have been used as the legacy to boost India's medal count in the discipline of weightlifting in the coming years. Alas! That was not to happen.

A total of 199 countries participated in the Sydney Olympics. Along with them came many doubters who had dismissed her as a forgotten chapter. But she made history. Prior to her departure for Sydney, one of India's premier news magazines had given her poor press. It had hurled allegations about her drinking beer. She was criticized for being overweight and weak of resolve. Consequently, her family called her up to probe, even questioning her eating habits. But the spunky Malleswari made the very same magazine eat humble pie by ensuring they gave her a banner headline eulogizing her achievement upon her return.

Only four of the forty-four Indian journalists who were there to cover the Games showed up to watch her lift. Only three Indian athletes who were part of the contingent went to cheer for her. On the contrary, there was a noisy throng when the hockey team played. Even while she was lifting, and her competition was on, just two hours away from her epic lift, she was a nobody.

And then, she won. And as if on cue, the neglect and derision were forgotten in a jiffy as the Indian officials accompanying the contingent started their chest-thumping, flocking around the champion, claiming 'we did it'. Did they?

And immediately, it's the irony that would lay itself bare for anyone who cared to see—people back home in medal-hungry India didn't even know about Malleswari's achievement for more than two hours after her lift to glory! Add to this the irony of India's national television telecasting a repeat of India's men's hockey match against Australia, while Malleswari fought for the glory of Indian sports!

Recalling this, Hansraj Tyagi, Malleswari's father-in-law, said in an interview, 'It was around one in the afternoon. Turning on the television to see if her event would be telecast, I sat through the repeat of the hockey match even as Malleswari went for the lift of her life. I did not have a number, or else I would have called the television channel to check.' Tyagi remembers lying in wait, exasperated at not being able to watch an event that would go on to shatter all stereotypes and create history in Indian sports. Tyagi managed to hear the news of Malleswari's epic feat later, and when Rajesh, Malleswari's husband, called a while later, Tyagi told him about her extraordinary feat and it took Rajesh some time to believe. 'It took us all some time for it to sink in', says Rajesh, such was the magnitude of what had been achieved on that day.

The morning of 21 September 2000 was like any other at the Games village. Except for one thing. The magic medal. The one that other athletes from her contingent wanted to touch. The reason why the prime minister had called and the faxes started flowing in. Yet, she seemed to be oblivious to it all. She didn't even wear her medal at the press conference after the final. It was wrapped around her coach Leonid Taranenko's neck.

Her medal was not with her during the press conference the very next day as well. Her reply to this was, 'It's lying next to the picture of my Bhagwan.'

Subsequently, there were occasions when she was seen wearing the medal. She wore it for the newshounds who maligned her without verifying their facts, at the time when all she needed was encouragement. She wore it for those very officials who had passed snide remarks, calling her a tourist. In a nutshell, she wore her medal for all those who were not convinced about her abilities.

Malleswari didn't really need to wear the medal for herself. She was fully convinced of her abilities. For ten years she had lifted weights, on a relentless pursuit, morning, afternoon and evening. With intermittent breaks totalling a mere twelve months out of the 120! During those ten years she went to bed each night with every muscle in her body complaining and every joint rebelling.

Pain is an inevitable part of weightlifting. Weightlifting as a sport has an inbuilt image full of ironies about itself. On one hand, we see the muscles of the weightlifters swell, expand and grow under the exertion of a lift—which looks alarming and is a moment of complete incredulity. The sport has as much charm as watching a clock tick. But then, lifting for glory isn't your regular sport. This was, and remains to this day, a sport of pain, of suffering; a sport for the remarkably tough. Bodies and minds go through never-ending torture and exhaustion to the point of giving in, till a champion is born.

But Malleswari carried herself through these times, confident of her own ability, with an impeccable work ethic that made clear her purpose and the effort behind the grind and sacrifice. Every weightlifter follows a ritual. They will walk to the bar, look at it, stare it down, breathe, grunt, rub their hands, contemplate, close their eyes, adjust their grip, bend, look up, breathe again and then heave. But not Karnam Malleswari.

Once she was asked, 'Why are you in such a hurry as you approach and why don't you feel the need to think, contemplate and visualize like others?'[1]

Her reply was, 'Arre, what's there to think? I do it every day.' And it's this attitude that made the woman who weighed 69.90 kg then lift 130 kg—which is almost the weight of two persons like herself—over her head. It's this confidence that made her the third-best female lifter in that weight category in the world. She won it. She had earned it. She knew her worth. Why would she need to wear the medal all the time to show her worth?

We set off for Yamunanagar in Haryana, her current location, to relive Sydney 2000. A shy soft-spoken kid, daughter of a cop from the boondocks of Andhra Pradesh who started her quest at the age of twelve, what made Karnam Malleswari the champion she became? We wanted to talk to her about The Moment. But more than the medal and the moment, we wanted to understand what it takes to be Karnam Malleswari.

The daughter of a police constable, Malleswari began weightlifting when she was not yet a teenager. Neelamsetty Appanna, who coached a young Malleswari at the Oosavanipeta village in Srikakulam district, northern Andhra Pradesh, said in an interview after her Sydney medal, 'She had the never-say-die

---

[1]Karnam Malleswari said this in an interview with DD Sports for the documentary *If I Can, So Can You* in 2014 in collaboration with the SAI.

attitude.' Opting for a career in weightlifting and giving formal education a go by may seem daring and unconventional to us. But for her it wasn't a difficult decision.

Lifting the barbells was a way of life in her village, and Malleswari, the third among six children, was born into a family of weightlifters. Of the five sisters, four have made their mark in weightlifting, while Karan Madhvi, the fifth sibling, has the regret of not taking up the sport, deep inside her.

However, from lifting weights in her village to a podium finish at the greatest sporting show was not easy. When she started off at Oosavanipeta, she had to make do with bare minimum equipment to practise, and it was no different even when she went to the town closest to it, Amudalavasa, a quaint little place situated in the Srikakulam district of the state of Andhra Pradesh.

She seldom had money to travel to and participate in national meets. District weightlifting officials came to her aid, though not often enough. The day before we were leaving for Yamunanagar to interview her, we had a chance meeting with a veteran sports journalist who has known her for years. He shared his memories of her being an introvert, some ten years before her moment of glory in the Sydney Games.

The teenage weightlifter used to go, with her sister Mahalakshmi, to a small room at the Karnail Singh Stadium so that they could train with other weightlifters. The sisters would train in the morning, rest a while in the afternoon, and return in the evening for more training. In between, they spent time cooking, washing and attending to chores.

But Malleswari made her mark soon enough. Nurtured under a special area games project of the Sports Authority of India (SAI), she would go on to join the national camp in 1990, and four years on she was a world champion in the 54 kg class weight category.

In the World Championships held in Turkey, she won the silver. And a quirk of fate intervened almost immediately as the gold medal winner, Chinese lifter Wang Shen, was disqualified for failing a drug test, ensuring that Malleswari won the gold medal itself. A world record followed at the Asian Championships held next, as she lifted 113 kg.

In 1997, she got married to Indian wrestler Rajesh Tyagi. Before she flew to Sydney to create history in 2000, she was already a two-time world champion with 29 international medals, including 11 gold, under her belt.

We had another obvious question on our mind—how did the state of Haryana react to its bahu's Olympic feat, one who had been born in Andhra Pradesh, and started her quest to glory from there?

'I still do remember that day vaguely, when she won the bronze medal for the country. My editor asked me to file a report from her home in Faridabad,' said veteran sports journalist Pravin Sinha. 'In fact, not many in the industrial town on the outskirts of Delhi were even aware of a household in the vicinity that was celebrating a historic first,' Sinha said. The owner of Milan Sweet Shop, which was a reference point to find our way to Malleswari's in-laws' place, wasn't even aware that his good friend, Rajesh Tyagi, was the champion lifter's husband.

Only on the morning after her victory, when he saw the papers, did he realize that it was Rajesh's wife who had won the medal, Sinha said. How did both of them come across each other and become life partners? Tyagi's family wouldn't have accepted Malleswari, if not for a last-minute reconciliation after a prolonged family quarrel.

A champion lifter himself during his university days, Rajesh Tyagi had met Malleswari at one of the training camps between tournaments. The shy Andhra girl who was then living with her elder sister in New Delhi had dreams of making it big. They connected, and in no time, fell in love, one that culminated in a happy marriage. Initially, though, the couple didn't have it easy, with Rajesh having gone against his family's wishes.

A first visit to his folks with Malleswari hadn't turned out well, but Rajesh had gone ahead, and after a three-year-long courtship, they got married. And with time, the concerns of the Tyagi family faded away as they took a great liking to their bahu.

The woman who was reluctant to get married often said that if not for the tension created by the delay in announcing the Olympics squad, she would have won the gold itself.

By the time Mr Sinha finished his story, we were almost at the door of the beautiful couple. They welcomed us with warmth and humility—something that is so special about all great sportspersons.

Malleswari and Rajesh were seated on the sofa. The much-anticipated question-and-answer session started.

How did it all start?

'My father was with the railway police. We used to stay in the railway quarters. You must be familiar with the way railway quarters are built, in a single line. The children in the quarters where we stayed were of an almost similar age group. We enjoyed our games together. We used to play kabaddi, kho kho, athletics and many other games. We used to study in government schools which had decent sports facilities at that time. For instance, in our school we had facilities for shot-put, discus throw and javelin. We had a ground where we used to play kho kho and kabaddi and we also had tracks for long jump. So we had enough space, both at our home and school where we used to play different sports.'

How did you get hooked to weightlifting?

'My relationship with weightlifting started because of my elder sister. Like so many other children in the railway quarters, she was into many sports. However, seeing her physique, the coach asked her to concentrate on weightlifting. There was a small gym where she started going regularly for practice. You know, when any girl used to go outside, be it for studies or for sports, a member of the family used to accompany her. In her case, as asked by my mother, I started accompanying her. There, six to seven girls used to practise for two hours, and I used to closely observe them.

'My interest in the sport started growing. One day, I approached the coach and requested him to allow me to join in as well. I was very thin then. He flatly refused, saying that I could not do weightlifting, and instead, I should focus on household work. I felt very hurt and angry. I decided that henceforth, I would never ever go there and not even accompany my sister. But then, my parents were insistent.

'The practice sessions in the gym used to start after school hours, and by the time the session got over, there was darkness all around. I had to go with my sister. I used to keenly watch my sister and her friends practising. After this, my sister left to participate in the national championships.'

After a brief pause, she started again, 'The secretary of the district where we lived had a gym. He was a tailor by profession. The gym was in a dilapidated condition, and so, was closed for a long time. However, there was weightlifting equipment stacked inside. I, along with my friends, approached him and requested him to give us the keys. He refused, saying that the roof of the gym could fall in any time. We assured him that we would take care of ourselves.

'We told him that it was a temporary arrangement and that the equipment in the gym would help in our preparation for other games. We somehow managed to convince him to give us the keys. In our school, every day, the last period used to be that of sports. We used to bunk sports and go to the gym for practice. It was there that I started practising seriously, to the best of my ability, with the help of the knowledge I had acquired seeing my sister and her friends practising.'

How much support did she get from her family?

Malleswari says, 'My mother was very supportive. We were five sisters and a brother. Even then, she never used to say that girls should not go outside. On the contrary, she used to encourage us. She used to wake me up early in the morning, at four, then make me study for an hour and a half and then take rounds of the quarters. She was very keen that we do physical activities. I don't know as to how she was so conscious about sports and fitness and its positive impact on health and upbringing then. She was very supportive throughout. If you get such support from your family, you don't bother about the rest of the world.'

What was the turning point?

'While I was practising, the selection trials of my sister for the 1990 Asian Games was on. My school was closed then because of vacations. As my parents were accompanying my sister for the trials, they took me as well. During this time, a delegate of Russian weightlifters had also come. It was trials as well as demonstration for the Russian weightlifters. I was keenly observing the demo—their approach, technique, temperament and their overall skill set. I had developed a deep interest in the sport overtime as I wanted to prove a coach wrong, someone who had once told me that I was not meant for weightlifting.

'The Russian coach Genedy Chitin, who was there for the selection trial, went to India's chief coach, Mr Salwan, and enquired about the girl who was watching them inquisitively. When Mr Salwan feigned ignorance, didi stepped in and told them that I was her sister and was accompanying her for the trials along with our parents.

Chitin then asked me, "Do you lift?" I said "Yes."

'When he asked me whether I had an interest in the sport, I again replied in the affirmative. Immediately, he asked me to give a demonstration. I was taken aback, as I did not have suitable clothes. I borrowed lowers from someone and a t-shirt from another. I don't know what he saw in my technique, but he immediately asked a senior official of the SAI, Mr A.V.S. Prasad, to include me in the camp. I had not participated in the district, state or national levels, and straightaway I was there in the camp. Things suddenly took off from there.'

'And then, how was the camp for you?'

'In the camp, our Russian coach trained us for eight months. And it was such a hard and rigorous training. I was fourteen years old then. I still do remember that at 5 in the morning, when it was extremely difficult for me to wake up, the coach used to literally drag me out of bed. He used to make me run uphill on a difficult terrain. After eight months of rigorous training, he left, but our training continued for another couple of months.

'This period in the SAI campus in Bangalore prepared me for the challenges ahead,' Malleswari says.

'What happened after this?'

'In 1990, in the Junior National Championships in Udaipur, I made nine national records. In clean and jerk, we get three lifts, and in each of my lifts I made a national record. I don't remember for how long these records stood. In the subsequent lifts, I surpassed my own records.

'For me it was a phenomenal achievement of sorts as I had not played at district or state level, and here I was, competing and winning at the national level. I was the junior national champion, with nine records and 3 gold medals in my name. Moreover, it was a vindication of sorts for me as that coach had said that I could not do weightlifting. After this Junior National Championships, coaches all across started saying that the future of Indian weightlifting had arrived,' Malleswari says.

'Henceforth, did you work with a specific target in mind? Was the Olympics your target?'

Malleswari replies, 'No, I did not work with any specific target in mind per se. One thing followed the other—from junior nationals to senior nationals, and then representing the country. I went into a sort of auto mode. I used to practise, prepare for the championships, then there would be another round of practice and then another championship tournament. It was not that I wanted to become world champion, Olympic champion or something like that.'

In the Asian level, China has been the dominant nation over the years. In order to do anything big here, one has to scale the great Chinese wall. So was the case with Malleswari.

'In our time, if any Chinese weightlifter was participating in any category, it was understood that they would get the gold, while silver and bronze would be shared by some other country.

The first time I broke the Chinese dominance was in the 1994 World Championships. I was competing against the Chinese weightlifters in their own country. I beat them and created a world record.'

And then came the historic event that made her a household name in India. The discussion veered around to the 2000 Sydney Olympics.

'Will you take us back to the 2000 Sydney Olympics? An Olympics in which you were confident about yourself, but no one else was?'

We could sense vindication, emotion, pride and hurt all at the same time, as she strained her eyes.

Malleswari says, 'When I was preparing for the Olympics, I was very strong. I had won enough medals and competitions in my name. I had a fair idea about my competitors. I was almost 100 per cent confident that I would win gold. Unfortunately, some of my coaches thought otherwise. For them it was enough to participate in the Olympics and to think about medals was too far-fetched. They used to tell my husband that "the fact that Malleswari is going to participate in the Olympics is big enough; don't expect a medal from her". I was of the firm belief that all contestants are in the Olympics for a medal, and it's altogether a different story that some win medals and most others don't. I was focused, and I knew where I stood.'

'How was the ambience and your feeling in the run-up to the competition?'

Malleswari says, 'During the competition, it's difficult to follow the opponents' game. The Games Village, however, is the best place to interact with your contingent and your opponents alike. After training, when we met for lunch, we used to shake each others' hands. Speaking to them sort of gave us an idea of the level of their training and preparation. Every country is allocated time slots for their training. I used to overstay even when our time was over, just to see the preparation and training of my opponents. But all this was before the competition. Once the event started,

I was totally focused on my game, with hardly any time left for the opponents.'

And then, we come to her ultimate lift that lifted the morale of the country.

'Do you still feel that you would have won the gold 9medal?'

'Of course—if you see the video clips of the Games even today, you will know that I had no competition there. I was so strong in the competition. I got bronze lifting 240 kg and the two girls from China and Hungary took gold and silver, lifting a little more than 242. Eventually, it was a difference of a mere 2.5 kg between them and me. If I would have had a better competition plan, the gold would have been mine for the taking. I was given the first lift of 125 in the first clean and jerk and then 130 in the second lift. I kept on insisting that they shouldn't give me such a low start and they should give me more weight in the beginning. I had a snatch of 110 and the Chinese girl of 112 kg. So, I would have easily done 5-10 kg more. I don't know what the rationale behind the decision was. Even in the last leg, if they would have given me 132 kg, I would have got gold, as I was lighter than my rivals. Even if it was 135 kg, we would have managed gold. But they gave me 137 kg, which was a sudden jump of 7.5 kg. If I would have managed that, it would have been an Olympic record.'

But was not getting the gold a priority, rather than an Olympic record? Did the thought of not winning gold still haunt her?

She says, 'I feel disappointed. I would easily have been the first Indian to win an individual gold medal. Earlier, whenever I used to see the video clips, I used to cry. I used to go through the competition over and over again in my dreams. I used to pray to God to let me relive the moment. But once a thing is over, it's over. It never comes back. Sometimes I feel that I would have managed 137 kg as well. In fact, as the officials (at Sydney) suddenly increased the weight by 7.5 kg, I approached them in haste and this hurt my neck. In the process, the nerves in my neck were affected I guess, and I had a blackout. Maybe it was my bad luck. Whatever it is, it was the moment that will haunt me till my last breath.'

She further adds, 'Personally, I was not that happy, but seeing the happiness in our contingent, I calmed down gradually. Everyone was congratulating me. But the anger within was not dying out. If I would not have deserved the gold medal I would have been content with the bronze medal, but that was not the case.'

Life, though, always has a bright spark to keep you going. Three years before the Sydney Olympics, Karnam Malleswari had almost decided to quit the game. If she would have, she and the country would not have got the much-coveted bronze medal.

We took her back in time.

'Was there any point of time in your life when you thought of quitting?'

Malleswari answers, 'Yes, surely there was one such instance when I had almost quit the game. The 1997 World Championships were happening in China. I had a bad tournament because of the back pain which started just a day before the competition. I had a back catch and it started paining immensely. After I returned home from the tournament, I had almost decided to quit the sport.

'You see, weightlifting is not an easy sport. Every day you have to put in hours of effort and lift more than 100 kg, at least fifty times in a day. While carrying 140 kg on your shoulders, you are going up and down. If you take a break of even ten days in between, your performance drops suddenly. It's not a joke. It's dangerous as well. I have seen the entire elbow of a weightlifter popping out while she was doing the snatch. I have seen the spinal cord of a weightlifter breaking. You put in such a lot of hard work and you put your life at so much risk. And then, just before the Games, you get injured and you are out of contention. I felt enough was enough and I would not do this anymore.'

Then how did it start again?

She replies, 'I was taking rest after the competition and

enjoying my time. My father-in-law asked me why I was not practising. My reply was that I had decided to quit. He said there was no fun in quitting after losing. "Win, prove yourself and then quit." So I started training again.' While she was answering this, her eyes were fixed on a picture of her father-in-law that was hanging on a beautiful frame on the wall facing us.

The state of Haryana, where she stays after marriage, and where her father-in-law came from, has a reputation. Haryana has this image of a society where the birth of a girl child is unwelcome, and if a girl child is born, she finds herself in a hostile environment throughout. Did the girl from Andhra Pradesh who got married into a family from Haryana share the same perspective?

'My father-in-law was very supportive. As I said earlier, in my home my mother was very supportive and my father used to tell us to focus more on studies. Here, it was the reverse. My father-in-law supported me throughout. In the families in Haryana, you know that the ghunghat system is prevalent, which is not there in South India. When some of the families here insisted that the bahu should be in ghunghat, my father-in-law opposed it vehemently. He used to tell them, "The entire world is seeing my bahu on TV, and at home you want her to be in ghunghat? There is no need of being in ghunghat. She is my daughter and so there is no need of ghunghat."

'It was because of that level of support and backing that I never had the feeling that I was in my sasural and they were my sasuma and sasurji. It was like my own home. And, of course, my husband has always been a huge pillar of support for me. A husband and wife's relationship is a very sensitive relationship. When he says no worries, we will see, and the assurance is actually needed, it means a lot to me. It gives me huge confidence. My husband was also a weightlifter, and he gave up his career so that my career could flourish. We had to start our family and nurture our home. If both of us would have continued, this would not have been possible. He took the onus of looking after the family and working in order to run the house upon himself and asked me to focus on my game.'

Our gaze turned to Rajesh, who was sitting on the sofa, facing her and listening to her with respect and admiration. 'See, when something has to happen, the circumstances shape everything in a manner that leads you to the destiny. She was destined to win the medal for the country, and from her home to our home everything shaped up in the manner that eventually led to it. As far as me sacrificing my career is concerned, I don't see it that way. I did the best in what I could and she did the best in what she could.'

An Andhra-Haryana pair, made for each other. In letter and spirit.

The girl who became the role model for the entire country sees her mother as her first role model. She was one among five sisters and a brother. Hers was a simple family. Her parents emphasized more on a good diet for the kids and a decent standard of living, rather than saving money. The neighbours often wondered at the attitude of the family with teenage daughters, living in the environment of complete freedom, not in any tearing hurry to get the girls married. But her parents did not buckle, and gave their children the freedom to grow and select their own path. 'This was God's gift to us,' says Malleswari. She dedicates her Olympic medal to her mother and her husband.

Does she remember all the coaches she had in life?

'Yes. The coach who told me that I was not made for weightlifting, as this egged me on to prove him wrong. He was the reason why I started pursuing the sport with passion. The Russian coach Chitin, without whom I would never have got into the camp. I met him again in 1996 in Iran and I still remember how proud he felt of my achievements. My coach, Mr Sandhu, and most of all, my Olympics coach Leonid Taranenko.'

Our journey from Delhi to Yamunanagar in Haryana to explore the journey of the Iron Lady of Indian sports took us through many unexplored facets of her personality. She is the daughter of Haryana now and she feels that there are many traits in Haryanvi society which can make it the epicentre of a sporting revolution in the country. 'The base of Haryana is strong. If you go to any village of the state, milk, curd and *ghee* (clarified butter) happens to be the primary diet. The physique of the girls from the state is strong. With the social media explosion, there is no dearth of sports-specific information. The mindsets of parents towards their daughters is also changing. The glass ceiling is being shattered, and with the likes of Sakshi (Malik) doing so well in wrestling, that was considered to be primarily a male sport, more and more parents are now opening up to their daughters taking up sports professionally.

Transcending the borders of Haryana, Malleswari wants to see more and more girls from across the country taking up sports and doing the country proud. When she made it to the podium in Sydney, the Weightlifting Federation of India at that time failed to make her medal count. Her feat encouraged many young girls to take up weightlifting. But lack of guidance and a proper system ensured they faded out early.

'Without hard work, concentration and individual planning, one cannot get anything in life,' says Malleswari. Perhaps still craving for the Olympic gold medal that eluded her, Malleswari is up and about, preparing the next generation. 'India has got huge talent. If we are able to create a proper system, we will not have to struggle for a single medal; we will win dozens of them. The aim of my academy is that my disciples get me the gold medal that I missed out on in Sydney in 2000. And...many more medals like it.'

The quest for that elusive medal has taken her back to the Srikakulam district of north Andhra again, where she runs her academy, 'The Weightlifting Academy', in association with the Sports Authority of Andhra Pradesh. And her most promising recruits—well, talented young lifters, especially from the north Andhra districts, that has produced many a champion lifter in the past. India didn't share her belief of winning the Olympic gold medal in 2000. Two decades on, it's time for a change in script. Karnam Malleswari is a true inspiration because of her dedication and the sacrifices she has made to reach the summit. She forsook all social and cultural norms, exuding extreme confidence for not just being comfortable with her body and image, but by using them optimally to reach the pinnacle of her sport.

FIVE

Anju Bobby George:
A Leap of Faith

A leap of faith, or a leap that transcended time and faith... into unknown, uncharted territory that no Indian had ever managed to venture into.

A leap that defied limitations, carried by the exhortations of the faithful few who were mindful of the possible spectacle that would take Indian sports to a hitherto impossible land. A family of seven brothers who welcomed a future star with open arms, egging her on to greater heights...

The constant support from a person who was a star in his own right and gave up his career to help catapult her to international fame and glory.

She leapt. And fell short. And she leapt again...

Propelled by faith, discipline and dedication, smacking of unbelievable talent, she delivered the jump of the century as far as India was concerned...

This is the story of Anju Bobby George.

Like its timeless traditions, there are certain abiding memories that need to be carried forward from one generation to another.

One such abiding memory amongst the connoisseurs of Indian volleyball is the image of a 6' 2" human spring, leaping high in the air and staying there longer than one usually can. This had caught the imagination of people within India and on the far-flung Italian shores—much before television and digital media had invaded our homes. Jimmy George, a legend of Indian volleyball, was the showstopper. The man had what many called 'the absolute jump'.

Volleyball is all about defying gravity. Jimmy made it look more stylish because he managed a little air rest where he could stop on a flight for a fraction of a second. Jimmy exemplified the power of mental strength. Jimmy was into meditation well before it became part of the Indian way of life in contemporary times. When he went back to the court after quiet thought, one could just see the stored energy explode. The mind and body became one when he jumped in the form of an arc. The Jimmy George phenomenon often made foreigners wonder, 'Where did that breakneck ace come from?'

This was at the time when we, as a country and a society, had a fixation for anything foreign. Jimmy rose to lofty heights in Italy. An indoor stadium at Montichiari, Brescia, was named after him. This was before Thiruvananthapuram offered its salutation with its own stadium. And a street off Coletto Club, close to Milan, has been christened Jimmy George. The legend died unfortunately and untimely—at the age of thirty-three—in a car accident in Italy. However, he left after having created a legacy, the imprint of which was felt in sports beyond volleyball.

Jimmy and his seven brothers—the eldest, Jose, Mathew, Sebastian, Francis Byju, Stanley, Winston and the youngest, Robert Bobby—even played as a volleyball team once. One of Jimmy's brothers, Sebastian, who played with Jimmy in his last match in India, carries with him tape compilations of his brother's games that he takes around to be distributed amongst schools and colleges. Sebastian does this with the hope that many budding careers in volleyball in the state and beyond are shaped, and his brother's legacy lives on.

Robert Bobby George gave up his career to focus on generating the longest jump in Indian athletics. Robert is a mechanical engineer and a former national champion in triple jump himself. There is an old saying, 'Behind every successful man, there is a woman.' If volleyball is about defying gravity, Robert Bobby George has defied this old adage and has gone beyond it like his late brother—behind the successful Anju Bobby George is the man named Robert Bobby George. Anju had the talent to give Indian athletics a big leap. However, her talent was caged by the limitation of laziness. It was then that Bobby George came into her life and became the catalyst that propelled the giant leap in Indian athletics.

We meet Robert Bobby George during one of our visits to the beautiful SAI campus in Bangalore. The handsome-looking man is busy giving tips to some of the budding athletes there. Once the training session gets over, we are introduced by a common friend. Immediately, we request for an extended interview session with Anju and himself, to which he readily agrees. He invites us to their home the very next day. The surrounding beauty and greenery of his house immediately appeals to us. But what strikes us is the equation the couple share and the warmth with which they welcome us. 'Sports is our passion, our way of life and our one true common love,' is the smiling Bobby George's introductory statement.

'Bobby has been my personal trainer, jump coach, nutritionist, cook, masseur, sports manager, travel planner, sports psychologist, friend and life partner, all rolled in one,' Anju puts things in perspective. And then, she takes us down memory lane to the years when the couple was Indian sports' biggest newsmakers.

Bobby used to start his morning as her trainer. Then the nutritionist kicked in, planning her day's menu. The coach used to take over from here, putting her through her training schedule. The afternoon was spent watching jump videos, visualizing enhanced performances, and setting a target for the evening, during which time Bobby became a sports psychologist. In the evening, Bobby the cook used to make her a cup of tea and drive her back to the stadium. Again, the coach took over and the couple worked hard on the track till 9 at night. In between, the masseur gave massages for recovery, and arranged sauna and ice baths. After Anju had her dinner and went to sleep, the manager began his night's work— which included corresponding by e-mail with contest organizers and journalists, checking her media coverage and downloading it for her for the next day, researching new jump strategies and planning her schedule.

'The undisturbed silence, peace and calm surrounding your house gives the feel of the leisurely pace with which you have conjured your dream. Do you think so too?' I ask them.[1]

Bobby replies, 'The multiple roles that Anju has attributed to me meant that for months, we hardly had time to do anything other than train. There were many days when I used to sleep only for four to five hours. Often I used to think that once she retired, I would take a whole year off for myself. By nature, I was not a workaholic—I had an interest in farming. I wanted to give myself enough time to attend family weddings, get-togethers and such things. Perhaps our home, which you see today, is the reflection of our pent-up desires and feelings from then.'

How was this formidable partnership formed? Did her husband become the coach or did her coach become her husband? I fire another question, this time at Anju.

She laughs, and then says, 'My coach became my husband. In fact, our affair started even before he became my coach. I was practising alone, and Bobby was practising alone. Then we started practising together. Later, we decided to marry and live together.'

'I met Anju at a training camp at the SAI campus, where both of us were training under national coach P.T. Joseph, in 1996. We became friends almost at once,' Bobby George elaborated. Bobby was also a model and a finalist at a Mr India contest. The fact that Bobby was a great looker appealed to Anju then.

Anju was training for the long and triple jumps. She failed in the selection trials for the 1998 Asian Games. It was then that Bobby, who had begun to care for her a lot by then, decided to take her under his wing to hone her jumping skills. Their personal relationship remained a secret for a while, until coach Joseph found photographs of Anju in Bobby's room. Bobby's sister, who

---

[1]Author Abhishek Dubey interviewed them during his visit to their home to shoot a documentary.

also lives in Bengaluru, broke the news to their father, George Joseph. George Joseph was an advocate living in Peravoor, about an hour's drive from the north Kerala town of Kannur. He was passionate about sports. When he brought seven sons into the world, he built a professional standard volleyball court at home. Jimmy George became India's first professional volleyball player. He died young in a car crash in Europe. Bobby too met with an accident in 1998. He busted his knee and had to have screws put into it. 'I think he could still have made a comeback as a jumper, but instead, he opted to become my coach. Bobby gave up his career to coach me. I have reached where I am because of his sacrifice. He is a mechanical engineer by training. He also did some modelling for Bengaluru style guru Prasad Bidapa. He aspired to enter model hunt contests, but once he took over as the coach, he gave up all that. He simply had no time.'

Bobby recognized that Anju had truly tremendous potential. She was winning gold medals here and there, but was not consistent. 'I got an instant feeling that if she would have got better financing, more systematic coaching and direction, she would have done far better at a younger age,' Bobby says.

Soon after Bobby became her coach, her career made a fresh start. In the year 1999, Anju set a national record for triple jump in the Bangalore Federation Cup, and won a silver medal at the South Asian Federation Games in Nepal. However, immediately after that, she suffered an ankle injury that threatened to end her career. She missed the Sydney Olympics and was out of competitive jumping for two full years. It was during this time that she married Bobby.

'Ours was finally a love-cum-arranged marriage, as our parents were quite happy about our match,' says Anju. Bobby is a Catholic, while Anju is a Jacobite. She became a Catholic after their marriage on 24 April 2000. Both Anju and Bobby come from rather religious and devout families. Anju, in her playing days, used to carry a figurine of the Blessed Virgin Mary in her bag, and her parents used to pray for her whenever she went to participate in competitions. After getting married, from one competition to another, the wife-husband team was on mission mode. Anju and Bobby worked together, almost as one person, with one goal in mind: winning a gold medal in the Olympics. Their formal athletics journey might have been assumed to be over, but the mission continued.

The sporting fraternity believed that they had seen the best of Anju. Bobby was convinced that it was not so.

'We read one of your father's interviews where he said that before you married Bobby, you were a very lazy person. It was only after marriage that Bobby made you train regularly, and hard. Is that true?' we ask.

Anju starts laughing and then says, 'So true! I am basically a very lazy and careless person. It was only because of Bobby that I started doing something. He used to push me to work hard. When I was young, it was my father who used to take me to competitions, and push me to work hard. I used to sleep as we waited for the arrival of the coach. What Bobby did for me later, Papa used to do then! Bobby's pep talks had tremendous influence on me.'

What did he say in his pep talks?

'Bobby used to often tell me, "You have so much talent, you should not let it go waste. There are many people with less talent than you but they work so hard to achieve something. Here you are with so much talent, but lazy. You are defying God. You shouldn't do this!" When he talked like this, I found it difficult to sit at home and laze around.'

'How difficult is it to have a husband who is also the coach? Is it not like a boss observing you both at home and office?'

Anju looks at Bobby, laughs and then says, 'Very difficult... On a serious note, without his pep talks, I would not even get up. I would either be sitting in front of the television or sleeping! It may be time to go for practice, but if there is a film on television, I just sit there and watch it. There were days when he literally had to drag me to the stadium!'

This surely is one turnaround story, and to understand this

overall process of transformation, we need to go back briefly to Anju's roots.

The year was 1977. Anju was born in Cheeranchira village in Kottayam, Kerala in a Syrian orthodox family, to K.T. Markose and Gracy Markose. She was initiated into athletics by her father.

K.T. Markose used to run a modest catering service. He used to wake her up early in the morning and take her on a bicycle to a playground about 10 km away for practice. Her interest was further developed by her trainer in Koruthodu School. From winning a lemon and spoon race at the age of four which she only vaguely recollects now, Anju won so many trophies in school and college that there wasn't enough space in her home to exhibit them. While the triumvirate of Usha-Valsamma-Shiny was setting the global sporting stage on fire, Anju, a small girl then, was staying at the residence of the younger brother of the father of Shiny Wilson, for her studies. She was studying at a sports school there. Her uncle was the physical trainer in the school. Because the girl was tall, Shiny's uncle had the feeling that she could achieve a lot. Gradually, the girl started aping and following Shiny everywhere. She became like a family member, a sister to her. When journalists would come to interview Shiny, they would meet the charming and innocent-looking girl. Some would jokingly offer to interview the girl as well. The girl was full of promise, but she was lazy. She was more interested in watching films and playing with other children. When she missed her practice sessions with regularity, she was often teased for not winning medals, despite having such a good height.

'It was only after joining the senior nationals camp in 1996 that I thought it was time to get serious,' she says.

When the raw talent of Anju got married to the seriousness and discipline of Bobby, the result provided method and direction to her immense potential.

The mechanical engineer in Bobby read up all that there was to read about biomechanics and did some research on jumps. In 2001, Anju started training thirty-five hours a week and bettered her own long jump record with a leap of 6.74 m, her best till date. In the same year she also won gold for triple jump and long jump in the Ludhiana National Games. Anju reigned supreme in the events at the Hyderabad National Games also. She won the bronze medal, clearing 6.49 m at the 2002 Commonwealth Games at Manchester. She also won the gold medal at the Asian Games in Busan. Anju made history when she won the bronze medal, clearing 6.70 m in long jump at the 2003 World Championships in athletics in Paris, thus becoming the first Indian athlete ever to win a medal in a World Championships edition in athletics.

'That feeling when I went up to the podium that day can't be expressed. I felt on top of the world. A bronze medal is almost equivalent to gold for us. At that point we all felt there was fair competition, but the recent findings tell a slightly different story,' Anju says.

Anju shares an incident that reflects the way our bureaucracy treated sportspersons in those days. 'Two months before the championships, I had to camp in Delhi for funds. My entire practice schedule got haywire then and I could not concentrate on my preparations. When I kept on following them, they asked me, "Will you win the medal if you get the funding?" I said yes and it was only then that the funds were released.'

Had the competition been fair and free of doping then, she would have bettered her opponents who sneaked ahead by a fair distance.

Anju, however, was increasingly becoming aware of the onerous task of bridging the gap between Indian and world levels for any aspiring youngster. The team of Anju and Bobby George had by then fully realized that excellence in the field of international athletics was 50 per cent about training and 50 per cent exposure to quality international events.

Anju says, 'To be world class, one should compete more in the European circuit, gain more Grand Prix points and improve one's ranking.' Ever since her historic win, there was no stopping her. A legend in the making had just stamped her authority on the international circuit. In the same year, Anju won her career's second gold medal at the 2003 Afro-Asian Games. Her jump of 6.53 m assured her a convincing gold medal over Lerma Gabito (Philippines), who could only manage 6.3 m. The year 2003 thus proved to be a watershed for Anju. By then, world record holder Mike Powell had joined the Anju-Bobby team. Realizing the importance of exposure in the West, they got in touch, after a great deal of difficulty, with Powell, who ran a California-based academy. This was a step ahead from P.T. Usha's time, who many believed would have done better if the Nambiar-Usha duo would have got help from a renowned foreign athletics trainer. In 2003, Anju had a nine-week stint with him, which, she says, transformed her mental make-up. The former long jump champion ironed out a few rough spots in her running action but, more importantly, gave her the confidence she badly needed to compete with the best. He made her realize the significance of relaxing before a race. One of the many important pieces of advice which Powell gave Anju included using cosmetics. In the West, looking good is a part of feeling good before the race.

Powell also introduced them to the sports management firm Hudson Smith International (HSI). Once HSI signed Anju, the doors to the world of elite and lucrative athletics opened for her. It was training under legendary American Mike Powell and participation in top European events that opened Anju's eyes to the world.

'The training methods were almost similar in the US, but Powell was a great motivating factor. He played the role of a psychologist more than that of a trainer,' she says. Anju gained confidence with each passing event in Europe. She was initially awestruck by just looking at the foreign athletes, but then, as she began to match them with her performance, her spirits began to soar. 'Now they are taking note that an Indian can also compete with them,' she said in an interview with *Outlook India.*[2]

---

[2]'We can do it too', *Outlook*, 16 September 2003

Anju's jump started making front page headlines. She was supposed to be the country's medal hope in the Athens Olympics. In the 2004 Athens Olympics, despite delivering her best performance, with a jump of 6.83 m, Anju could only manage a fifth place after the disqualification of American Marion Jones. In September 2005, she won the gold medal in the women's long jump at the 16th Asian Athletics Championships in Incheon City, South Korea, with a leap of 6.65 m. She went on to win the silver medal at the IAAF World Athletics Final in 2005 with a leap of 6.75 m. 'I consider that as my best-ever performance,' she says, reflecting on her career then. She won the silver medal in women's long jump in the 15th Asian Games 2006 at Doha. In 2007, Anju won the silver medal in the 17th Asian Athletics Championships at Amman with a jump of 6.65 m. With this, she qualified for the Osaka World Championships in August 2007, where she finished ninth. Anju started her 2008 season with a silver medal in the 3rd Asian Indoor Championships in athletics at Doha with a jump of 6.38 m. She improved her distance to 6.5 m by winning gold in the 3rd South Asian Athletics Championships at Kochi.

She also contested in the 2008 Beijing Olympics, but failed to qualify for the women's long jump event, fouling in all her three attempts. She was once ranked world no. 4. Anju's journey to success from rank 61 in 2001 to rank 6 in 2003 within the short span of two years was full of sheer hard work and intensive planning. She received the prestigious Arjuna Award in 2002-03 and the country's highest sporting honour, the Rajiv Gandhi Khel Ratna award, in 2003-04 after her success in the World Athletics Meet. She was conferred the Padma Shri, India's fourth-highest civilian award, in 2004. Anju's athletics career was almost over by the 2008 Beijing Olympics. However, her best was yet to come.

The dawn of 2014 saw Anju Bobby George becoming the first Indian track and field athlete to win a gold medal in a major world event after international governing body IAAF upgraded her second place finish at the 2005 Monaco World Athletics Final to the top spot. This was following a dope violation by a Russian competitor, Tatyana Kotova. When asked about this, she says, 'One can say that I became World Champion nine years after it was due. And I am very happy that we have got a world title. If we would have got the medal that day, I would have been happier. It's always great to hear the national anthem of the country on foreign soil. Still, we could celebrate after nine years. I felt really happy and the wait was worth it.'

Strange situations occur in athletes' lives. In the case of Anju Bobby George there have been stranger ones. Perhaps a few more await her in the future.

In 2013, Russian Tatyana Kotova was caught for doping after her samples collected during the 2005 World Athletics Championships in Helsinki were found to contain traces of a banned substance. The IAAF had re-analysed samples of the 2005 World Athletics Championships in line with the International Olympic Committee's decision to re-test eight-year-old samples, dating back to the 2004 Athens Olympics, to deter dope cheats. The 2005 Monaco World Athletics Finals (9-10 September), which had the top eight athletes of that time, was held a few weeks after the 2005 World Athletics Championships (6-14 August) in Helsinki. So, Kotava's result in the latter event was deleted from the record books. 'During my time, there were three Russians ahead of me, and they were winning almost everything. But they have been suspended now and we have a better picture of how they achieved the feats. I still feel that I was more talented than those Russians who won three medals at the 2004 Athens Olympics. We are still awaiting one in athletics. Hopefully, that day will come soon,' says Anju.

How soon is this possible?

In 2004, during the Athens Olympics, Anju Bobby George was placed fifth, with fellow athletes, Australia's Bronwyn Thompson and Britain's Jade Johnson, placed fourth and sixth respectively. The trio believe that they have been denied the medals that they rightly deserved, and have asked the sports authorities to investigate the matter. Even though the medallists in the women's long jump event at Athens, Tatyana Lebedeva (gold), Irina Simagina (silver) and Tatyana Kotova (bronze) passed the dope tests at the time, all three Russians have subsequently failed the prerequisite drug tests in other competitions.

As per a *The Times of India* report, 'At the 2004 Games, Anju made the finals and broke the national long jump record with 6.83 m, which still stands. If all goes well, Anju Bobby George could very well find herself with a silver Olympic medal before the country moves on to the 2020 Tokyo Olympics.'[3] In the same report, Anju's husband has said he firmly believes that the drug scandal in Russia runs deep, and the trio (Anju Bobby George, himself and the Athletics Federation of India) have a solid case.

Bobby says, 'It's a conspiracy. More than 128 samples kept in Russian labs were spoiled after that. The Russian government is also involved in it. There are connections with the Russian mafia. Interpol has made arrests and it was found that money was channeled through Singapore. I believe there are people sitting in some corner of the world with solid evidence to prove that we have a clear case, and we are confident of getting some advantage.

'Once it comes to the international media's notice, someone sitting in Australia or England or maybe Russia itself will come forward, I feel.'

If Bobby's word is proved true and the Athens Olympics medal comes to her, it will certainly pitchfork Anju Bobby George as the greatest all-time Indian athlete. However, there are many within the Indian sports fraternity who strongly believe that Athens medal or no medal, she is already the greatest-ever Indian athlete till date.

Anju Bobby George's achievements are often overshadowed by the number of medals won by two other Indian greats, namely, Milkha Singh and P.T. Usha. It's interesting to note that while Milkha Singh and P.T. Usha had most of their success in the Asian

---

[3]'Anju Bobby George might end up with an Olympic silver if an investigation is launched into the 2004 long jump results', indiatimes.com, 29 March 2017

Games and at the Asian level, on the other hand, Anju Bobby George has had a greater range of victory in terms of international competitions, as she has won various medals in five different competitions.

Anju Bobby George has won 7 medals across five major competitions. On the contrary, P.T. Usha has won the highest number—10 medals amongst the three, but all of them have come at the Asian level. Milkha Singh has 5 medals in his name, all gold, 4 in the Asian Games and one in the Commonwealth Games. 'We used to believe that the Asian level was everything. We used to celebrate an Asian medal like it was an Olympic gold. We set a mental barrier for ourselves. Bobby trained and motivated me to go beyond this,' she says.

These statistics speak volumes about the mental strength possessed by Anju Bobby George, and her ability to not only perform but also win big consistently on the world stage. However, the significance of Anju's feats goes beyond this statistics, and in many ways, she was the real game changer.

Anju, who at one point of time, was ranked no. 4 in the world, was the first to be signed by HSI, a top sports management firm, the first to receive appearance fees at the top global meets and the first one who endorsed a multinational apparel and shoe company in a lucrative deal. If Milkha Singh and P.T. Usha brought Indian athletics tantalizingly closer to the finishing line in the highest global sporting platform, Anju Bobby George actually was the one who crossed that finishing line. The Government of India in recent years has adopted a systematic approach for sending Indian athletes for foreign exposure and training as preparation for the main events like the Olympics and Asian Games, but the trend was initiated by Anju and Bobby George. After their success, the sports fraternity in the country realized the importance of this.

If the Flying Sikh and the Payyoli Express gave 'so near yet so far' moments to Indian sports, Anju Bobby George gave Indian sports lovers the 'we are there' moment. However, these 'we are there' moments would have had a phenomenal cascading effect had the trio of Russians not robbed her of the medals on the spot in marquee world level competitions i.e. World Athletics Championships, the Athens Olympics and the World Athletics Finals. However, the final chapter of her contributions beyond her personal glories is yet to be written.

Anju and Bobby George have been contributing in varied capacities even after hanging up their boots. The duo runs their academy in Bangalore. 'Athletics is everything for me, and my mission is to help Indian athletes win the Olympic medal. Even at my academy, I ask every athlete to aim for an Olympic medal, as thinking big makes a difference,' says Anju, who is one of the observers of the 'Khelo India' project. Some of her trainees have won medals at the national level.

'It is really fantastic to see my trainees winning medals in the domestic championships. I feel such results will keep me motivated to work hard even further.'

Can Indian athletes make a mark on the world stage?

Anju answers, 'We are not able to find big talents now. Maybe in future. Athletics, as you all know, is the mother of all sports. We have to really work hard. There are lots of things involved. We need real talent and real support, and competitive management is where we are lacking. We have to take part in competitions not only in India, but also overseas, in Europe, and for that we have to be in the top 12 in the world.'

She further explains the road ahead when she says, 'Actually, we are doing only the training part, which is 50 per cent. But peaking in high-level competitions like the Grand Prix and the Diamond League is not happening in India. We still believe that we can train hard in the country and go for the World Championships or the Olympics. That is not the correct way. That is not going to give us a medal in the Olympics or the World Championships. That is not how the Americans and Europeans are doing it. You may have to take part in other top-level international competitions. I was doing it that way, which is why I got success at that level.'

Asked who will sanction the funds for taking part in these

top-level international events, she says, 'Sanctioning money is the government's job, but it is also about athletes acting like professionals. You are a professional athlete and your manager or coach should take care of everything...your travel, your training, your schedule, etc. You have to do all these things; it is all about bringing professionalism in yourself. It is not the federation's job. The Americans and the Europeans, they are professional athletes, and they are all going to these events on their own.' She further adds, 'The process of coaching needs to evolve, and it should be customized as per the athlete. For instance, Bobby used to give me training not from the heart but from the brain. He knew me very well. He designed a training pattern only for me. I was prone to injuries on my right leg or take-off leg. I injured my right leg when I was nineteen years old. He knew how to go about it. That's the trick.'

Can our country produce a Usain Bolt one day?

'He is a big machine (laughs). He's born for athletics, an extraordinary human being. You cannot compare him with anyone.'

Sports flows in the genes of Anju Bobby George's family. But would she try to let her daughter Ami be an Olympic medallist in future?

She says, 'It's too early to say this, as she is just three-and-a-half years old, but I wish to help her win a medal at the Olympics. If not, I would like her to be an excellent human being and succeed in whichever field she chooses in her journey.'

From Sachin Tendulkar to Anju Bobby George, whenever any legendary sportsperson is asked about their child being a future sports prodigy, the answer comes along these predictable lines. Perhaps one of the major things that sports teaches them is to take life as it comes and play the game with full spirit. However, there are bitter and harder lessons as well, which need to be learnt from these legends' experiences. This also explains why top performers in sports in our country refuse to be a part of the system of sports administration after their retirement.

The ace athlete was appointed president of the Kerala State Sports Council. Hurt by allegations of corruption levelled against her by state sports minister E.P. Jayarajan, India's lone athletics World Championships medal winner resigned from the post on 22 June 2016. Announcing her decision to quit, the celebrated long jumper said it was not proper to continue at the post after allegations were levelled against her and misunderstandings cropped up. The fighter in her was there for all to see. Anju famously said after the episode, 'Anybody can kill sports, but nobody can defeat a sports star.'

Besides the iconic athlete, thirteen other members of the council, including noted volleyball player Tom Jose, also resigned. In an interview she said, 'It started when we went to meet the newly-appointed Kerala sports minister E.P. Jayarajan. The way he responded to us was not what we had expected. All the transfers and appointments we had suggested were being questioned and we were called corrupt. He accused us all of being directly elected members of the previous government. His demeanour was totally wrong. It was not our fault that we were appointed by the previous United Democratic Front government. We are only sportspersons—we do not belong to any party. Sports is our party and our religion. It was the Kerala government that invited me to become the president of the Kerala Sports Council. They told me that having a high-profile athlete like me would be very beneficial. And I felt it was my duty to help the cause of sports in Kerala.'[4]

When asked what her contributions in this period were, she says, 'I was only appointed in December 2014. We lost two months due to elections. One of the main things I tried to do was implement an Ethics Commission to probe irregularities, because after some digging, we found irregularities in many files. But we faced lots of problems in implementing that commission. From Kasaragod to Thiruvananthapuram, we went on district visits

---

[4]'I don't need a post to serve Indian sports: Anju Bobby George,' scroll.in, 26 June 2016

and tried to identify and solve issues that athletes faced, like lack of proper accommodation, infrastructural issues and the need to provide proper nutrition. My aim was to create a three-level structure that would help in administering sports in the state.'

Anju took Indian athletics to the world level. Her achievements can better be understood if we consider that she achieved all these with the minuscule government grant of ₹15,00,000 throughout her career. The duo of Anju and Bobby George had to plan and prepare and manage the rest of the amount from sponsors and individuals. To add to this, where her competitors used banned substances to enhance their performance in a clinical manner, she achieved all this while adhering to clean sports. One can just imagine what her final medal tallies in the world meets would have been if she would have got the type of support top-level athletes get and if the ecosystem around the sport she pursued would have been free of banned substances.

Journalists who used to observe Anju and Bobby training together often portray this vivid picture. There was a piece of green twig that her husband, coach Bobby George, used to pluck from a nearby tree and plant on the far side of the sand pit. It was like a ritual. For years, a twig—actually a marker placed at 7 m—used to be her treasured quest, her holy grail. The twig used to remain tantalizingly elusive. Still, Bobby used to drill ambition into her, the desire and daring to dream big. The 7 ft twig remained elusive for her. But a continuous and scientific effort to scale that enabled Anju to long jump from Asia to the world stage. There is a lot of potential in the fertile sporting soils of Kerala. Unfortunately, there are hurdles galore too, as is clear from the experience of Anju Bobby George from her stint in the State Sports Council. If Kerala and India have to stamp a universal image of triumph on the global sporting landscape, like Jimmy George's absolute jump, they need to position themselves above the narrow net, and plan and execute accordingly.

SIX

M.C. Mary Kom:
A Fistful of Glory

The 2012 London Olympics had many firsts to its credit. But when we arrived in London to cover the Games, we, as Indian journalists, had our eyes set on a unique first. Women's boxing was introduced in the Olympics for the first time. Women's boxing goes back to the eighteenth century, and though it emerged during the 1904 Olympics in a demonstration bout, it was not introduced as an Olympic sport until 2012. This extraordinary person, by then already a legend in world boxing and six-time world amateur boxing champion, Chungneijang Mary Kom Hmangte, was going to represent the country in the 51 kg flyweight category. There is something special and unique about boxing as a sport. Boxing is more about defiance than aggression, more about the outburst of the pent-up angst and the mapping of the strategy of the opponents than deftness and subtlety, and more about the toughness of the mind than physical toughness. When a boxer sets the stage on fire, it is a sort of fast forward of all that one has gone through in their journey of life till then, demonstrated through their punches and their defence. During one summer in London, there was double defiance by these special classes of boxers. There was Nicola Adams' and M.C. Mary Kom's defiance against their tough journey of life till then. It was also the defiance of these two protagonists against the so-called masculinity attached with boxing as a sport. There was China's Ren Cancan as well. But if sports is about the series of actions leading up to the most actionable defining point in one's career, the battle was between the 'believe' mindset of Adams and the 'unbreakable' character of Mary Kom. What was the 'believe' (also the title of the autobiography of Nicola Adams) against which the 'unbreakable' (the title of the autobiography of M.C. Mary Kom) was pitted?

It was faith that led a young girl to tell her mother that she was going to win a gold medal in boxing in the Olympics. People love Nicola Adams today, for she is technically gifted and also ballistic, she dances like a pint-sized Muhammad Ali, she is an accidental role model who, without any fuss, revealed that she is bisexual, and she has got a luminous smile which makes her a life force. But when she had believed that she would be an Olympic champion in boxing, her claim had been more of a fantasy than an ambition. Women's boxing was not even an Olympic sport. In England, boxing for women was banned for more than a century, on the grounds that premenstrual syndrome made women unfit for boxing. It wasn't until November 1996 that the Amateur Boxing Association of England controversially voted in favour of lifting the ban, allowing girls as young as ten to compete and spar in gyms. Adams had her first fight a year before the ban was lifted, aged thirteen, at a working men's club in Leeds.

The odds were heavily stacked against her. The young Nicola was a frail little thing, waylaid by asthma, allergies and eczema. When she was five, the doctor told her mother she had better not let her run around, lest it triggered her asthma. Adams wasn't having any of it. Her parents got separated when she was eleven years old, after her mother had put up with a lot. In her autobiography, Adams describes an incident that happened when she was around four, when her parents were arguing.

'I just wanted to get between them and stop it, so I jumped in front of my mum and tried to protect her with a plastic sword. I thought I could keep my dad away. My mum reckons that, even then, I was brave.'[1]

---

[1]Nicola Adams, *Believe: Boxing, Olympics and my life outside the ring*, Viking, Penguin, pg 67

From the age of eight, she started begging her mother to leave her father. Three years later, she did. This gave them freedom, but forced them to come out of their comfort zone. In her early years, Adams' family was comfortably off, both her parents were working and every summer they left Leeds to spend six weeks in New York with relatives. After her mother left her father, she had to take on two new jobs, working day and night to make ends meet, and her black uniform went grey with rewashing. Nicola had every such moment captured in the subconsciousness of her mind, frame by frame.

A year after her parents separated, Adams started boxing. She said, 'At the time, I enjoyed boxing because it was the place I could go, to escape. All the kids in the gym had problems, and it was a place you didn't have to think about them.'[2]

At the age of fourteen, there was another family crisis. Dee, her mother, contracted meningitis and almost died. Adams called the ambulance when she found her mother could barely walk, and her speech was slurred. And it was Adams who demanded that something urgent had to be done when she was left for three hours at the hospital. This was when she grew up and became strong, for she had to look after both herself and her brother.

'I was by myself in the hospital cafeteria and I just broke down. I didn't ever let my brother see me cry, because I didn't want him to think things were really bad. I stayed strong for him. And I had to stay strong for my mum.'[3]

To complicate matters further, at the age of fifteen, Adams was diagnosed with attention deficit hyperactivity disorder (ADHD). Many would have taken this as the last nail in the coffin, but not Nicola Adams. She took this positively. She says, 'I think it helped my training. I never get tired. I have always got energy. It helps

---

[2]Nicola Adams, *Believe: Boxing, Olympics and my life outside the ring*, Viking, Penguin, pg 69

[3]Nicola Adams, *Believe: Boxing, Olympics and my life outside the ring*, Viking, Penguin, pg 70

with my shots. I am always trying new things.'[4]

There is something common about these woman champions. They know how to change the course of an adverse current in a favourable direction.

When did it all start?

When she was twelve, her mother had gone to an aerobics class. Her babysitter had cancelled at the last moment. She did not want to leave her two children home alone, and took them with her to the gym. It just happened that there was a children's boxing class on that day, which Nicola fancied. And that was that. In 2001, she became the first woman boxer to represent England. In 2003, aged twenty, she became an English amateur champion. She had hoped that women's boxing would be introduced as an Olympic sport in 2008, but it wasn't to be. In fact, 2008 proved a disastrous year for her. She slipped on a boxing bandage, fell down the stairs and cracked a vertebra. For five months, she had to wear a body cast plastered to the top half of her body. She didn't box for more than a year. But in August 2009, she received the best incentive to get fit again. It was announced that women's boxing was going to be included in the next Olympics. Nicola Adams' Olympics moment had finally arrived.

And here she was, in the ExCeL arena, for the 2012 London Olympics.

Her opponent was unbreakable. She was M.C. Mary Kom. When one goes through the previous pages of her life, before London 2012, one wonders how she had managed to reach where she had. Every moment in her journey asked the question how, of all sports, she had come to represent her country in women's boxing. Her autobiography, aptly titled *Unbreakable: An Autobiography*, tries to uncover this.

She writes, 'My years of hard work, the refusal to give up, pushing every boundary, the thrill, the joy of winning, the success.

---

[4]Nicola Adams, *Believe: Boxing, Olympics and my life outside the ring*, Viking, Penguin, pg 7

The Olympic bronze, my most prized possession. And boxing, the sport I gave myself to. All of it is real. I was the David who took on the Goliaths in the boxing ring—and I won, most of the time.'[5]

These lines and her autobiography in totality define her only partially, not fully. Mary Kom is a living legend on whose life a biopic has been attempted. The dialogue which defines the biopic and Mary Kom per se is, '*Kabhi kisi ko itna mat darao ki darr hi khatam jo jaaye.*' (Don't scare anyone so much that they are not scared anymore.) But then, such is the enormity of the aspect of unbreakability in her character that no one dialogue or biopic can encapsulate the whole meaning of being Mary Kom. A film could at best be a mediocre account of the magnificent life of Mary.

After closely following her Olympic moment in London, we follow her to her village on the outskirts of the town and to her home in Imphal to understand the meaning of being Mary Kom. As we make yet another attempt to absorb her true meaning and prepare to leave the SAI regional centre in Imphal, which has been more than her second home, she gifts me (Abhishek Dubey) a signed copy of the book *Unbreakable: An Autobiography*.

As she gives me a copy of the book with the hands that are notorious for landing uncomfortable punches on people, she says, 'I have to make the second Mary Kom, the third Mary Kom...I just want to contribute for my state, for my country and for the younger generation...I want to produce more and more Olympic champions.'[6]

Mary Kom's desire to make the second, the third and the fourth Mary Kom resonated in my ears for many days and months after I returned to Delhi. And every time, I felt that India could produce many more boxing champions in the future. Some of them may go on to win world championships and medals in the Olympics. Maybe the colour of their medals would be better than

---

[5]Mary Kom, *Unbreakable: An Autobiography*, HarperCollins, introduction
[6]The interview was conducted by Abhishek Dubey for a documentary made on Mary Kom's life, after filming in her farm, village, home, the town, her academy and the SAI centre.

that of Mary Kom. But, it would be difficult, if not impossible, to produce another M.C. Mary Kom.

Why? What is the meaning of being Mary Kom?

Mary Kom's homeland, Manipur, has, for years after Independence, been far away from development. Almost the entire state has been affected by insurgency. The United National Liberation Front (UNLF), founded in 1964 with the objective of seeking independence from India, was the first insurgent group. Over time, many more groups with different goals, and deriving support from diverse ethnic groups with links in other states and countries like China and Myanmar, have risen. These insurgent groups used to run a parallel government, with illegal tax collections, extortions and robberies. The government had to respond by inducting the much-hated Armed Forces (Special Powers) Act— (AFSPA). The armed conflict between the insurgents and security forces has caused great hardship to the locals. Poor security situations have hampered economic growth, trade and tourism. Manipur is a landlocked state with poor road and rail connectivity. The limited lines of communication are susceptible to blockades by insurgents, creating shortage of essential commodities and increasing the hardships of the local population. The population has grown rapidly and there has been no corresponding increase in jobs. Policies of the central government have traditionally paid little regard to local opinion and sentiments. Of late, the situation has improved, but there are still miles to go before even a normal condition could be arrived at.

Mary Kom, for many, is un-Indian in her looks. This is especially true for those who have their own definition of Indians as per their accepted norms of physical appearance. Mary Kom's village is hardly 100 km from the Burmese border. Her looks resemble, as do so many people's in her state, those of neighbouring countries. Mary Kom says, 'My looks are different and I look different. I look like the Chinese, the Japanese or the Thai...(she laughs) and people are often surprised on seeing me, and at first look like they don't think that I am an Indian.'

She has elaborated on this further in her autobiography where she writes, 'I was not always recognized as Indian in my own country. Because of our oriental looks, people from the north-east are often mocked in other parts of India. We are called Nepalis, or "Chinkies"...people call us names... Whether or not I look "Indian", I am an Indian and I represent India, with pride, and all my heart'.[7]

Mary Kom belongs to one of the six most recognized tribes of Manipur. In the state of Manipur, they constitute around 45,000 people and are scattered in the foothills of all the districts. Mary's great grandfather, Pu. M. Khupneitong, was the chief of the biggest Kom village, Sagang, in the 1940s, from which subsequently around thirteen villages sprang up. His chieftainship was the glory days for the Koms. Her grandfather was also a legend among his contemporaries and was acknowledged for his hunting skills. In comparison, Mangte Tonpa Kom, the father of M.C. Mary Kom, had to face difficulties. In the 1980s, he decided to shift to his adopted village, Kangathei, another Kom village. However, here he was treated as an unwelcome guest. Life is tough for the poor. It gets tougher for those who become poor after having been rich. Her family had to face hardships as the situation at home turned adverse.

Mary Kom says, 'I was five years old when my father shifted here. Papa came here as grandfather refused to give him land in his village. As we were amongst the poorest in the village, people used to run away from us.' Thus, Mary Kom's family had to go through a great deal of hardship and economic deprivation when she was a child.

Mary Kom's family and surroundings did not even have a remote connect with competitive sports. The only connect, if any, was her father being an enthusiastic wrestler in his younger days. Mary Kom's parents, Mangte Tonpa Kom and Mangte Akham Kom, were poor farm labourers. Despite this, she was named Mangte Chungneijang, which means 'prosperous' in her local

---

[7]Mary Kom, *Unbreakable: An Autobiography*, HarperCollins, pg 11

dialect. Perhaps the seeds of rebellion were inadvertently sown in her character with this move.

Subsequently, Mangte Chungneijang named herself Mary for two reasons. Firstly, it was easy to pronounce. Secondly, it underlined her Christian faith. Even today, Mary is a religious person. She regularly goes to church and prays before every bout. She goes to sleep with the Bible under her pillow.

'When I was a child growing up in this village, I dreamt (she takes a long pause) of having all the basic things. I never dreamt of a huge building, but a beautiful and cute-looking basic home,' she says as she opens the door of her village home in Kangathei. She gets emotional, and we see her nostalgic demeanour when she says, 'It's good that you have come to my village... Not even a single shot of the film based on my life could be filmed in my village. In the soils, farms and fields of my village, many of my childhood stories, my struggles and time spent playing and fighting with my foes lies buried. I always go through several kinds of emotions whenever I come here.' The plans to shoot the film on Kom in her hometown were dropped due to safety concerns. *Mary Kom* was shot in Dharamshala and Manali, where a major portion of Manipur was recreated.

She starts preparing tea for us. As it gets ready, she takes us through the collage of photographs that adorn the wall of her home in the village. The child in her suddenly comes alive. She says, 'This is the only photograph of my childhood—it looks so cute; it looks like my mummy-papa did not take any other snap of me while I was a child.' Her other favourite photograph from the collage is the one where she wears the Olympic medal round her neck. And yet another one is her wedding photograph with Onler Kom.

Mary Kom's gender and ecosystem had nothing conducive or natural to shape her up as a legendary boxer. She first went to Loktak Christian Model High School where she studied up to class VI. After this, she moved on to St Xavier Catholic School. As a student, she displayed keen interest in athletics and used to participate in sports like football. But she never took part in boxing. She may have had a fondness for the sport, but family circumstances meant that it was the last thing on her list of priorities. She quit studies before completing school. 'In my family, I was the eldest one; I had younger brothers and sisters, and so I had to get a job and earn money for my family,' she says.

Far from encouragement, when she took up boxing, she had to hear taunts like, 'What is a girl doing in a man's world?'

Mary says, 'For the first four-five years, people used to tease me. "You are getting into boxing; this is crazy!" But I always challenged them whenever they used to laugh at me. "I will prove all of you wrong one day," I used to say then. After I became five-time world boxing champion, they all became quiet and started respecting me.'

As soon as she started to find her feet in competitive boxing, Mary Kom got married. She tells me, 'We were dumbstruck, lost for words, aghast at the thought of inevitable marriage. How? What are people thinking? Why marry at twenty-two? Is there a future for me? Is it all over? Is this dream run over? A million questions, with no answer, at that moment.' Such were the thoughts going on in Mary's mind before taking the plunge. After her marriage, Mary took a short hiatus from boxing. She and Onler had two children, Khupneivar Kom and Rechungvar Kom.

Mary then decided to answer all the questions in her mind with more than a befitting reply. The flurry of medals that include 15 gold, 2 silver and 1 bronze was a way to proclaim that she was still in business.

Boxers are supposed to be ruthless and unforgiving. But Mary Kom has a humane side to her. 'When in the ring, I am all alone. Even my coach is not with me. My entire focus is to bring my opponent down. In the process, they get hurt and start bleeding. I feel very bad. More often than not, in such cases, after the bout, I go to them and enquire about their condition. Sometimes I feel bad...but then this is an inherent part of boxing.'

Boxers are supposed to be feisty and muscular; Mary Kom

has her feminine side as well. She is a fashionista. She likes to wear western ensembles, paint her nails in bright colours and buy cosmetics when she is abroad for tournaments. Rajat Tangri, who did the research on Mary Kom for styling Priyanka Chopra in the film, says, 'There are so many tribes in Manipur, and each has its own symbol and colour palette. Mary Kom belongs to a tribe that descended from the Thai people. While she stayed in Manipur, she would help her parents on the jhum fields. She mostly wore a traditional phanek—a comfortable wraparound skirt with a shirt or a top.'[8]

As part of his research, Rajat Tangri worked on the clothes she wore as a child, as a teenager, during her early twenties and later. He worked on how Mary dressed when she took a sabbatical from boxing after marriage. Rajat says, 'Being an athlete and a five-time world boxing champion, she always preferred comfort over trendy or fashionable clothes. She has very simple tastes in fashion. However, now, on account of all the media attention, she is glamming up a little bit. The designers too want to work with her because she can really carry off so many styles with her athletic look.'[9]

Boxers are supposed to be tall. Mary Kom is shorter when compared to most of her opponents in the ring. This is supposed to be a disadvantage in the sport. 'Sometimes I wonder how I sustained my passion, given that I had neither exposure to the possibilities nor opportunities,' says Mary Kom.

Being born poor, living in a remote village with absolutely no facilities, with a diminutive frame, Mary Kom, a David, had to defeat so many Goliaths in her life. 'David is so small but he still kills Goliath! I am small too. And I come from a small state. But, like David, I have full faith in God who has gifted me with a special talent,' she says.

It is against this backdrop that the meaning of being Mary

---

[8]Anjali Jhangiani, 'The Mary Kom Style', *The Indian Express*, 9 September 2019
[9]Ibid.

Kom may be truly understood. But then, what is there in this David that has led her to come up triumphant against all these Goliaths?

The answer lies in the history of Manipur. Throughout its history, women have played a dominant role in society. In 1891, when the British seized this former kingdom, it was the women who led the revolt. Be it the fight for human rights against the army, the police or the insurgents, most of them were led by women. Ema Bazaar or Nupi Keithel, literally meaning Mother's Market or Women's Market, lying in the heart of the city, is the living symbol of this spirit. Here, only females are allowed to sell products. The market may just be a symbol, but the history of the state is full of stories encapsulating the resilience, the mental and physical toughness and never-say-die attitude of Manipuri women. Mary Kom is a strong Manipuri woman and in her case boxing became the medium to channelize her angst against the problems and situations she confronted in the different periods of her life.

The turn of the century was critical in the context of the social milieu of the state. The early 2000s was the time when defying curfew, women activists stripped during a demonstration before Kangla Fort—the headquarters of the Assam Rifles. They were protesting against the rape and killing of young women by the security forces. This was also the time when Irom Sharmila was already on her iconic fast. As L. Ibomcha Singh, the man who is credited for bringing modern boxing to the state, tells me, 'The strong and brave women around me convinced me that they would make excellent boxers. Whenever I passed by the Ima Keithel (Ema Bazaar), this belief became stronger. But then I did not have a set template. Women's boxing had not taken off in other parts of the country, and there were no examples to follow as such or any particular direction to go in. Getting a nod from the state government was was also testing my patience. Manipur didn't have any formal state association, even for men's boxing. The state's bodybuilding association was rechristened to a more formal boxing body.'

The man who has produced as many as thirty-eight international medallists, including boxing champion M.C. Mary Kom, L. Sarita, N.G. Dingko, P. Narjit, S. Suresh and M. Suranjoy amongst others, further adds, 'I was desperate to bring about some sort of kranti, some revolution. I went to schools, directly approaching the parents, and also to kung fu and taekwondo classes. The idea was just to convince them that if their children did well in sports, this could be the start of something really great for all of us.' Mary Kom, a strong girl herself, was one of the finest products of this wave.

The answer to queries regarding Kom's success lies in the rootedness and related values imbibed by Mary Kom from her family and the society she comes from. Mary Kom's relatives, especially her father, are all a picture of great humility. They would never turn to the other side, but stay in servitude for the betterment of society. Mary Kom's father could have ridden the wave of success, acquiring bungalows and fancy cars. But he chose to ride a cycle rickshaw and wear the same second-hand but dignified apparel bought from shops selling Moreh goods. The thrill and the camaraderie aside, the community she comes from contributes in terms of pooling in their resources. Everyone from all walks of life—laymen, farmers, doctors, engineers, teachers, police personnel, lawyers, church leaders, chiefs, social workers, students and housewives, from the old peers to the young energetic youth, everybody in the Komrem community has, in one way or the other, contributed to her success.

During a training session at Bangalore, Mary had lost all her belongings from her room, including all the money she had. She cried like a small child. Dr Angam Limai, a Tangkhul surgeon, travelled 40 km and gave her ₹5000. On another occasion, during a lightning training session at SAI Chandigarh, in preparation for the World Boxing Championships at Hungary in 2002, she had lost everything, including her passport, while travelling on the train. Again, an Assamese gentleman, who was the regional passport officer, issued a fresh passport for her in a record single day. This ensured her participation in the World Championships at the eleventh hour and she came back with a gold medal. The many prayers, fasts, in Komrem and other communities and associations, have also not remained unanswered. The Komrem fraternity of Delhi braved cold winter breezes, baked in the hot summer sun, waiting for hours at Delhi's IGI airport every time their sister Mary returned from her sojourns abroad. All the prayers, love, sacrifice, assistances and contributions in every way have moulded Mary into the 'Magnificent Mary' of today. The different types and degrees of adversities M.C. Mary Kom had to face in the formative years of her life would have made any other person bitter. But Mary is positive and full of warmth because of the family and the community she comes from. Like the state of Manipur, the life of Mary Kom also took a new turn with the dawn of the year 2000.

The seventeen-year-old girl, on a fine December morning of 2000, participated in the 7th East Open Boxing Championships. She was gifted ₹500 and a Kom Ponvei, a traditional wrap-around skirt for women. She was requested to wear the Ponvei on the victory podium, with the state in the grip of the Dingko Singh fever. Though the state government's awareness of women's boxing was next to non-existent, it was Dingko and his exploits outside the ring that inspired Mary to take up boxing as a profession.

Mary Kom's first coach, Konthoujam Kosana Meitei, said, 'I do still remember that when she came to me, she appeared to be from a poor family. The clothes she was wearing were a torn t-shirt and torn track pants. I thought that she was slightly short and she should be taller to compete in the sport. Then, she was also lean and thin. I started thinking which event we should fit her in. But soon I realized that she had strong willpower and firm determination and whatever I used to say, she used to do that.'[10]

---

[10]K. Kosana Meitei said this in a television interview with DD North East.

Mary Kom did not share the fact that she had started boxing, even with her parents. Her father said, 'We heard from someone that a girl from the Kom tribe was boxing. So I started thinking who it could be. Who was good at sports from our tribe? And then I saw the photo of Mary in the newspaper. My wife went to ask this person and then she bumped into Mary with the medals in her hand. I don't know what to say, but maybe it was a gift of God, I felt. Even when she was young, she was fast and strong like boys. So maybe God gave her this talent for boxing.'

His reasoning behind the cause notwithstanding, the overall situation around her made him apprehensive about his daughter taking up boxing as a career. His biggest worry was that his daughter might get hurt in the bout and become disfigured. Who would marry her then?

In Onler, Mary Kom got the life partner that every woman, particularly one who wants to buck the trend, needs in her life. How did this partnership start?

Mary's better half, Onler, is the third son of the chief from Samulamlan village. The meeting between the two, however, was an accident. Back in the year 2000, an unknown Kom girl from Manipur took a train to Bangalore for the national boxing camp. Having lost her wallet in a previous train journey, she strapped her suitcase, carrying her passport, money and other worldly possessions to her wrist with an iron chain. She woke up to find that the suitcase was gone.

'I had a very difficult financial background. Money was always tight and it had taken a lot of work to get my passport made. There I was with nothing in my hand but the chain. I have been a fighter by nature but that was one moment when I actually contemplated ending my life. I was tired of the struggle and the troubles a stolen suitcase entailed. I was most worried about my passport, as I had my first international tournament within a month or so,' Mary says, as the tea gets ready and all of us start sipping it in the winter chill. Onler, then, was the president of the northeast students' body in Delhi. He heard what had happened and offered to help.

In the early 2000s, Onler Kom was in Delhi on the instruction of his father who had asked him to sit for the UPSC exams. He was studying, and at the same time was the president of the Manipur Students' Union. Onler speaks less, and like most of those who speak less, whenever he speaks, he speaks sense. As we move out of their house to an open area in the village, he says, 'I first met Mary at the Jawaharlal Nehru Stadium in Delhi. I saw this girl; she had short hair and a lot of gumption. I knew she wanted to become a boxer against all odds. We were a student community from the northeast. I told her if she needed anything, starting from financial help to home-cooked food, she could tell me. She once came home for dinner. We became friends,' says Onler.

After this, Onler became Mary's local guardian for all purposes. 'We stayed in touch. Whenever she needed to go to the ministry for a meeting, or shopping, she would call. I would accompany her, or send one of my friends. We established a good rapport, a friendship.' It was a relationship that developed slowly. At first, Onler was only concerned about helping her.

Mary's parents lived in the village and she was struggling single-handedly. And as a woman boxer, Mary had many hurdles to cross. She won the silver medal at the World Championships in 2001. It was celebrated in Delhi, but there was little effect in Manipur. When she had to go to Turkey the next year, she had very little money for the trip. She had gone to the US with ₹2000. The Manipur Students Union and some Manipuris in government service decided to help. A fund-raising project was initiated to fund her on her trips for her competitions. Only when she won the gold medal at the World Championships did she become a known name in her home state.

With time, Onler and Mary both started realizing that there was more to their relationship than just friendship. But the decision to get married was not an instantaneous one. After a long pause, Onler starts again, 'We were friends for four years... Besides, I was almost engaged to another girl at that time. I had to decide between the two. I thought about which of them needed me more. The other girl was from a middle class family; her father was doing well. Mary, on the other hand, was still struggling, with no support at all. I felt empathy for her, felt her suffering as she travelled alone for her competitions. Sometimes, during the long bus journeys from Imphal to Guwahati and from there by train to Delhi, she would lose her luggage or be teased by boys and men at bus stops. Also, there were all the negative comments about a girl boxer; at that time it was not a popular sport at all and people looked at her as if she was some strange creature. I felt protective, and I think my feeling evolved from there.'

After the feeling had developed, they had to confront numerous problems. Onler Kom had left his job in Shillong to try for the civil services in Delhi. It had not worked out. He could not get married till he had a job. By 2004, when he decided to marry her, she was already the winner of a silver medal and a World Championships title. She had plenty more medals to win and wanted to keep on boxing. 'We had known each other for four years now and she knew she could depend on me for any help. At that time, there were many boys pestering her with proposals and offers of marriage. She had become a star. It was a source of annoyance to her, a disturbance. I told her, you better get married to me and leave all these proposals behind. Once you are engaged to me, no one will bother you and you will be in my care,' he says.

Before talking to her, Onler had already approached her parents. 'Her father (smiling) nearly killed me. He said that it was not the way to come with a proposal; we had our traditions and customs. I tried telling her mother that Mary needed to be cared for, that I could do that, protect her, help her financially, and said everything that I could say. She had no access to finance to improve her boxing. I had played national football when in Meghalaya and I knew how to deal with the management. But nothing worked, and so I spoke to Mary directly,' he says.

When Mary heard the entire thing, she agreed to get married. Onler approached her parents again, but was rejected. 'Mary then said, "Let us elope. We will go to Delhi, Shillong or somewhere. Let us stay separate from our families, on our own, and we can have a court marriage." I told her not to get emotional. She was the eldest daughter and I was the youngest son, and everything we did would affect our families. In fact, her mother too came to visit me and requested me not to take her daughter away. She assured me that she would convince her husband to let us get married,' says Onler.

There is a ceremony amongst the Koms wherein the boy's parents carry food and tea to the girl's house, and if the girl's parents drink the tea, it means the proposal is accepted. If they don't, then it is a refusal. When Onler's parents visited Mary's home for the first time, they did not even let them pour out the tea. But when they understood the magnitude of the resolve of their daughter, they invited Onler's parents and drank the tea. The wedding was fixed. It was 2005.

As the entire conversation related to her marriage ends, she takes us to the middle of the field. She starts digging with the available tools so that our camera can capture the scene. The children huddle around their father. The picture of Mary ploughing the field exemplifies her grounded and rooted nature, which has kept her hunger alive despite one success after other. The children huddling around their father reminds us of the man who has always been a source of support for the successful woman.

Onler is the person who knows Mary best, perhaps even better than her parents. He knows that sometimes she is very short-tempered with the children. When she becomes tense, then it is difficult to cool her down. Sometimes she is shy and distracted and says things to the media that are blown out of context. She has problems with English and communicating with the press. 'But now, after so many interviews, she is even better than me, in English,' Onler says with a palpable sense of pride in his voice.

What is the one defining quality of Mary Kom?

Onler says, 'I see her as the perfect woman. Whatever she does, she does perfectly and with full concentration, be it boxing, watching television or even sleeping. She is never half-hearted in her approach. When she watches serials, she gets so engrossed that she starts crying.' After a long, thoughtful pause, Onler says, 'She is still firmly rooted. Nobody thought she would still clean the toilet, or wash clothes, but she is still the same. She does what she did before, with the same energy and dedication, both at home and in boxing. She looks after the children the same way.'

Whenever she finds time, Mary Kom likes to cook for her family. Although she mostly eats boiled food, she can also whip up finger-licking fish and rice dishes.

As one closely interacts with Onler, one gets the sense that he is mature beyond his age. One also feels his broad-mindedness that defies the time and circumstances in which he grew up. The calmness in his demeanour speaks volumes about the restless phase he had to go through when he lost his father.

Onler Kom lost his father to violence. Unidentified gunmen, numbering about six, shot his father Rekhupathang Kom dead, between the villages of Samulamlan and Turinphaijan. Rekhupathang had been beating the winter chill with a meiphu (charcoal/wood burner) inside the house after dinner, when, around 6:30 p.m., a Kom dialect-speaking youth showed up and asked the village chief to show him the Chinglangmei village road. Meanwhile, four to five accomplices loitered at the entrance gate. Moments after Rekhupathang moved out of the house with the meiphu in his hand, a gunshot was heard in the vicinity and then the villagers found the victim lying motionless by the roadside. As per local sources, the killing was either connected to a land dispute or Rekhupathang preventing his daughter-in-law Mary Kom from attending a recent felicitation programme. The couple withstood this crisis as well and continued with their responsibilities with renewed energy and vigour.

Mary Kom has been a prolific sportswoman who has demonstrated a relentless passion for the game. This has been reflected in the results over the years. She won a total of five national championships from 2000 to 2005. Between 2001 and 2006, she won a silver at the Association Internationale de Boxe Amateur (AIBA) World Boxing Championships in India. In the same year, she boxed at the AIBA Women's World Boxing Championships in China where she earned the gold medal—her fourth successive gold medal at the Championships. In the following year, she went to Vietnam, from where she returned with a gold medal at the 2009 Asian Indoor Games. In Kazakhstan, Mary won the gold medal at the Asian Women's Boxing Championships in 2010. Then she proceeded to Barbados to register a career milestone— her fifth consecutive gold at the AIBA Women's World Boxing Championships. The feat makes her one of the best women boxers the world has ever seen. She competed in the 51 kg class in the 2010 Asian Games and won a bronze medal. Again, at the Asian Women's Boxing Championships in Mongolia in 2012, she participated in the same weight category and won the gold. She bore the Queen's baton in the opening ceremony of the 2010 Commonwealth Games in Delhi. She became the first amateur to surpass several professional athletes in terms of earnings, sponsorships and endorsements. Her agility and sharp reflexes have become part of boxing lore. During a national camp at Delhi's Indira Gandhi Stadium in 2002, she killed a snake. During another camp at Hisar, she was seen catching squirrels in and around the camp area. A tally of 30 gold, 2 silver and 1 bronze medal were attached to the CV of M.C. Mary Kom, in national and international competitions, as she boarded the flight for the 2012 London Olympics.

The stage was thus set for the big bash between Nicola's 'Believe' and the 'Unbreakable' trait of M.C. Mary Kom at the 2012 London Olympics. There could not have been better opponents representing women's boxing in its debut Olympics. Before heading to London, Mary Kom won her world amateur titles in the 46 kg and 48 kg categories, but the lightest of the three weight brackets at the Games was 51 kg. The 5 ft 2 in., five-time champion, Mary Kom, started her campaign in style. She chopped down the much taller Pole Karolina Michalczuk—herself a former world champion, as women's boxing finally made its Olympic debut. The ferocious twenty-nine-year-old flung many hooks at the head of her upright opponent, cheered on by a sizeable Indian contingent.

'Every athlete wants to participate in the Olympic Games and for twelve years I have been waiting and waiting, asking when it would be included here. It's very special. I am crying because it is my twins' fifth birthday. It is emotional because I cannot be with them to celebrate their birthday, but I am here at the Olympics, and I am fighting and winning,'[11] she told us as we stood there to get her first reaction after her win.

In the quarter-final the following day, she defeated Maroua Rahali of Tunisia with a score of 15-6, and with it, the bronze medal was assured. With this, she became the third Indian woman after Karnam Malleswari and Saina Nehwal to win an Olympic medal. In the semi-finals, she was up against the local favourite, Nicola Adams. She could not proceed further as she went down fighting in her pre-summit bout. She displayed heart, but was no match for Adams, who won comprehensively, by 11-6.

'I want to tell all Indians that I am sorry I could not get a gold medal. But I am satisfied. I gave it my all. My dream of an Olympic medal is fulfilled. It has been such a long wait for this medal. I am happy,' she told the waiting Indian media. We had tears in our eyes as we thought of her incredible achievements against all odds. The unbreakable Mary Kom may have lost out on the colour of the medal, but hers was a phenomenal achievement nevertheless.

Even eight years after the medal in the London Olympics in 2012, the fight in Mary Kom has not died. Perhaps her resolve has strengthened with each passing year. Whenever life starts punching and pushing her, she stages a major comeback. She is the only woman to become World Amateur Boxing Champion for a record six times. She is the only woman boxer to have won a medal in each one of the seven world championships. She is

---

[11]'Kom stars on historic day-London 2012-boxing', olympic.org, 5 August 2012

the first Indian woman boxer to get a gold medal in the Asian Games 2014 in Incheon. She is confident of competing in the Tokyo Olympics in 2020.

On 26 April 2016, Mary Kom was nominated by the president of India as a member of the Rajya Sabha. As an MP, Mary Kom has even better attendance than someone as sincere as Sachin Tendulkar. Moreover, the stretch of road leading to the National Games village in Imphal has been renamed MC Mary Kom Road.

When she started on her quest, she started all alone. After years of perseverance and hard work, she has paved the road for women of future generations—to follow her road to success. If she could remain unbreakable after facing so many hurdles, so can we, following her example.

SEVEN

Sania Mirza: Changing the Game

There have been two distinct stages in her tennis career. She is the most popular and most talented tennis player in India. But many argue about the 'underachievement of her potential'. She doesn't care. She is a woman of New India who believes in speaking her mind.

Her marriage was a love marriage. Controversy's favourite child dared to go for a marriage that had cross-border ramifications. She had to go through gruelling off-the-court battles after this.

She is Sania Mirza, the charm of the city that houses the Charminar.

There is something in tennis that sets it apart from other sports in terms of the emancipation and empowerment of women. The history of the game has been full of contradictions. The game has been fought and won against aristocracy, colour, gender bias and, most importantly, the monopoly of the resources. There are events in the history of the sport that are so bizarre that they don't quite seem true after a point of time.

The nationally-televised 1973 Battle of the Sexes match in which twenty-nine-year-old Billie Jean King beat fifty-five-year-old former champion Bobby Riggs in three straight sets was one such occasion. Thirty-four years after this, when a film was made based on the event, the screenwriter Simon Beaufoy said, 'The actual match was pure pantomime, outright silly. Yet what was going on underneath was incredibly serious. That win had a huge sociological effect.'[1]

That match at the Houston Astrodome in front of 30,000 spectators attracted a televised audience of around ninety million people. Riggs was a former Wimbledon singles and doubles champion who had retired in 1951 at the age of fifty-five. In an act of male chauvinism, he announced that he was still better than any female player, and could beat any woman on court. Riggs managed to challenge and beat the women's no. 1 player, Margaret Court, 6-2, 6-1. It was then that Billie Jean King stepped up.

The match had its impact beyond sports. The event management was wonderfully choreographed, befitting the occasion. In the $100,000 winner-take-all match, King was carried into the arena on a throne carried by four men dressed as slaves, while Riggs was brought in on a rickshaw pulled by barely-clothed women.

As Billie Jean King remembers, promoter Jerry Perenchio had suggested the absurd entrance.

'He said to me, "I know you are a feminist. So you probably won't get on this Egyptian litter, will you?"
'I said, "Yes, I love it! Let's go."
'He was shocked. I got on it, and we walked out.'[2]
King found out that Riggs, who was paid $50,000 to wear a 'sugar daddy'-inscribed jacket during the match, intended to give her a giant 'sugar daddy'-inscribed candy on a stick. Perenchio had a small pig for King to present him in exchange.
'I named it Robert Larimore Riggs, Bobby's formal name, and put a little ribbon around his neck. It was so cute,' King still remembers. She made Parenchio promise that the pig would

---

[1] Nation Now, '"Battle of the Sexes": How accurate is the movie about the infamous tennis match?', 13wmaz.com, 24 September 2017
[2] 'Battle of the Sexes': How accurate is the movie about the infamous tennis match?', KGW8, 24 September 2017

never end up 'as ham on a table'. 'Let it live a long life at a farm. They gave it to an Oklahoma farmer.'[3]

King's actual match apparel is still housed at the Smithsonian National Museum of American History.

Riggs was leading the first set by four games to two. But the tie swung in King's favour as she adopted a baseline game and wore down her opponent by forcing him to run. As a result, she eased to victory in three straight sets, 6-4, 6-3, 6-3. She won the $100,000 (£75,000) winner-takes-all prize, presented by world heavyweight boxing champion George Foreman. But more than the prize money and who gave away the prize, the match had its impact on tennis, sports and beyond the boundaries of sports in many ways.

As a report in the *Los Angeles Times*, dated 2 October 2017, says, 'In a key scene late in *Battle of the Sexes*, the new tennis movie about the landmark Billie Jean King-Bobby Riggs match, an icon is reminded of her power to influence. "Times change," King, played by Emma Stone, is told by a confidante. "You should know—you just changed them".'[4]

The 1973 exhibition was certainly a study in contrasts—the trailblazer and the showman, the chauvinist and the progressive, the old guard and the new world. What has the match left as legacy for the times to come? In the context of Indian sports, Sania Mirza has been the torchbearer of the legacy of the epochal match.

Firstly, at the heart of professional tennis lies a paradox. The sport has always had a more progressive reputation than its counterparts. It boasted top-flight female professionals decades ahead of most team sports; it counts social activist pioneers like Arthur Ashe amongst its ranks. And tennis was a global mélange of cultures long before the NBA and MLB moved in that direction.

---

[3]Bryan Alexander, '"Battle of the Sexes": How accurate is the movie about the infamous tennis match?', *USA Today*, 21 September 2017
[4]Steven Zeitchik, 'How tennis' Battle of the Sexes did—and didn't—change the game', *Los Angeles Times*, 2 October 2017

And yet, to play the game is to require resources. Historically, the champions used to come from money and more than often were white. Now, the Williams sisters have ushered in a new era of fans and competitors. The idea of tennis as a sport for the aristocracy has eroded too, as champions like Andy Murray and Novak Djokovic, along with the Williams sisters, come from more hardscrabble backgrounds.

Sania Mirza represents tennis's non-aristocratic background in India. As she says, 'One of the reasons people think I have not struggled as much as other people have struggled is because we don't talk much about it. We definitely were never in the position where we had to struggle for food. But this does not mean that our struggle was anywhere else. My sister, who is seven–eight years younger to me, must have been one year old when I was nine. My father, mother, sister and myself used to travel in our car which we converted from petrol to diesel because that was the cheapest fuel at that time. To reach in time for matches and avoid hotel stay expenses, we even drove from Mumbai to Trivandrum, which used to take twenty-four hours.'[5]

Her non-aristocratic tennis background is also evident from the manner in which the entire family optimized their thin resources for their daughter so she could live her tennis dream.

'At the age of four or six you don't understand why you cannot afford to play tennis. Now, of course, I can understand the reason. At that time it was difficult for me to reconcile with the fact that my cousins could play the game and I could not. In fact, the first time I held a tennis racquet was in the US. I was bullied on the court by my cousins who said, "You are a girl and you cannot play tennis." Certain things are destined. Had I not come back from America, I would never have been able to afford to play tennis. The first thing that my mom told me once we were back was—let us play tennis and swim and do all the

---

[5]Sania Mirza said this in an NDTV interview with Shekhar Gupta, for *Walk the Talk*.

things we were unable to do.'[6]

Secondly, the Battle of the Sexes match in 1973 didn't happen in a vacuum—King and other women players had been waging a fight for equal pay on the tour. When King accepted the challenge from Riggs, it was to popularize the equal pay cause and pressurize tournament organizers, particularly at the Slams, to bring gender alignment. Prize money at the majors is now equal. However, the Battle of the Sexes did not change everything overnight. It took some of the Slams decades to award equal prize money to men and women; Wimbledon, the last tournament to do so, didn't change its policy until 2007.

Sania Mirza, in this sense, represents the generation of women tennis players who have played in the era of equal pay for women and men players. There are still murmurs of discontent. Recently, the tournament director Raymond Moore said, 'If I was a lady player, I'd go down every night on my knees and thank God that Roger Federer and Rafa Nadal were born, because they have carried this sport.'[7] But thanks to the legacy left behind by the Battle of the Sexes match, players like Sania Mirza have been witness to equal prize money for both male and female players.

Thirdly, as King rightly said then, 'The biggest thing that came out of the match for me was the girls in the stands who felt self-empowered and encouraged. Fathers came up with tears in their eyes. And many of their daughters started playing tennis.'[8] Sania has given that hope to thousands of daughters across the country. 'If I can, so can you,' has been her seminal message for them.

Lastly, and most importantly, what's striking in the post-Battle of the Sexes era is how much of a cult the personalities of the principal players became. As renowned tennis expert Jon

---

[6]Sania Mirza said this in an NDTV interview with Shekhar Gupta, for *Walk the Talk*.
[7]Ian Anderson, 'Tennis boss apologises after saying women players should 'thank God' for Federer and Nadal', stuff.co.nz, 21 March 2016
[8]Steven Zeitchik, 'How tennis' Battle of the Sexes did—and didn't—change the game', *Los Angeles Times*, 2 October 2017

Wertheim aptly puts it, 'Rod Laver was great, but I don't know that anyone was saying that I am a fan of Rod Laver, and that means something.'[9] On the contrary, rooting for Riggs or King said something about what you stood for—politically, culturally and philosophically. The trend has continued with renewed vigour since then. Federer fans see themselves as graceful purists, Nadal supporters relate to all-out passion and Murray enthusiasts champion the grit and working-class sweat.

India's Sania Mirza, too, has a strong representation. She is a woman from a Muslim family in India. From her birth to her marriage to a Pakistani cricketer, she has done a tightrope walk. She has done all this without a particular role model to look up to. She has fought controversies all along her way. And, unlike the Battle of the Sexes match of 1973, which was well-choreographed by the promoters of the game, she had to react to the situations in her own way, naturally, as and when they arose.

Sania Mirza was not even born when the Battle of the Sexes match was played in 1973. She was born thirteen years after this, in 1986, in Mumbai. She was born to Hyderabadi Muslim parents—Imran Mirza, a builder, and his wife, Naseema, who worked in the printing business. Shortly after Sania's birth, her family moved to Hyderabad, where she and her younger sister Anam were raised in a religious Sunni Muslim family. Sania is a distant relative of former cricket captain Ghulam Ahmed of India, and Asif Iqbal of Pakistan. She is an Indian Muslim woman, and for people who claim to be intellectually aware and sincerely dedicated to their religion, her sportsstar status does not prevent them from pointing their finger at her. Sania, in her career, has notable wins over Svetlana Kuznetsova, Vera Zvonareva, Marion Bartoli, former world number one Martina Hingis, Dinara Safina and Victoria Azarenka.

She is the highest-ranked female player ever from India, peaking at world no. 27 in singles in mid-2007. She has achieved

---

[9]Jon Wertheim said this in an interview with *Sports Illustrated*, May 2006.

a number of firsts for women's tennis in India. She surpassed US $1,000,000 in career earnings, she has in her bag a singles pro level title and six major titles—three each in women's doubles and mixed doubles, and she won the WTA Finals in 2014 alongside Cara Black and defended the title the following year partnering with Martina Hingis. She has a total of 14 medals in her name, which include 6 gold at three major multi-sports events, namely the Asian Games, the Commonwealth Games and the Afro Asian Games. Sania registered 41 straight wins with her partner Martina Hingis, to be crowned the no. 1 doubles pair in the world of tennis.

But keeping aside the accolades, trophies, prize money and titles, we should concentrate on Sania Mirza's contribution, in the way she has fought the stereotypes throughout the formative years of her life. Times change, but Sania Mirza should know that she has changed them in Indian women's sports. How much these changes can alter the future of tennis in the country will depend on the responsiveness of the tennis ecosystem in the times to come. Thus, broadly speaking, there are two Sania Mirzas to understand. First, the Sania Mirza about whom the best in the game said that they acknowledged that she had great potential early in her career. As her singles journey was reaching the takeover stage, she changed track to doubles and set the stage on fire. The second is the Sania Mirza who responded to the controversies she found herself surrounded by, defining what she represents in tennis.

The tennis journey of Sania Mirza started when it took Krishna Bhupathi less than forty-five minutes to realize that she was the undisputed owner of India's most outstanding forehand in tennis. Not long after he'd shepherded son Mahesh's career, Bhupathi Sr's keen eye had spotted this wicked weapon in another prodigy—a shot that could be hit clean and accurate on any surface. The twenty-one-year-old Hyderabadi girl, however, came up in the national headlines in 2003, when she, along with her partner Alisa Kleybanova of Russia, won the girls' doubles final and registered their triumph at the mother of all Grand Slam venues—Wimbledon.

This marked the beginning of the journey of an ordinary girl with not-so-ordinary ambitions in her life. She knew what she wanted in life and it reflected in her on-court aggression. Her attitude and determination were compared to legendary German tennis ace Steffi Graf. Krishna Bhupathi often talks about a press conference in 2005-06, where he remembers Mirza fielding questions and then walking off when she was done, leaving behind a dais full of startled celebrities, including a southern superstar.

'That day, I knew this girl was something else,' he says, with a touch of pride.[10]

The girl was not going to be content being just a many-time national champion at the Delhi Lawn Tennis Association grounds, and aimed higher to find a place on the international stage.

Sania says, 'Ten years before I started, there was Nirupama (Vaidyanathan). Then I started playing well, and suddenly went from no. 200 to no. 31 in the world, and no one expected that. After that, for so many years, I have moved from one Slam to the next in doubles, I don't think of it as something unique. But it gets lonely since there's no other Indian girl out there,'[11] she says.

'I came at a time when there was no girl in any sport, and the last icon was (sprinter) P.T. Usha. People were shocked and surprised to see me, but I guess it was boring to speak about just the forehand and my serve. Some of the controversies were so pointless. At eighteen, you are supposed to know how to party or bunk college, not how to be politically correct. But I'm calmer now while handling such things,'[12] she says. Shivam Naik puts it aptly:

> Great forehand, a decent backhand, poor service and no volley—that's where Sania's game stood when she woke up one day, wracked by unbearable pain. In one of her last singles tournaments at Brussels in 2012, Mirza would beat three Top 100 players. And wake up the next morning with

---

[10]Shivani Naik, 'Breaking back: Sania Mirza gets through it all', 2 November 2014
[11]Ibid.
[12]Ibid.

painful swollen knees. 'I am double-jointed and suffer from hyperlaxity, a genetic problem not many are aware of. It causes chronic pain, and my joints are vulnerable to freak injuries. It's like having arthritis in your teens,' says Mirza.

Hyperlaxity affects athletes the worst when going through rapid growth spurts, and since it wasn't detected earlier in her case, the pain ended up being severe. 'People kept saying she should have done this or that, but they refused to understand that my body had its limitations,' she says. It was a tough decision to switch to doubles. I had to make the right call and since it worked, in hindsight I can say that it was the right thing to do.' Nevertheless, Sania missed playing singles all the time and is confident she was among the top 100 players of the world.

Sania still remembers the nightmarish 2008 Australian Open doubles finals, where she teamed up with Mahesh Bhupathi, and lost the match. Loaded with painkillers, Mirza had wondered aloud to her apprehensive partner if she'd ever be able to play another final. A year later, she would win the same tournament with him. 'I'll never forget that feeling. Mahesh had managed my career when I was young. It was almost like winning with family,' she says.[13]

Krishna Bhupathi, who first spotted the spark in her, now says, 'Though I was disappointed that her singles career didn't work out, I'm happy she's doing well in doubles.'[14]

As her tennis graph showed an upward curve, so did awards and recognitions. National awards brought laurels to Sania. She was named the 'best young female achiever' and received the award for the 'most outstanding performance in tennis' in the year 2004. Sania was the first Indian sportswoman to make it to *Time's* Asia edition cover, which described her as a role model for Indian women and the fastest rising star in the year 2005.

---

[13]Shivani Naik, 'Breaking back: Sania Mirza gets through it all', 2 November 2014
[14]Ibid.

In the list of heroes, Sania shared space with Chinese actress Zhang Jingchu, South Korean footballer Park Ji Sung and Japan's Ken Watanabe. Later, in 2005, she was presented with the Rajiv Gandhi Khel Ratna award. Apart from her performance on the court, her gracious presence on the circuit was also being noticed. In 2006, she was ranked amongst the top 10 most beautiful tennis players of all time by Chinese news agency Xinhua, which had her up next to Russians Anna Kournikova and Maria Sharapova. Fame gives birth to foes, and for Sania, this happened quite early.

Her on-the-court appeal, short skirts and fondness for piercings were always under the kind of scrutiny she might not even have been aware of. In the book *Ace Against Odds*, she says, 'If it was the t-shirts at Wimbledon, it turned out to be the nose ring at the US Open. Everything I wore was interpreted to be a symbol of rebellion. Maybe it was that the foreign media had never seen a young Indian girl on stage before. Maybe I did not fit the American idea of a typical Indian woman.' She further adds, 'The ring soon became a symbol of a cult status I was quickly gaining in public consciousness. It began to be marketed in India as the "Sania nose ring" and the tiny piece of jewellery became a rage amongst young girls.'[15]

In the year 2005, Sania saw her freedom being snatched away. And this was done on the basis of religion, something she sincerely abides by. A fatwa was issued against Sania which highlighted her 'indecency in dressing up' for a job she is best at. Hasheeb-ul-hasan Siddiqui of the Sunni Ulema Board protested against her sense of dressing and feared other young Muslim girls would follow this flamboyant sportswoman. There was a threat to Sania's game, demanding she change her on-court dressing. She was given special protection at the Women's Tennis Association Sunfeast Open Tournament in 2005.

Later, she flaunted a cheeky slogan on her t-shirt, 'Well-behaved women rarely make history.'

---

[15]'Sania Mirza's battles on court and off', rediff.com, 19 July 2016

Sania Mirza's self-belief not only reflected in her dressing or game but also in her thoughts. She said that whether before or after marriage, the most important matter was that sex should be safe.[16] Zealots accused the nineteen-year-old of defending Tamil actor Khushboo's reported remark that it was all right for women to have sex before marriage as long as they took precaution against disease and pregnancy. When she was asked about the Khushboo controversy at a function in Delhi, she said, 'So, there are basically two issues here—safe sex and sex before marriage.'

Commenting on the first issue, she said, 'You don't want me to tell you that you should have safe sex, whether it's before or after marriage. Everyone must know what he or she is doing.'[17] Interestingly, in the same function in the capital, Sania had also taken a pot shot at critics of her short skirts. 'As long as I keep winning, people should not bother whether the length of my skirt is six inches or six feet.'[18] Following her statement on sex, there were protests against her in Andhra Pradesh and people burnt her effigy. Sania cleared the air saying her words were misquoted and she never meant to hurt anyone's sentiments.

In a long statement, Sania said, 'I would like to clearly say on record that I could not possibly justify premarital sex as it is a big sin in Islam and one which I believe will not be forgiven by Allah.'[19]

There are critics who say that Sania had to take her statement back after the pressure by radicals and that she should have held her ground. But the girl from Hyderabad had made her point known to those she had intended her statement for, before taking her words back.

Sania Mirza's family doctor was threatened through e-mails and letters that if he treated her, he would have to face heavy

---

[16]Omer Farooq, 'Sania smashes 'hurtful' sex quote', BBC, 18 November 2005
[17]Sania Mirza said this at a function in Delhi, where she was invited as one of the chief guests.
[18]Shalini Langer, 'The long and shorts of it', *The Indian Express*, 24 October 2017
[19]'Mirza insists she opposes premarital sex', ESPN, 19 November 2005

consequences. In December 2007, a Mecca Masjid ad shoot landed her in a soup, when she and the camera team were accused of entering the premises without permission. Sania apologized for the same and that put a halt to the much-hyped issue. But the one that hurt her most was the one related to the national flag. On New Year's Day in 2008, Mirza was spotted sitting with her feet resting on a table next to an Indian flag.[20] She said that the pose was accidental. A case was filed in the Chief Judicial Magistrate's Court under Section 2 of the Prevention of Insult to the National Honour Act of 1971, by a Hyderabad-based lawyer.

Sania, if found guilty, could have faced a penalty of three years in jail and a fine. The flag controversy pained her so much that later on, she admitted in one of the press conferences that she had even thought of quitting the game. 'I think a lot of thoughts went through my head in the last couple of weeks. One of the thoughts was to quit the sport, but I wouldn't say it was serious enough that I am going to quit now,'[21] she said.

Mirza further added, 'I just know that I would not do anything to disrespect my country. I love my country; I wouldn't be playing in the Hopman Cup otherwise, but besides that I am not allowed to comment.'[22]

There comes a time in every sportsperson's life when they graduate from being a good player to a sporting stateswoman. For Sania Mirza, that moment came on the eve of India's participation in the 2012 London Olympics. Sania Mirza, in a press statement, said that although Mahesh Bhupathi would have been her first choice, she was ready to partner Leander Paes in the larger interest of the country.[23] But she had made her reservations known to the

[20]'Sania Mirza "considered quitting",' BBC, 15 January 2008

[21]Sania Mirza said this at a press conference in Melbourne on the eve of the Australian Open, 15 January 2008.

[22]Simon Cambers, 'Mirza admits she considered quitting over flag row,' Reuters.com, 15 January 2008

[23]PTI, 'I have been treated as bait by AITA: Sania Mirza,' The Times of India, 26 June 2012

power centres in tennis before agreeing to this.

'As an Indian woman belonging to the twenty-first century, what I find disillusioning is the humiliating manner in which I was put up as a bait to try and pacify one of the disgruntled stalwarts of Indian tennis,' Sania said in an apparent reference to Paes.[24] The twenty-five-year-old also hit out at the way she was 'offered in compensation to partner one of the feuding champions purely in order to lure him into accepting to play with men's players he did not wish to play with. This kind of blatant humiliation of Indian womanhood needs to be condemned even if it comes from the highest controlling body of tennis in the country.'[25]

In her statement, Sania was also critical of Leander's father, Dr Vece Paes, who had asked her to give a written commitment to pair up with his son. 'To Dr Vece Paes, who has on camera asked me to give in writing about my intention of partnering his son for the mixed doubles event at the Olympics, I would like to point out that my commitment is to my country. For the sake of India I am committed to play with Leander Paes or Mahesh Bhupathi or Rohan Bopanna or Somdev Devvarman or Vishnu Vardhan or any other person that my country feels I am good enough to partner. There should never ever be a question on this, although if asked, I am entitled to have my preferences. I will do everything I possibly can to win a medal for India.' She did not stop here. She said, 'To Leander Paes, I would like to point out that Vishnu Vardhan is an extremely talented player, who I had the privilege of partnering. We went on to win a silver medal for India at the 2010 Asian Games, when all the three male stalwarts of Indian tennis had opted to stay away from Guangzhou. I am convinced that he can go one better when pitted with someone as good as Leander as partner. For Leander to consider partnering with Vishnu only if he has a written assurance from me to play mixed (as Vece Uncle has suggested in his television interviews) is, I think demeaning

---

[24]'India's Sania Mirza: I was used as a bait in player row', BBC, 27 June 2012

[25]Amarnath K. Menon, 'Sania takes offence to AITA's disregard for her commitment to the sport', *India Today*, 7 July 2012

If we talk of one female athlete who performed and transformed the Indian women's sporting scenario forever, it has to be P.T. Usha.

Photo courtesy: Debashish Datta (Aajkaal)

Ashwini Nachappa: She ran like the wind, gazelle-like strides carrying her far away from hustling opponents as she beat the clock with ridiculous ease.

Photo courtesy: Ashwini Nachappa

And she does it! Blue ribbon coiling down to a bronzed sphere that she clutches in her hand. Karnam Malleswari with her medal at the 2000 Sydney Olympics.

Photo courtesy: Karnam Malleswari

If Milkha Singh and P.T. Usha brought Indian athletics tantalizingly close to the finishing line in the highest global sporting platform, Anju Bobby George actually was the one who crossed that finishing line.

Photo courtesy: Seshadri SUKUMAR

Far from encouragement, when she took up boxing, Mary Kom had to hear taunts like, 'What is a girl doing in a man's world?'

Photo courtesy: Debashish Datta (Aajkaal)

Sania Mirza is the highest-ranked Indian female player ever, peaking at world no. 27 in singles in 2007.

Photo courtesy: Seshadri SUKUMAR

'Yes, I am mentally tough. Maybe this is because of my roots. My mother never gives up, and she has ingrained the same quality in me. When I was nine, she used to say, "Saina, you have to win an Olympic medal".'

Photo courtesy: Debashish Datta (Aajkaal)

The architect of the Great Indian Badminton Story, P. Gopichand, with Saina Nehwal, Parupalli Kashyap, Jwala Gutta and Ashwini Ponnappa.

Photo courtesy: Debashish Datta (Aajkaal)

P.V. Sindhu is the first Indian to have become a world champion in badminton.

Photo courtesy: Debashish Datta (Aajkaal)

Like every good partnership in life, the Jwala-Ashwini partnership has had its share of ups and downs. But it is the most consistent and effective partnership in the Indian badminton story.

Photo courtesy: Debashish Datta (Aajkaal)

Sakshi Malik became the first woman wrestler from India to win a medal in the Olympics. Sakshi's rise was not a bolt from the blue. Rather, it was the result of the strong undercurrent at work in the wrestling centre of the country.

Photo courtesy: Debashish Datta (Aajkaal)

Deepa Malik's determination paid off, and she was able to bring home the first ever female Paralympic medal for India in 2016. She also became the first and the oldest woman para-athlete to win the prestigious Rajiv Gandhi Khel Ratna award.

Photo courtesy: Debashish Datta (Aajkaal)

Dipa Karmakar: 'Gymnastics is the sport that is based on courage. And Produnova, which I do, needs courage.'

Photo courtesy: Seshadri SUKUMAR

'I am happy that people now recognize there are sportspersons other than Mahendra Singh Dhoni, who have emerged from Jharkhand. I take pride when they say that I am a daughter of Jharkhand.'

Photo courtesy: Seshadri SUKUMAR

Dutee Chand was born to Chakradhar and Akhuji, a weaver couple who could barely sustain their family of six daughters and a son on a daily income of a hundred rupees.

Photo courtesy: Seshadri SUKUMAR

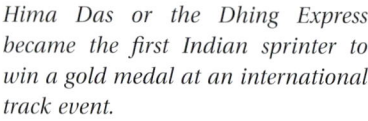

Hima Das or the Dhing Express became the first Indian sprinter to win a gold medal at an international track event.

Photo courtesy: Seshadri SUKUMAR

The Indian story on the fight to run starts from Santhi Soundarajan. The middle distance runner, her quick rise and fall, had rocked the athletics world years ago.

Pic courtesy: Santhi Soundarajan

for me, Vishnu and Leander Paes.'[26]

Sania also did not spare Bhupathi, and said the veteran had 'sacrificed' his commitment to play with her at the Olympics after their French Open title. 'Mahesh Bhupathi has firmly stood by his commitment to play together with his men's doubles partner, Rohan Bopanna, as he genuinely believed it was good for India. However, in the process, he sacrificed the commitment he made to me to try and win an Olympic medal together for India,' she added.[27]

Sania, in this manner, not only ripped apart the male patriarchy entrenched in the sporting system but also hit at the roots of aristocracy which has stunted the lateral growth of Indian tennis over the years. This, too, is a reflection of the Battle of the Sexes match in her personality. If Sania Mirza was playing the role of Billie Jean King, the Bobby Riggs pitted against her was the entire Indian tennis aristocracy, who had, on more than one occasion, used the establishment for their narrow self-interest.

Sania's controversies also relate to her personal life. Some of them are filmy in a typical Bollywood style.

In July 2008, twenty-eight-year-old Mohammad Ashraf, a civil engineering student, was arrested for allegedly making threatening calls to Sania and creating a nuisance at her residence demanding that she cancel her engagement to Sohrab Mirza. The youth claimed to be madly in love with her and was allegedly sending messages and making threatening calls. Ashraf went to Sania's home in Banjara Hills and allegedly entered into an argument with her father over the issue. Some of Sania's life stories are common ones that happen in many of our lives. But in her case, they became headlines, as she happened to be Sania Mirza.

Sania's engagement to Mohammad Sohrab Mirza was called off citing incompatibility. Sania said, 'We were friends for half a decade, but found ourselves incompatible during our engagement

---

[26]Sania Mirza's full statement on the tennis selection row, *India Today*, 26 June 2012
[27]'Sania Mirza lambasts AITA and Leander Paes after wild card', *India Today*, 27 June 2012

period. I wish Sohrab the best in life.'[28]

Sania's father, Imran Mirza, confirming this, said, 'Sania has already said that there was incompatibility between the two. They came to us and informed us. The families have known each other for half a century, so the decision was mutually agreed upon.' Asked if the break-up could hamper her career, he said, 'Of course it could. But she has to fight out of it. It would hurt Sohrab, and he too has to come out of it.'[29] In situations like this, getting into a family huddle has been her most soothing balm. She again did this and came out reinvigorated. The stage was now set for the most daring step in her personal life.

Sania Mirza decided to marry a cricketer from Pakistan, just when the ties between India and Pakistan were at a historic low. She represents the thought process that being in love means that no boundary or line of control can keep you apart; they just become shadow lines for you. Sania Mirza met Shoaib Malik for the first time in 2004, but the meeting lasted for only two minutes at a restaurant in Hobart. The very next day Shoaib, along with former fast bowler Waqar Younis, went to watch her match where she found the 'all-rounder Malik very simple and attractive' in her own words. It was soon after her engagement with Sohrab Mirza was called off.

'It was decided from both sides,' Sania Mirza said.[30] The celebrity couple kept their courtship secret and decided to marry in an intimate function.

How well aware was she of the likely repercussions of her marriage with the Pakistani player?

Sania said, 'Yes, we were aware that the two countries didn't have the best of ties. But as far as we were concerned, it was a marriage between two individuals. We have not opted for the marriage thinking that it will bring about a change in the two countries' relationship. Today, I am as much Indian as I was

---

[28]'Sania Mirza's engagement called off', *Hindustan Times*, 29 January 2010
[29]'Sania's break-up was mutual, says father', *India Today*, 28 January 2010
[30]Sania Mirza said this in an interview with news channel IBN7.

before I decided to get into this relationship. Shoaib is as much a Pakistani as he was before. I will keep on playing for India and India will remain my country, no matter whether I marry a Pakistani, an American or an Englishman.'[31]

When she was asked whether she hesitated during the courtship as her lover was from Pakistan, she said, 'Honestly, there was never a hesitation, so to say. If you want to stay with someone or someone wants to stay with you, everything takes a back seat. We are not trying to make a political statement; we are not trying to bridge things, and we are not trying to do anything of that sort. If that happens, that is good. I don't think any woman thinks along those lines while getting married. It's the same with me.'[32]

As news reporters then, we distinctly remember the way in which her marriage was scrutinized from every possible angle. Throughout, she and her family requested for privacy in the most private moments of their lives. But this too was asking for the impossible. The couple had to stay closeted in a hotel for four days after their marriage, when, as a young couple, they must have longed to go out and party.

Considering the fact that she has always been under pressure and faced the attention of the media throughout her life, will there be an added pressure on her to prove her patriotism all the time now that she is marrying a Pakistani?

To this, she said, 'I don't know; I don't think so far. But what I know is that whenever India will play Pakistan, I will continue supporting India. I am a big fan of Sachin Tendulkar and I will keep on supporting India especially when Sachin is playing.'[33] But there were more problems in store for Sania.

Sania Mirza was appointed the brand ambassador of the newly-carved state of Telangana. The chief minister of the state, K. Chandrasekhar Rao, presented her with a cheque

---

[31]Sania Mirza said this in an interview with news channel IBN7.
[32]Ibid.
[33]Ibid.

of ₹1,00,00,000. Questioning her credentials for becoming the brand ambassador of Telangana, a political leader called Sania a daughter-in-law of Pakistan. The Indian tennis star broke down in her interviews to news channels after this. 'I was really sad yesterday. It was really upsetting for me. I don't know if this happens in any other country. I don't know how many times I will have to justify my Indianness.'[34]

She further said, 'This is such a horrible thing. Is this happening because I am a woman or because I am married to a man from another country? Why am I picked on? I got medals for India after I got married. If someone questions my roots and my family even after that, I won't let that happen. I am representing Telangana and India when I am playing and I will continue to do that. I will remain an Indian until the end of my life.'[35] Later on, in a press statement, she said, 'I am married to Shoaib Malik, who is from Pakistan. I am an Indian, who will remain an Indian until the end of my life.'[36] The storm subsided, but comparisons continue. In 2016, after P.V. Sindhu got a silver medal for the country in the Rio Olympics, the Pakistani bahu rhetoric for Sania Mirza was replaced by the 'Sindhu In, Sania Out' slogan.

Out of the many posts addressed to the state, there was one by Venkata Ramana Vanteru from Hyderabad to K. Chandrashekhar Rao and his son, Telangana industry minister K.T. Rama Rao, that read: 'We don't want a brand ambassador who doesn't know Telugu and its culture (Bonalu, Bathukamma) and who doesn't live in Hyderabad (current ambassador lives in Pakistan/Dubai if I am not wrong), I have never seen her promoting the brand of Hyderabad. But still takes crores of rupees in her account. Plz tell me, which name reflects Telugu nativity "Venkata Sindhu" or "Sania". "Pusarla" or "Mirza". If you still want that the community votes, let her be their ambassador. This is the request by all the

---

[34]'A tearful Sania Mirza: Can't keep proving my patriotism', *India Today*, 5 November 2014
[35]Ibid.
[36]Ibid.

people from Hyderabad/Telangana.'[37]

Several others were even more pungent and emphasized on the Telugu and Telangana identity of Sindhu to run down Sania. Almost all of them, as visual evidence, used the photograph of Sindhu participating in Bonalu, a festival indigenous to Telangana.

But there were voices opposing Sindhu as Telangana brand ambassador as well, harping on her 50 per cent Andhra roots. While her father P.V. Ramana hails from Adilabad in Telangana, her mother is from Vijaywada in Andhra Pradesh. What if another Telangana prodigy defeats Sindhu in future? Will saluting the rising star be done at the cost of the past legend? But the characters of the best are forged in such testing circumstances. It's the same with Sania Mirza.

What is it about Sania Mirza that makes her what she represents?

When Doordarshan, approached her for an interview for the show that was being made about her being a youth icon, she said, 'Other channels started following me when I had become a champion. DD Sports has been part of my making as a champion.'

While talking to her family and close friends, it becomes clear that she has set her razor-sharp vision on the top. Elaborating on this, she says, 'I have taught myself to be strong despite the criticisms and hardships I have faced over the years. And there are no shortcuts; you need to work hard—whether you want to or not—to get to the top.' Such rigorous work could not be consistently sustained without passion and love for the sport.

Sania explains this and says, 'With thousands of people watching me play, there is bound to be intense pressure. And that is why it's important to enjoy the ups and downs in a game. I love working under pressure because it fuels me to give my best. There will be times when you will feel overwhelmed, but it's important to truly enjoy what you are doing, to be able to succeed. Tennis

---

[37]'With Sindhu's rise, a clamour to dump Sania as Telangana ambassador,' *Huffington Post*, 20 August 2016

truly is my passion.'

In modern sports, which include tennis also, adaptability is the key. Times have changed and the sportsperson of the modern era needs to be adaptable. Sania Mirza has got the great power of adaptability. She made a seamless transition from singles to doubles when required. She is the master of adaptability in her personal life as well. If you follow her social media account, you will find her active there too.

She says, 'The trick lies in being willing to adapt to the ever-changing circumstances. Be it on or off season, I have no specific pattern because my schedule is very unpredictable, and apart from practice, I have a lot of other commitments to fulfil. And to be able to survive and still deliver your best, you need to mould yourself.' And the eternal charm of the girl from the city of the Charminar has been 'being true to herself'.

Be it her unique fashion sense, her game or her views on different issues, she has never taken a back seat when it comes to speaking her mind.

'I have always been taught to be true to myself and I ensure I am true to this teaching. In our part of the world, when children are supremely confident, they are labelled arrogant. If you don't bend down to what everyone says, it's considered to be bad attitude. Coaches discourage self-confidence in children, and that hampers them when they have to stand on the court and match strokes with the big players,' Mirza says. Any tennis pro will tell you that humility and politeness are all very good, but best left behind in the locker room.

She has been able to do this over the years because of her unflinching family support. Sania says, 'I have always done what I have felt is correct and done justice to what my parents have taught me. And, they are the ones who have always got my back and helped me be who I am today.'

Sania Mirza represents a new India with this attitude of fearlessness, which is what people in India today connect with. Life is always a struggle for them. Life has been a constant struggle for Sania as well. From managing money and resources earlier to managing commitments, routine and injuries now, the transition makes her believe in enjoying rather than cribbing about the struggles.

Sania has won her Battle of the Sexes match in India in what has been a riveting three-setter, for she represents the legacy of the 1973 epochal match, in letter and spirit.

EIGHT

Saina Nehwal: The Promise of a Bountiful Summer

She turned up on stage as Jawaharlal Nehru for a fancy dress competition, saluted, and then got tongue-tied, as stage fright gripped her, in a packed auditorium.

Her parents gently got her off stage, only to send her back up again, for another competition.

And she forgot what to say. All over again.

Playing before large audiences was still years away.

She woke up at 4 every morning, hopped on to a bus with Papa for a 25-km ride to the stadium. She trained from 6 a.m. to 8 a.m. Then she rushed to school, barely on time, sometimes even getting late. She left school with Mummy at 3.30 p.m., sometimes even earlier, for the stadium.

Train. Practise. Practise. Train. Repeat.

She finally went home for the day at 9 p.m., sometimes even later, with Papa and Mummy, in an auto. Or sometimes on Papa's scooter, falling asleep on the way. Exhausted. Drained. Her body in a constant state of soreness. Still, dreaming...

All this hard work would go on to fortify her resolve to keep moving ahead, despite the numerous injuries and other difficulties that would be constants in her life in the coming years.

She forced herself off to Guntur for the junior nationals, and became the youngest ever to reach the finals, even as she struggled to cope with news of Mummy in a critical condition after a serious accident...

She gave up the delicious aloo paratha, paneer butter masala, jalebi... She planned new moves and angles, with visualization exercises, erasing old follies on court... No films. No parties. No outings. Just practise and train. Repeat. She got used to non-stop travel, alone, criss-crossing continents, in pursuit of glory. She staved off career-threatening injuries and took on the fearsome Chinese at their own game.

A dream team aided her dream. Selfless parents and a handful of experts helped chip away the rough edges. Not the ones who would trudge along, but the ones who believed she could go faster. Stronger. Higher.

Papa quietly took out his savings from his provident fund account to meet her expenses. Even if it seemed like an impossible situation, he kept guiding her to find her way around life.

Mummy initiated her into the sport, instilling in her the belief that it would be hard work, but only then would she find what she wanted from life.

Fans and the media at first appreciated her hard work, and then doubted her abilities at every loss, challenging her legacy with every unfortunate injury.

Yet she kept rising.

And continued to play for gold, glory and excellence.

As she strode out onto the court, her racquet swishing in anticipation of another conquest, she stopped to hear it.

'Ladies and gentlemen, Saina Nehwal, from India.'

Fifteen years after the birth of Karnam Malleswari, a girl was born in the state where the Iron Lady got married. Destiny called Saina to Hyderabad, the then capital of erstwhile Andhra Pradesh and the home state of Malleswari. She went on to emerge as one of the lead protagonists of the Indian badminton story, the story of the strong narrative of the emergence of great Indian badminton stars one after another, starting with Saina Nehwal. The nerve centre of the story is the famed Pullela Gopichand Badminton Academy in Gachibowli, Hyderabad. And the film is produced and directed by P. Gopichand.

Saina Nehwal, the second daughter of Harvir Singh Nehwal

and Usha Rani Nehwal, was born in a Hindu Jat family in Hisar. Hisar is the steel city of Haryana. And this girl from the city of Hisar, Saina, had a steely resolve and determination to conquer the best in the world. There are good players and there are great players. What separates the great players from the good ones are their resolve and determination to bounce back when they are down and out, both on the field and off it.

Saina Nehwal possesses this ability in plenty. Perhaps the genesis of this steely resolve runs in her family. Both her parents were badminton players. Her mother hated losing. And Saina got stuck with badminton as she loved winning. Compared to her mother, her father was not so expressive on the court. But off the court, in real life, he never allowed his thin resource base to come in the way of his and his daughter's common dream.

It's often said about people living in Hyderabad, 'Once a Hyderabadi, always a Hyderabadi.' The typical Hyderabadi Hindi dialect, the laid-back attitude, being a complete foodie and enjoying even a small portion with a bunch of friends is what differentiates a Hyderabadi from other Indians. But of late, the city has added one more defining aspect to its overall character. As per the Brookings Institution Report, over the past decade or so, it has turned into a hub for thousands of students aspiring to enter the prestigious Indian Institutes of Technology. Between 2008 and 2012, it sent over 26,000 students to the US, most pursuing a science, technology, engineering or mathematics degree. The city attracts talent from all across, and fine-tunes and shapes them to be world-beaters. Hyderabad fine-tuned the inherent talent in Saina Nehwal and transformed her into a world-beater.

Andhra Pradesh and Haryana, in this sense, forged a unique symbiotic relationship in giving Indian sports two incredible women of substance—Karnam Malleswari and Saina Nehwal. Both defeated the Chinese to emerge as world-beaters. However, on one hand, Karnam Malleswari still bears a grudge about her federation's inability to build on the momentum after her 2000 Olympics success. On the other hand, after the phenomenal success of Saina Nehwal, the Indian badminton story has gathered momentum. P.V. Sidhu has taken the baton from her and has carried the legacy further. Taking a cue from the girls, the boys have picked up too.

Kidambi Srikanth, B. Sai Praneeth and H.S. Prannoy are recent poster boys of the Indian badminton story.

Badminton, as the game we know today, was inspired by a game played by the Greeks called battledore and shuttlecock centuries ago. This ancient game was then refined by leisurely British army officers settled in Poona in the 1800s, and took up the form that is currently being played. So, like cricket and hockey, which have been India's sporting identity in the outside world, badminton also has a colonial legacy. Badminton has been a household sport in India, and going by a random assumption, after cricket, it's the most played game in the country. The sport requires little investment, needs no special facilities, is gender-friendly and asks for as much effort as one is willing to put in.

The game attracts all and sundry. For instance, the sport is a hit amongst ageing gentlemen who do not wish to accept the fact that they are ageing. On the contrary, the game demands a lot of physical fitness, endurance and stamina as a competitive sport. And when we talk of competitive sports on the global stage, India had nothing much to boast about until 1980, when Prakash Padukone won the All England Open Badminton Championships. 'Even on the day of the final, I had taken the train, carried my kit, and walked to the court,'[1] says Prakash Padukone, with a twinkle in his eyes and in a matter-of-fact tone.

These words from this iconic player of his time took us back to the journey he undertook thirty-seven years ago, in the fourth week of March, from the YMCA in central London to Wembley, about a twenty-five-minute ride on the tube. The match was the

---

[1]Prakash Padukone said this in an interview with author Abhishek Dubey when he was sports editor with IBN7.

final of the All England Open Badminton Championships. On 23 March 1980, Padukone silenced his arch-rival Liem Swie King of Indonesia, winning the coveted title. King was the defending champion, having won the title in the previous two years, and as world no. 1, he was the clear favourite to win and thus score a hat-trick of All England titles. Moreover, King had even decided to skip the European tour events to arrive fresh to this tournament. And then history was made. 'It was the greatest win for me and Indian badminton. It was historic.'[2]

After Prakash Padukone, only one Indian has won an All England Open Badminton Championships—Pullela Gopichand, in 2001. Gopichand beat the then world no. 1 Peter Gade in the semi-finals and proceeded to defeat China's Chen Hong 15-12 and 15-6 in the final match to lift the trophy. 'In a lot of ways, Prakash sir's win at the All England Open Badminton Championships inspired me as a young sportsperson. His win was important to the country.'[3]

Gopichand was different—his family and close friends knew. But the country came to know how different this personality was from others when he rejected the brand endorsement offer from a soft drink company after his win. 'It was just a personal decision. Since 1997, I have stopped drinking these soft drinks. After seeing the reports, as well as studies on the health hazards of these products, I stopped their consumption.'[4] More importantly, unlike how most of us would be, he was not pompous about his decision. Only his family members and friends were aware of the offer from the cola brand and his decision.

But after a few months, when his friend Amala Akkineni broke the news to the children present at a function organized by her NGO, the media came to know about this. When specifically asked

---

[2]Prakash Padukone said this in an interview with author Abhishek Dubey when he was sports editor with IBN7.

[3]P. Gopichand said this to Abhishek Dubey in an interview with IBN7 during the 2012 Olympics in London.

[4]Ibid.

about the reasons behind turning down the offer at a time when badminton was underrated and when the brand was the chance to appear before millions of people, Gopichand says, 'I could not go against what I believed. If you like, you can call it ethics.'[5] That the man was different was obvious by now. But what difference it was going to make to Indian sports was to become clear in the following years.

There are great players and then there are great players who go on to become institutions in themselves. When we talk of the Indian sporting horizon, we have had great players in Sachin Tendulkar, Vishwanathan Anand and Leander Paes. However, there are others like P. Gopichand and Rahul Dravid who are gradually transforming themselves from sporting legends to living institutions in themselves. They are the real sporting statesmen of our times in a country like India that aspires to be a sporting superpower.

In 2001, while he was caught in a traffic jam in Delhi after returning from the UK following his famous victory, Gopichand first thought about setting up an academy equipped with training facilities that matched the best in the world. The Pullela Gopichand Badminton Academy, a badminton training facility in Hyderabad, was founded in 2008. To set this up, he mortgaged his house and later found funding from Nimmagadda Prasad, an industrialist from Hyderabad. 'We built the academy with passion. It scares me to even think about it now. There was a lot of bullishness, we didn't know if it would succeed, but we gave it our best. Nobody believed that the academy could be a path-breaker unless we proved it. Those days were more difficult, and I am very happy that it worked,'[6] recalls Gopi.

---

[5]P. Gopichand said this to Abhishek Dubey in an interview with him in 2014 in the Pullela Gopichand Badminton Academy, Hyderabad, when they were making a documentary on the real achievers in Indian sports.
[6]P. Gopichand said this to Abhishek Dubey in an interview with him in 2014 in the Pullela Gopichand Badminton Academy, Hyderabad, when they were making a documentary on the real achievers in Indian sports.

In its almost decade-long existence, the academy has foreseen the future of the country's badminton sensations. The academy, which started with only twenty-five players, has grabbed over ten hotspots in the top fifty badminton players in the world. It offers full scholarships for over 50–60 per cent of its players.

Gopichand says, 'There are a lot of players from the lower strata/economically-challenged backgrounds, and we are making space for them. We believe that a lot of talent emerges from that strata of society. When we started the academy in 2004, we only had twenty-five players. The oldest was Kashyap and the youngest was Sindhu. In time, at least ten of them played the top fifty in the world. I have loved my roles as player and coach. The innate need for success, or to support players, is rather childlike. I am very happy with the way things have gone for me,'[7] he sums up the key to the phenomenal success of the academy.

Gopichand says, 'World badminton changes, opponents change, conditions change and the formats change. It's important that we keep abreast. It's important that we evolve ahead of the competition.'[8] More than the skill set and technicalities, what Gopichand has been able to imbibe in his protégés, starting with Saina Nehwal, are beating the odds, fighting adversity, but never for once losing their balance, or equanimity.

The architect of the Great Indian Badminton Story, Pullela Gopichand, credits his success to the female superpowers in his life. Gopichand's mother and wife have stood behind him and his dreams through his initial days and continue to do so. His wife P.V.V. Lakshmi, also a badminton player, represented India at the Atlanta Olympics in 1996. A former national champion herself, Lakshmi is spearheading the administration at the Pullela Gopichand Academy. It was again a female superpower, Saina Nehwal, who was destined to catapult the P. Gopichand Academy to its lofty heights in the coming years.

---

[7]Ibid.
[8]Ibid.

If Gopichand's eleven-year-long journey is often cited as the reason that ended China's dominance in the sport, Saina Nehwal was the first one who successfully showed that this could be accomplished. 'Saina's victories were important to propel badminton forward in India. Thanks to her, other players are looking at the Chinese in a new light; that they are beatable. The beauty about Saina was her self-belief. That belief was important to be the first to beat the Chinese. Today, others are also pushing to beat them, but the first one always has it toughest,'[9] Gopichand says.

The eight-year-old Saina got her first lessons in toughness on the roads of Hyderabad. On an average, she used to travel 50 km before retiring for the day. Saina still cherishes the days when her father used to drop her to school on his scooter. But more than the scooter, the autorickshaw used to be an inseparable part of her life during those days. And when the autorickshaw becomes an inseparable part of one's life, often an affinity develops between the passenger, on one hand, and the autorickshaw and its driver on the other.

Saina says, 'For almost four years, travelling has been an inseparable part of my life. There were some days when my father used to drop me to school on his scooter. But it was mainly by autorickshaw. My day started at 4:00 in the morning. I had to travel from my home at Rajender Nagar to the Lal Bahadur Shastri Stadium, which is roughly 25 km.'

The little girl used to battle out the tiredness, fatigue and pain for her passion. And the passion was not badminton. Rather, it was winning. As a child, Saina used to play all sports. She used to play cricket with boys while she was in Haryana. In hindsight, it seems badminton pulled the family to Hyderabad.

Saina's father got a promotion. He had the option of choosing among five different places in the country. Harvir Singh finally

---

[9]Pullela Gopichand said this to Abhishek Dubey in an interview with him in 2014 in the Pullela Gopichand Badminton Academy, Hyderabad, when they were making a documentary on the real achievers in Indian sports.

decided to settle in Hyderabad. While the family was trying to find their place in the city, he enrolled his daughter in karate classes. She won a brown belt in karate, but wanted to do something relatively less rigorous. Saina says, 'When we came to Hyderabad from Haryana, we used to stay in Rajinder Nagar. I had no clue initially what to do after school. My father's friend's son used to play in the Lal Bahadur Shastri Stadium. He suggested to my father to enrol me there as well. And that is how the to-and-fro journey of 50 km started. Initially, from one hour of practice every day, it became six-seven hours, and then up to nine hours. As I spent so many hours in the stadium practising, recuperating and again practising, the stadium became my home.'[10]

The deep connect between her and the stadium can still be felt.

But for certain interesting turns in events at the right time, this connect would not have happened at all. Or it may have got severed before it became firm. Saina says, 'I have a strong emotional connect with this stadium. I used to come here regularly till 2002. In the month of May in 1999, my father requested P.S.S. Nani Prasad Rao to enrol me in the summer camp. However, he expressed his inability, saying that the deadline was over. My father requested him to see me play, and then take a call. Nani sir saw me play and he was so impressed by my smash that he included me in the camp.'

After this, there was one final twist of fate which made her association with the stadium and badminton definitive. 'There used to be matches after the summer camp; there was this final in which I lost. In the final match, a player from Nagpur in Maharashtra defeated me. She could not join the academy permanently as she had to return to Nagpur—where her family was staying and where she was doing her schooling. I thus got the chance in her place. I still remember her, because it's because of

---

[10]Saina Nehwal said this to Abhishek Dubey in an interview with him in 2014 at the Pullela Gopichand Badminton Academy, Hyderabad, when they were making a documentary on the real achievers in Indian sports.

her that I got my career.'[11]

The girl from Nagpur must have felt distraught then. But the distraught girl of those days must be feeling proud today of Sania's achievements. Saina loved winning. She started winning frequently on the badminton court. As Saina aptly sums it up, 'Today I realize that I was able to do all this because I loved winning. Since I loved winning, badminton became my way of life. I imbibed the habit of winning from my mother who hated losing. Winning became my habit. Badminton became the way of my life.'[12]

While on her quest of winning, as she measured the distance she travelled in kilometres in the city of Hyderabad, she must have seldom thought that her passion would give her name and fame miles away from the city. Her popularity soared with every passing year, and today her exploits are talked about and admired globally. Despite all this, today the city also helps her relive her past. One of such places is her home at Padmanabha Nagar in Hyderabad. After all, her father had bought this house with his hard-earned money. One can feel the deep sense of belonging Saina feels with the house. The family doesn't stay there anymore, but the house is full of photographs, some of them rare ones, which take us down memory lane and understand the child in her. 'Papa bought this house with his salary. We get emotional about this house. I have memories of eating my food while watching television and fighting with my sister. All my trophies started coming when we shifted to this house. This house has been lucky for us.'

The house is full of trophies, and has sweet memories associated with it. The place is witness to the small steps that led her to finally stand where she is today.

But seeing the trophies, one wonders if she had time for herself as a child as she chased one trophy after another. Looking

---

[11]Saina Nehwal said this to Abhishek Dubey in an interview with him in 2014 at the Pullela Gopichand Badminton Academy, Hyderabad, when they were making a documentary on the real achievers in Indian sports.
[12]Ibid.

at the pictures on the walls, she gets emotional and says, 'Yes, sometimes I do feel that I missed some pleasures of childhood. Playing with dolls and playing pranks on people. In my teenage I was so engrossed in my game and practice that I did not have many friends. I had to sacrifice a lot of food that are a part of any child's menu. But then, how many people get the chance to represent the country? How many get the chance to be part of the Olympics, win a medal for the country, and see the country's flag flying high and hear the national anthem in a foreign land? It's like being in the service of the country, and everyone doesn't get this chance. When I think of all these things, the sacrifices I had to make in my childhood and teenage feel too small and insignificant.'

Any individual's success story is the cumulative result of the efforts put in by their support team. The team comprises family and friends, the coaches and the entire sporting ecosystem. When the sporting ecosystem is found wanting, the onus on the immediate family and the coaches becomes more.

Saina's mother Usha Rani Singh has been part of each and every moment of her life—good or bad. She has been the mirror that has reflected her talent. More importantly, she has never been satisfied and has continuously raised the bar for her. Usha Rani says, 'I never think that she has reached the peak. I am always a firm believer that there is lot more hard work to do.'

The moment she says this, Saina comes up with an instance which further elaborates this. Saina says, 'When I was playing the under-10 nationals, I lost the finals in Thane in Maharashtra. My mother came to the court and slapped me in front of everyone. I felt very hurt. I felt bad. Not because she slapped me, but because she slapped me before everyone. Deep down in my heart I decided that one day I would show everyone what I was capable of.'

For ordinary people, this may be akin to putting pressure on a child. But for an extraordinary person like Saina, this made her battle-hardened for future challenges. The toughness and the self-belief that her coach Gopichand often talks about lies in this attitude of hers. The hands of her mother that slapped her have also provided her with ointment and a soothing balm whenever required. And, like other families, there is the sense of caring, sharing and possessiveness too. This is reflected in the bonding Saina shares with her sister Chandranshu Nehwal. Chandranshu says, 'She used to play cricket and love all sports. She used to often tease me, saying, "You study and let me play". She had attractions for the things that generally boys like.' Saina still has got the upper hand in terms of teasing. After her huge win at the Malaysian Masters Grand Prix in February 2017, and on returning home, Saina started posting several pictures and videos of her family on social media.

She posted one video on 9 February 2017 that doesn't feature her but her 'mad sister' as she put it. It showed Chandranshu laughing uncontrollably. The video also featured Saina's father and the family dog Chopsy. Like the infectious laughter of her sister in the video, the chemistry between the two is infectious as well. The great vibes the two share can easily be felt.

'My sister used to love me so much. When we were children, my mother tells us, she used to say that she would leave me with the maid when she had to go somewhere. Whenever such a discussion used to come up, my sister opposed it tooth and nail. "When I am there to take care of her, how does the question of a maid come up?"'

The family bonding is typical of Indian families with a middle-class background. As most of these families come up sharing the thin resources, more often than not, a bonding of this nature stands the test of time.

Saina did her schooling in Hyderabad at the Bhartiya Vidya Bhawan, Vidyashram. This was the school where she studied from class IV to class X. As we do a tour of the school, we see a wing named after her—Saina Nehwal Classroom Block. The school must have taught her many valuable lessons in life. She stands as an inspiration and an example for all the students studying here today. Hundreds of them get inspired by her name itself. To achieve so much, so early in life, is truly incredible.

'The naming of the block after me was very surprising. But it was a special feeling for me. I have many memories of the school. They will eternally remain etched in my mind,' she says.

The girl who was awarded the Padma Shri at the age of nineteen on account of her amazing performance in the field of sports understands and emphasizes on the value of education in one's life. She says, 'I have changed many schools. I studied at the Campus School, Hisar in Haryana from lower KG to class III. Then from classes IV-X, I went to Bhartiya Vidya Bhavan's Vidyasharam School and the National Institute of Rural Development School, Rajendra Nagar, also in Hyderabad. I was quite shy in school. I was studious and paid attention to my studies. Even if you take up sports seriously, don't leave your studies. It's crucial for your personality development and the growth process,' she sums up the importance of education in one's life. As we leave the boundaries of the Bhartiya Vidya Bhavan school, we visualize that the shy girl who used to come here years back has turned out to be the role model for the students studying in hundreds of similar schools spread across the country.

In the journey of life, the making of Saina Nehwal's destination can be credited to the Gopichand Academy in Hyderabad. One gets the feeling of excitement and anticipation as one enters the gates of the academy. There is a sense of joy and curiosity in the probing eyes of the children and contentment and anticipation in the walk and demeanor of the parents accompanying them. There is a buzz all around. Children of all age groups are dropped off by their parents. The sounds of the shuttlecocks meeting the racquets and shoes rubbing the surface are all around. Amongst the various girls practising, sweating profusely, one can visualize the teenage Saina at the age of eighteen—with either of her parents dropping her off every day.

'The academy changed my life forever. My life is all about the right things happening at the right time and place. Gopichand sir had retired after his historic All England win. He had been there and seen it all, he had the experience and knowledge of what it takes to be a champion. The coaches before I joined the academy had made my basics strong. And everything took off from there. I am what I am because of the P. Gopichand Academy,' Saina says. 'My first international title came at the age of sixteen in the Philippines. In that event I was nowhere in the ranking chart and I went on to beat the no. 3. I never expected to win. More than the title, this victory gave me the confidence that I could compete and beat the best in the world,' she further adds.

The year 2006 saw the dawn of Saina Nehwal. She became the under-19 national champion and created history by winning the prestigious Asian Satellite Badminton tournament twice, becoming the first player to do so. In May 2006, the sixteen-year-old Saina became the first Indian woman and the youngest player from Asia to win a 4-star tournament—the Philippines Open. The same year Saina was also runners up at the 2006 Badminton World Federation (BWF) World Junior Championships, where she lost a hard-fought match against top seed Chinese Wang Yihan. She did better in 2008 by becoming the first Indian to win the World Junior Badminton Championships by defeating ninth seeded Japanese Sayaka Sato.

She became the first Indian woman to reach the quarter-finals at the Olympic Games when she upset world no. 5 and fourth seed Wang Chen of Hong Kong. She, however, could not get to the podium as her campaign was cut short after she lost a nail-biting three-gamer to world no. 16 Maria Kristin Yulianti. In June 2009, she became the first Indian to win a BWF Super Series title, the most prominent badminton series of the world, by winning the Indonesian Open. She beat Chinese Wang Lin in the final. The echo of her statement given immediately after her victory still reverberates in the ears of sports lovers, 'I had been longing to win a super series tournament since my quarter-final appearance at the Olympics.' The country had by then realized that it was only a matter of time before she would win a medal in the Olympics. And the moment came in London in 2012.

On 4 August 2012, she won the bronze medal at the London Olympics when China's Wang Xin retired from the match after an injury, at 18-21, 0-1. I (Abhishek Dubey) have my personal memories attached to that day. 4 August happens to be my birthday, and along with select reporters, we were waiting for her to come outside with the medal around her neck.

'This medal is very valuable to me. I wanted this for my country. But it has not been an easy task for me. Badminton is physically a very demanding game. It requires lots of hard work and training. Both off the court and on it it requires hard training for the upper body and the lower body. One needs to continuously improve the strokes and prepare both tactically and physically. But now I feel it is all worth it. It's difficult but not impossible. Whoever is physically and mentally strong and willing to push hard could go for this game,' she said, every word of hers full of emotion.

'Has the game changed from what it was before?' I ask.

'The game has become very fast and long, especially amongst girls. If we compare it to tennis, badminton requires faster reflexes, as one doesn't get enough time to think in between. For girls it has become longish, as one has to play for an hour or an hour and a half. So it has become very demanding physically. Thanks to Gopichand sir...he had prepared me for this day.'

What is the secret of your mental toughness—does this have something to do with the fact that your roots are embedded in a Jat family in Haryana?

She is a bit taken aback at my question. And then with a contented smile on her face, she says, 'Yes, I am mentally tougher. Maybe this is because of my roots. My mother also never gives up, and she has ingrained the same quality in me. When I was nine she used to say, "Saina, you have to win an Olympic medal."

I used to laugh it off at that time. I used to think that no one had got an Olympic medal till then, so maybe she must be joking with me. But now I do realize that she had a dream for me, and whenever I used to get tired, she used to push me hard. Gradually, this became my habit.'

'And, the role of the coaches in your life?' I ask haltingly.

Other reporters were waiting for their turn for an interview. She replies, 'I was fortunate to get the right coaches at the right point of time in my career and all of them have contributed immensely. S.M. Arif sir, he used to make me do lots of physical training, which helped me with my basics. If one does such a rigorous training at such a young age, the effects remain till the end of one's career. Perhaps his training has given me such a high level of endurance and strength.

'After this, it was Govardhan sir, who taught me the skill sets on the court. And finally, Gopichand sir, who has been the pillar of my success. Once I started training under him, I defeated Aparna Popat and then marched ahead in my career.'

With her Olympic dream accomplished, expectations from the champion player are soaring. But players' lives are full of battles— more within than outside. So is the case with Saina.

Like any other player, she has had her share of injuries. Another talented player from the same academy, P.V. Sindhu, has started doing well. The comparisons keep happening in the media. But again, what is striking is her self-belief.

'If I keep training like this, my turn will definitely come again. It's said that if you set a goal, love, like and follow that goal passionately, the goal itself doesn't have any other option than coming to you,' she greets us in the present day with this introductory statement.

What about your injuries? Are you getting back to your best?

'When you start at such a young age and compete with the best in the world, it's difficult to maintain the same level of fitness for so many years. A toe fracture made me sit out for six weeks.

After this I had a difficult time with a knee injury and I had to practise and play through the tapes. And then an ankle injury, which made me sit out again for 5–6 weeks. However, I am not the exception. The same happened with the world no. 1 player. After starting the season brilliantly, she had to sit out.'

And what about the Saina vs. China phenomenon in badminton?

She starts laughing and then says, 'The Chinese are my favourite rivals as they give a tough fight to the rest of the world. They have such a good training system and the best of the coaches in the world. They plan very well. It's good to see players always improving in China. India, too, has started catching up and doing well at the world stage. Our assembly line of players is also increasing. But what separates India from them is that whereas we have only two world-class academies, they have so many. They have so many world-class coaches and sponsors. With government backing, things are improving at a faster pace in India now. Resources, and not talent, is the thing that separates India from the leading sporting nation of the world.'

As we start descending the steps of the academy, this realization starts sinking in.

As Saina's father Harvir Singh says, 'I was an officer, but even then had limited resources. With limited resources, it was tough. But then I thought, as parents buy books for their children and many of the books are costly as well, why should I not utilize the same resources for Saina's sport, as she enjoys playing? She was passionate about sports. I asked for money from my close friends and they helped me too. After all, the cost of one racquet was ₹8,000 and it was not easy for me to arrange for that sort of money.'

When Saina is asked about this, she gets emotional. She says, 'My father never told me that he used to take money from his friends and use up his provident fund savings. It was only later on that I realized this. I wanted money, he gave it to me. I wanted a racquet, he gave it to me. I wanted to tour, flight tickets were there for me. Now I realize what getting all this for me entailed.'

She further adds, 'As a nine-year-old, I never knew what money was all about, but I certainly knew what winning was all about. I wanted to play to keep on winning.'

If we want more and more Saina Nehwals, we need to have more and more Harvir Nehwals. If India has to do well in sports, the country needs change in the mindsets of people, along the lines of Harvir Singh Nehwal. And to make the path of the potential Saina Nehwals easier, the country needs to have more and more centres of excellence like the P. Gopichand Academy. P.V. Sindhu has taken over from Saina Nehwal. The time has come when academies, at least in the potential sporting hubs of the country, get inspired by the P. Gopichand Academy and try to give such facilities to its sportspersons.

Saina Nehwal's on-field achievement is phenomenal. Off the field, she is settled now. In the closing months of 2018, the star shuttlers Saina Nehwal and Parupalli Kashyap tied the knot. The wedding took place at Saina's residence in Orion Villas in Cyberabad. She has been active on social media of late. Saina posted a photograph with Kashyap announcing her marriage. 'Best match of my life,' she wrote on Twitter.[13] Saina and Kashyap, who met at Pullela Gopichand's academy, have been in a relationship for quite some time now. She had confirmed the news of the wedding in October 2018 itself. However, a hectic international badminton schedule kept them busy. Saina will be giving her best shot in the upcoming 2020 Tokyo Olympics, but her mental toughness and tough work culture coupled with tactical acumen centred on optimizing her potential, will make her a formidable coach once she hangs up her racquet.

---

[13]Saina Nehwal, 'Best match of my life', Twitter, 14 December 2018, 3:42 a.m.

NINE

P.V. Sindhu: The Toast of a Nation

Abronze each in the 2013 and 2014 World Championships and a silver each in the 2017 and 2018 World Championships. A silver in the 2016 Rio Olympics. A toast of the nation for so many, she was dubbed a choker in the finals by some. On 26 August 2019, at the Centre Court in Basel, Sindhu didn't let the aggression dip for thirty-eight minutes, and let her opponent Nozomi Okuhara suffer a shocking defeat in one of the most one-sided finals in the history of the sport.

She finally won gold...

She is the first Indian ever to become a world champion in badminton. After the great Zhang Ning, she is only the second woman in the world with five World Championships medals. She has won the Rajiv Gandhi Khel Ratna award, the Padma Shri and the Arjuna Award. She made it to the Forbes list of the highest paid female athletes of 2018-19.

She is only twenty-four years old.

She might be on her way to becoming the greatest-ever Indian sportsperson in an individual sport.

She is P.V. Sindhu.

But this is not the success story of P.V. Sindhu alone. In sports, we always talk of the process and structure for consistent results. Finally, in badminton we now have the world's finest academies that follow modern and up-to-date processes. Badminton has given us the structure that other sports could emulate. Today, the Great Indian Badminton Story is not merely a story. It has turned into a reality show. It isn't merely about an academy, it is an attitude. Hyderabad has added another stalwart, reinforcing its identity as the badminton capital of the country. Saina Nehwal is still going strong. And P.V. Sindhu has taken it forward from where Saina is yet to leave. And there are men like Sai Praneeth, Satwik Rankireddy and Chirag Shetty who are doing the catching up—taking inspiration from one of the all-time greatest women badminton players. There are many who play the game of badminton across the globe. But there are only three pairs of legs that get to stand on the Olympic podium after every four years. Saina won the bronze medal at the London Olympics in 2012.

This set of processes and structures of the Great Indian Badminton Story can be better appreciated with the help of a case study. Let us study how the entire team worked together for the podium finish of P.V. Sindhu in the 2016 Rio Olympics. This was followed by two major blips in other finals. Learning from the mistakes and working on them is how Team Sindhu regrouped and worked behind the scenes round the clock to give India the title of world champion. Let us start with Rio 2016. Gopichand was convinced that Sindhu had it in her to win a medal in Rio. He started work on 'Operation Rio' a year in advance. A weight trainer and a physical fitness expert were given the specific task of working on Sindhu. The aim was to build stamina and strength so that the twenty-one-year-old could last more than an hour on court and engage in long rallies to tire out opponents in tight games. The semi-final match against Nozomi Okuhara proved how useful that tactic was.

Gopichand considers Sindhu a natural talent. As per the architect of the Great Indian Badminton Story, her body type and the fact that her parents were sportspersons played a huge part in her game. The only issue was her reluctance to be expressive on court, to scream and to display an aggressive body language. After all, international competitive sports is not only about skills. Ramana, Sindhu's father, was drafted into Gopichand's plan by the end of 2015. Gopichand could think of no one better than her father, given her credentials as a sportsperson of international repute, to advise Sindhu on how to work on one's mind.

Ramana, who works with the railways, took eight months of special leave to spend all his time with the Olympic debutant. The journey to and from home and the academy would see father and daughter engage in banter. Ramana, with a hand on Sindhu's shoulder, would drill into the young mind the responsibility the Indian flag put on her shoulders. The idea was to make Sindhu dream big. Gopichand's son, Vishnu, who also plays the game, was the surprise addition to Team Sindhu. He too would come to the academy at 4:30 a.m. with his father for dribbling practice with Sindhu. 'Dribble' is a unique Indian term that means a shot that sends the shuttle spinning over the net tape, ensuring the opponent is unable to pick it up. Sindhu owes her exquisite net play throughout the Rio campaign to her young partner.

Here, selflessness is critical. Here, everyone breaks bread together, sweats it out together, enjoys each other's success and lends a shoulder when the chips are down. It's the modern version of the ancient gurukul—in letter and in spirit.

The cumulative result of all this was that, as P.V. Sindhu was charting a historic course in Brazil, both her parents opted to cheer her from their suburban residence around 20 km from Hyderabad. But what they have done in terms of preparing Sindhu for the Rio Olympics and her career in general, needs to be valorized as an example for all Indian parents to follow.

Sindhu's father was on a sabbatical before Rio, to finish the task assigned to him by coach Gopi. Her mother was her constant companion in the tough months leading up to the Olympics. A mother knows her child best, in terms of physical and emotional needs. She ensured that Sindhu followed a proper diet. She was her counsel when she used to be down.

Together, they mentally prepared their child for the toughest and often irrelevant questions posed to her. Who's better? Is Sindhu better than Saina? Will she be able to better Saina Nehwal's bronze medal performance in the 2012 London Olympics? Are there problems between them? Right from the beginning, like every aspiring sportsperson's parents, they have got used to confronting one of the most difficult questions frequently posed in social circles. 'What is your daughter doing?' 'She plays badminton,' is still not a very acceptable answer. Playing badminton is fine, but what is she preparing for—medical, engineering, management, what?

But they persisted with her choice and the results are there for everyone to see. The results may have come in 2016, but the victory in Rio de Janeiro was plotted by the Almighty in 2004 itself. Gopichand had turned coach around the same time, when the daughter of two Indian volleyball players, P.V. Ramana and P. Vijaya, nine-year-old Sindhu, was more than enamoured by the flight of the shuttle. Considering her height, volleyball would have been an easier option, and her parents were accomplished players in the sport as well. Gopichand liked what he saw in little Sindhu, especially how her legs moved on court. Gopichand and Ramana go back a long way together. Coincidentally, both of them received the Arjuna Award together in 2000. The two friends and their families have played a huge part in her success story.

'We used to stay in Secunderabad. It is 27 km from my house to Gachibowli. Sometimes we used to go up and down twice a day (108 km). Then I started staying back and returned home only late in the evening. We did that for about two and a half years when I was small. Later on, I spent about a year and a half living at the academy. I used to return home for the weekends. A few years down the line, my parents bought a house near the academy, so now it's only five minutes away,'[1] says P.V. Sindhu.

A regular student till class VIII, Sindhu studied at the Auxilium High School, Hyderabad. The school was supportive of her sporting endeavours. Sindhu's father used to drive her from Secunderabad to Gachibowli for her training while she took naps in the back

---

[1] P.V. Sindhu said this in an interview with Abhishek Dubey while they were making a show named *Hyderabad—The Badminton Capital of India*.

seat. Besides attending school, completing school work and getting trained, Sindhu spent four hours every day commuting, and it began to take a toll on her.

When her parents made Sindhu join the academy hostel, she started missing home to an extent that it affected her performance. Finally, Sindhu's family moved to Gachibowli in 2010. She values the sacrifice and all the efforts put in by her parents from the core of her heart.

'My parents gave me all I wanted. Both of them used to work in the railways and yet they accompanied me every day to the academy and back home. It was not easy. When we shifted near the academy, it was tough for them to cover such a long distance to the office. They took voluntary retirement so that I could concentrate on my career.'[2] Perhaps their conviction led to them giving complete freedom to their child to pursue her passion. Also, being sportspersons themselves, they must have sensed that she was a special child in terms of sporting talent. Though she is the greatest-ever Indian badminton player today, there was a time in her life when she thought of joining some other profession.

When we watch Sindhu hitting speedy strokes and cross court returns, we hardly realize that the same person once thought of becoming a doctor. The inspiration behind this was Sindhu's elder sister, a national-level handball player who gave up the sport to pursue medicine. Nonetheless, Sindhu chose badminton and this proved to be a blessing for her. More importantly, the decision turned out to be crucial for a nation eager to establish its sporting footprints beyond cricket globally. Such a career story is bound to be full of success and sacrifices. Her father narrates the list of the things she had to miss to focus on the game: missing the class X board exams, missing her sister's wedding and missing out on personally receiving the Arjuna Award. There are many more, but these top the list.

---

[2]P.V. Sindhu said this in an interview with Abhishek Dubey while they were making a show named *Hyderabad—The Badminton Capital of India*.

But teenaged Sindhu was very particular about not missing a single badminton practice session. 'Sindhu would cry if I did not take her to the academy even for a day. In the morning as soon as I said, "It's 5, let's wake up and go for training," that was it. I did not have to repeat the same thing even once after that,'[3] says Ramana. During his playing days, Ramana was one of the best smashers on the Indian side. 'She smashes like me, albeit on a different court,' he says jokingly. Ramana was a part of the bronze medal-winning Indian volleyball team at the 1986 Asian Games.

Perhaps one of the most often-repeated and the most boring questions that Sindhu has faced in her life is, 'When your parents used to play volleyball and you had the height to go for it, why did you opt for badminton instead?'

'I had seen a video of Gopichand somewhere. I was inspired by his success at a young age,'[4] says Sindhu. Gopichand's victory at the 2001 All England Open Badminton Championships inspired Sindhu to pick up the badminton racquet. Little did she know that Gopichand would become her coach in two years and take her to an Olympic medal victory.

Ramana says, 'I was in a team game. I had realized that however well I played, the result would be dependent on the entire team's effort. But here, in the badminton singles, the entire onus of doing well or poorly lies solely on you.'[5]

This statement answers many a question. As a child, Sindhu did not get a lot of chances to play with senior players. So, she was advised by renowned badminton coach Mehboob Ali to do wall practice 'till the paint peeled off'.

She made that advice the dictum of her professional tennis life. She learned the basics of badminton on the courts of the

---

[3] P.V. Ramana said this in an interview with Abhishek Dubey while they were making a show named *Hyderabad—The Badminton Capital of India*.

[4] P.V. Sindhu said this in an interview with Abhishek Dubey while they were making a show named *Hyderabad—The Badminton Capital of India*.

[5] P.V. Ramana said this in an interview with Abhishek Dubey while they were making a show named *Hyderabad—The Badminton Capital of India*.

Indian Railway Institute of Signal Training and Communications in Secunderabad under the guidance of Mehboob Ali. She, too, like Saina Nehwal, was trained by other renowned coaches, including S.M. Arif and Govardhan Reddy. In 2005, the ten-year-old Sindhu caught the eye of the national coach P. Gopichand, who convinced her parents, her father being his friend, to get her enrolled at his academy. Gopichand believed in Sindhu's potential and planned to use her height to her advantage.

He invited trainer Christopher Paul to his academy to create a training regimen for Sindhu. Paul worked on her muscle strength while Gopichand worked on her speed and agility. The talent was now well-groomed and all set to take off. Sindhu's grit and perseverance, along with her parents' support and Gopichand's mentorship, started getting her widespread recognition at the domestic level.

Sindhu played her first international tournament at the 2009 Sub-Junior Asian Badminton Championships. She won the bronze medal. She lost to the second-seeded player at the 2010 Junior World Championships to reach the quarter-finals. Sindhu later won the match against Carolina Marin from Spain to finish fifth in the tournament. She won the silver medal at the 2019 International Badminton Challenge in Iran. She also found a place in India's national team at the 2010 Thomas and Uber Cup.

Sindhu missed her sister's wedding in Hyderabad to participate in the 2012 Syed Modi International Grand Prix Gold event in Lucknow. She wanted to make this count, and that she did. Sindhu didn't lose a single set before the final and finished as the runner-up, taking her world rank to 19.

On turning eighteen, Sindhu was employed by Bharat Petroleum as an assistant sports manager. She won her first Grand Prix Gold title at the 2013 Malaysian Open. She also became India's first medallist in women's singles at the 2013 Badminton World Championships. Sindhu ended the year by winning the 2013 Macau Open Grand Prix.

In the same year, she was honoured with the Arjuna Award

by the government of India. This was a very special moment for Sindhu and her family. Her father had won the Arjuna Award for volleyball long into his career. Sindhu says, 'When I got the Arjuna Award at the age of eighteen, my father was so proud and happy—happier than me. He got the award at the age of thirty-seven. Perhaps the day I got the award was one of the happiest days of his life.'[6]

The two Arjuna Awards won by the father-daughter duo occupy a place of pride in the home and hearts of the family. While our television camera was filming the trophies in their home, the family specially requested the team to focus on the two Arjuna Awards. The family upped the bar after this. Sindhu's father said, 'Her wish is to be number one; she wants a medal in the Olympics and the Asian Games. She wants to win the All England Championships.'[7]

Like a mature father who has played sports at the highest level, Ramana wants his daughter to give wings to her desires. He doesn't want his list of desires putting added pressure on his daughter.

2014 turned out to be a crucial year in Sindhu's life. She clinched the bronze medals at three major events—the Asian Games, the Glasgow Commonwealth Games and the World Badminton Championships. She became the first Indian to win back-to-back medals at the world championships. In March 2015, she became the youngest recipient of the Padma Shri award, one of the highest civilian honours in India. Later that year, Sindhu won her third successive title at the 2015 Macau Open Grand Prix Gold event. P.V. Sindhu's fairytale tryst with Macau—winning three times in a row—involves a ferry. An hour's ride from Hong Kong, it's the only way to get to the island.

'Yeah, it's something between Macau and me. I have made it a sort of habit to land at the Rua de Ferreira do Amaral address

---

[6] P.V. Sindhu said this in an interview with Abhishek Dubey while they were making a show named *Hyderabad—The Badminton Capital of India*.
[7] Ibid.

where the Grand Prix Gold is held, on the back of a bumpy season. And I return from there as the winner. My friends also ask me what is so special between me and Macau.' Her eyes and the smile on her face convey her attachment to the place. She goes on to elaborate her connection with all those places that have given her special moments in her life.

There is a moment in every champion athlete's life which defines their career. P.V. Sindhu's Rio Olympics moment was approaching. She said at that time, 'The biggest dream that I am chasing now is an Olympic medal. I remember watching Saina in London. Then I was ranked world no. 25. I always longed to be there and I am all excited to represent India in Rio.'[8] At the 2016 Rio Olympics, she became the first Indian badminton player to reach the finals. She defeated the world no. 6 and world no. 2 on the way.

Sindhu could not win the final against the world no. 1, Carolina Marin, from Spain, but won a billion hearts by winning the silver medal for India. She made history by becoming India's youngest athlete, first female athlete and first badminton player to win the silver medal at the Olympics. In August 2016, Sindhu was conferred with the prestigious Rajiv Gandhi Khel Ratna award along with other Indian success stories from the Rio Olympics, including bronze medallist Sakshi Malik.

Immediately after the Rio Olympics, we had the opportunity of meeting the legend of our times in the P. Gopichand Badminton Academy in Hyderabad. The eight courts of the academy are witness to the sweat and blood and the effort she has put in to find her place on the Olympic podium. The staff at the academy still carry vivid memories of the small girl coming there for practice every day, watching her seniors practice from outside the court with her watchful eyes and giving them back the shuttle when it crossed the lines.

---

[8]P.V. Sindhu said this in an interview with NDTV, a few months ahead of leaving for Rio Olympics 2016.

If one sets one's priorities right, one's dream does come true. 'When I started playing badminton, I never dreamt of playing in the Olympics. The effort and focus then was towards becoming a good player who can win titles at the national level. But after I joined Gopichand sir's academy, I started looking at things differently. Slowly, my goals started changing with every passing month. I am glad that I am in the best academy and under the best coach, Gopichand sir. I am fortunate to have someone like him as my coach,' she says.

'Your coach Gopichand had the hunch that you would win a medal. Did you ever feel the same, that Rio was the best chance for you to win a medal?'

'When I reached Rio, my aim was to take one match at a time, which is my normal approach to any event—nationals, the super series or the world championships. The important thing here was that the preparations were very good before we left for Rio. There were many areas that Gopichand sir worked on, with valuable inputs from our physio Kiran and the SAI athletics coach, Ramesh sir. I knew the draw was very tough, but I always had the feeling that nothing was impossible if I stayed focused and played to my full potential.'

'Do you regret having missed the gold medal after coming so close to winning it?'

She replied, 'I don't take it that way. True, gold would have been a huge thing as it is every athlete's dream at the Olympics. But at the end of it all, as Gopichand sir pointed out, I just forgot that loss and kept thanking my destiny for the silver, which, I believe, is a huge achievement in my maiden Olympics.'

The answer was a clear indicator that her best was yet to come.

P.V. Sindhu is like any other girl who has just crossed her teenage. In terms of converting her potential to performance, she may be yet to touch the greatest heights, but the first thing that attracts attention is her height. As opposed to the 1.65 m tall Saina Nehwal, 1.73 m tall Sania Mirza and 1.78 m stature of Jwala Gutta, Sindhu is 1.8 m tall. 'I am taller than my mom. My sister and I are of the same height. My father is 6 ft 3 in. tall. I would not like to be as tall as him,' Sindhu says with a mischievous smile on her face.

This was what Gopichand used to Sindhu's advantage in the badminton court initially. But competitive and professional badminton is a tough world. This advantage of hers has been sorted out by the players and coaches all around the world. 'Height is not always an advantage. As I am tall, opponents don't give me the chance to attack. Being tall, it takes me time to bend when compared to other players. That is why my prime focus these days is on tightening my defenses.'

As Sindhu moved up the ladder, opponents started mapping similar weak links in her game and taking advantage of them. This is routine in competitive international sports. She made it to the finals of three major events in three years. At the 2016 Rio Olympics, she lost to Carolina Marin of Spain in the women's singles final in three sets in an eighty-three-minute match. In August 2017, she reached the finals of the BWF World Championships. In the final, she lost to Nozomi Okuhara in a nail-biting encounter. This final match is still regarded by many former badminton greats as the best-ever women's singles final in any World Championships match. In 2018, she again made it to the finals of the BWF World Championships. This time, she lost to Carolina Marin 19-21, 10-21. This, again, was a closely-fought match.

Sindhu clearly was a world champion in progress. But instead of seeing the glass as half full, a section of the media focused on the empty part. She was dubbed by some as a 'choker' in the finals. The English daily, *Hindustan Times,* published an article on her. An excerpt of the article read:

> A top athlete is expected to show nerves of steel, produce that additional ounce of stamina and demonstrate that extra edge to kill the opposition. Sindhu failed on all three aspects... In the last one year, Sindhu has played seventeen matches that stretched to the third game. She won ten and lost seven. Six of those seven losses have come against players who were unseeded or seeded below her. A top-5 player of the world

certainly has to have a better record than that.... When Sindhu won the silver at Rio, it was a unique occasion—an Indian woman had claimed the silver medal for the first time at the Olympics. Given India's poor returns from the world's greatest event, it was worth celebrating. But how long will India celebrate being second best? And why shouldn't she feel the pressure? She is representing India and not any club. She is expected to play in adversities and come out on the top. P.V. Sindhu is undoubtedly one of the top sportspersons of our country but till she does a Marin or an Okuhara, she will not be pure gold standard.[9]

The sportsperson who came to the limelight after defeating Li Xuerui, an Olympic gold medallist and the world no. 1, at a World Championships match, had to fight off the tag of a choker. For an aspiring champion in any sports, there is no other tag that hurts more. One can feel this, going through the range of her emotions when we ask her to take us through the two extreme matches of her career.

We ask her to take us through the match against Li Xuerei. She gets very excited as she starts to recount the details of the match.

'Firstly, I didn't think I would win because she was an Olympic gold medallist. The coaches told me—just go and play your game; you have got a chance to play against a senior player. Don't get tense; you are a good player, play your 100 per cent. When we started, I won the first game. It gave me a bit of confidence, but then I lost the second game very easily. In the third game, you know, we were going level before I took the lead and won. Even while leading, I was thinking, she is a senior player, she has got the experience and she can bounce back. So I was taking one point at a time, and eventually I emerged victorious.'

Four years down the line, when asked about losing two crucial close final matches at the Olympics and World Badminton

---

[9]Sandip Sikdar, 'Why choker P.V. Sindhu is still not pure gold standard', *Hindustan Times*, 29 August 2017

Championships, she says, 'The World Championships was one of the longest matches and the fact that I came so close and I gave everything meant that nothing more could have been done. In any match one loses or one wins; I happened to be on the losing side on that occasion. I felt bad for a few days, but taking positive lessons from this was the key.'

Her coach P. Gopichand elaborates this further when he says, 'From the outside, these close matches may look similar. But she has beaten four big players and lost to one. As an insider, it will not be a wise thing to forget the four big winning matches and stick to the one in which she lost. It's too easy to get into negativity. We need to take the positives. She was not well physically, and despite this, she fought for ninety-four minutes on the strength of her reserve energy, which was simply amazing.'

Team Sindhu again regrouped, not with the negative mindset of fighting the 'choker' tag, but with the positive mindset of raising the bar.

P. Gopichand's hands were full and he had to give attention to a galaxy of champion players. He wanted someone to specifically focus on P.V. Sindhu and Saina Nehwal—both of them being in the crucial stages of their respective careers. The SAI took Kim Ji Hyun, a former international star from South Korea, on board. In March 2019, she landed in Hyderabad to train the champion duo. Saina Nehwal, however, decided to prepare with her husband, P. Kashyap, and Kim got an opportunity to exclusively focus on Sindhu. Kim started working on Sindhu's game based on a coaching schedule prepared by Gopi. Sindhu gradually started trusting Kim as coach, counsellor and motivator. Kim closely analysed her game and started working on her weaker links. One of her initial observations about Sindhu's game was that she was not smart enough—something so critical to becoming a champion player. Moreover, her game was increasingly becoming predictable to her opponents. Step by step, Kim started working to fine-tune her skills—particularly her net skills and deception in terms of changing tactics.

In the 2019 World Championships final match, Sindhu let her racquet do the talking. She was aggressive right from the word go in the final match against Nozomi Okuhara. She did not allow her to even settle. This newfound aspect of her game was a pleasant surprise both for Kim and Gopichand. They wanted Sindhu to be aggressive right from the word go and this made the job easier.

Another challenge before Team Sindhu was to put her body in the best possible shape for the big event. In 2017, Srikanth, who works at Suchitra Badminton Academy in Hyderabad, was introduced to Sindhu and her father by Praveen Raju. He's the owner of the academy and has been closely following her game for years. Impressed with Srikanth's approach, Ramana asked him to get her ready for the World Championships in 2017. However, he got just twenty-four days to prepare her for the Championships. In those twenty-four days, he did a Strengths Weaknesses Opportunities and Threats (SWOT) analysis of her body and fitness. Her major strength was that her body recovered thirty seconds after strenuous exercise, and this was truly incredible. However, there were a few weak areas as well. Some of the muscles in her body were affecting her front court movement. In each individual, muscles are structured in a different manner. In the last forty-five days before the Championships in 2019, she followed the rigorous fitness regime of Srikanth. For this, Sindhu used to travel around 60 km every day, navigating the dense traffic of the city. The physical conditioning coach worked on her weaker areas as per the structure of her muscles. He also worked on improving the body mass of Sindhu. All these led to the deadly exhibition of smashes in the 2019 World Championships. The team is now gearing up for the 2020 Tokyo Olympics. One gold medal there will make her the all-time greatest Indian sportsperson ever.

The tall, dusky girl, however, has a life outside the badminton court. She doesn't think solely about badminton, 24x7. She is conscious of her attractive looks.

'People say that on the court in my sports dress I appear to be on the healthier and heavier side. But off the court in my normal clothes I look slim and attractive. I say, "Excuse me...",' and she laughs it off. Taking the discussion further, she says, 'People do say that I have a good height and body structure. I am tall and dusky and could give the best of models a run for their money. My reply has been that I should focus on badminton for now. Yes, we do get the opportunity to do photoshoots and walk on the ramp. All the top badminton players like Gopichand sir, Jwala, Saina and I walked on the ramp once. People were stunned seeing me in a saree. Whenever I do photoshoots, I love wearing different dresses. I like wearing good clothes and trying out different dresses. As far as make-up is concerned, while playing I am my normal self. I don't believe in heavy make-up unless required.'[10]

Sindhu's hectic practice schedule, tournaments and travelling don't give her time to go to parties or make friends. The days when she goes on vacation are also few and far between. 'Our day at the academy starts at 4:30 in the morning—4:30 to 6:00, then 7:00 to 8:30. We have a midday session from 11:30 to 12:30 and one in the evening between 16:00 and 17:30. We do multiple forms of training—playing opponents, on-court drills, weights and endurance. Sometimes we do agility, shadows, running and core ab work to strengthen the abdomen. It is important to have strength and endurance. Stamina is very crucial in badminton as there are too many rallies and long matches. We do stretching, because otherwise body parts become stiff and our legs don't move and they start paining. We get cramps, so we need to do proper stretching and relax ourselves. Sometimes our physio gives us a massage; it depends on the state of the body really. Amidst all this, I get a day in the week for rest. I prefer to use this time relaxing and sleeping at home and spending time with my family members,' she says. After she missed her class X board exams, she appeared for them the next year, in the supplementary section.

After graduating from school, Sindhu pursued her bachelors in commerce from St Ann's College, Hyderabad. As she didn't attend

---

[10]P.V. Sindhu said this in an interview with the Youtube channel iDream Sports.

classes at college and only took the exams, Sindhu couldn't make many friends. Most of her friends today are her fellow players at the Gopichand Academy. 'From my LKG days, I have had a friend called Nandralini—from when we used to stay at Secunderabad. She is two years senior to me. Till date we keep in touch with each other by phone. It's not that I share everything with her. My sister is the only one with whom I share everything. A few years back, I got in touch with one of my class X friends. She introduced me to our school friends' WhatsApp group. They used to keep pestering me as to why we didn't meet. And then we met one day. It was real fun.'

When asked about her favourite pastime, she is candid enough to say that she doesn't enjoy reading books. 'I had been gifted two books—one on Dr A.P.J. Abdul Kalam and the other one an inspiring story of a para athlete. The moment I open a book, I feel sleepy. But one day, I intend to finish both these books.'[11] Not a great reader, Sindhu, however, loves travelling and listening to music.

One of the frills in the life of an international athlete is the constant travelling throughout the year. As former Indian cricket team coach John Wright, whose regime saw the Indian team doing well overseas, once said in a television interview, 'One of the keys to their success is how well they take to travelling. An athlete who enjoys travelling has got much more chances of success on the field.'[12]

Ditto with P.V. Sindhu. She says, 'I enjoy travelling. Though spending longer hours on the flight is a problem, other than that I love every aspect related to travelling. On the flight, I spend my time listening to music, watching films and sleeping in phases. Once you come out of the flight, you realize that every country is different—somewhere it's chilly, somewhere it is sunny, somewhere it's cloudy and somewhere windy. I simply love and

---

[11]P.V. Sindhu said this in an interview with the Youtube channel iDream Sports.
[12]John Wright said this in an interview with Abhishek Dubey on IBN7.

enjoy these different shades of the weather.'

Perhaps this is one of the main reasons why she acclimatizes well overseas and does well before foreign crowds on a constant basis. Apart from travelling, she enjoys her own personal space. 'I love listening to music and watching films—Telugu, Hindi and English. I go to cinemas, where the lights are off, so that I can enjoy the film without any disturbance. We tend to leave the cinema the moment the film is over, to avoid the crowd. Amongst the Telugu actors, I like Mahesh Babu—he is known as the prince. Everyone likes him as he is good-looking and handsome. Amongst Hindi film actors, I like Hrithik Roshan and Ranbir Kapoor. I also like Deepika Padukone and Anushka Sharma,' P.V. Sindhu says. After a brief interruption she starts again, 'Like every girl, I love shopping. I like all sorts of dresses. I don't like sticking to any particular format in terms of dressing.' She is certainly not someone hooked to badminton day in and day out. 'When on court, I give my best. Off the court, I have my own life,' she sums up.

One more aspect of sadhana for an athlete is their remarkable discipline in terms of eating.

The issue becomes all the more challenging when one happens to be from Hyderabad—a city famous for its gastronomical delights. 'We have to follow a strict dietary regime. But once in a while I love eating junk food. When we win, for a day we are given the liberty to eat sweets, ice creams and chocolates. I do love biryani—Paradise biryani—and I can eat it the whole day. I also love Italian food like pasta and pizza. I love eating my mother's home-cooked biryani, keema and fish. I am a foodie in this sense. But to achieve something, more often than not I have to forego many of my favourite foods.'

One of the ironies of the modern athlete's life, other than managing with the paucity of funds in their days of struggle, is how to cope with the funds when they do come in plenty. And especially when all this happens during the early and formative years of one's life. 'When I pocket huge sums of money, it's my parents who handle my account. Both my dad and my mom handle my account. I don't have any clue—whatever I ask for, they give me. People often tell me, "You don't even know that you are a crorepati." This is how I am. I have never done any calculation,'[13] the simplicity of the girl in her early twenties comes out with this statement. Another important challenge for an athlete of her age is coping with the fans, particularly the crazy ones.

P.V. Sindhu has got many of them, both male and female. They belong to every age group and are spread across the globe. 'I have got one crazy fan in Indonesia. We almost go there every year for the tournament. She wrote a long letter to me expressing her admiration and fondness for me. She also asked for my t-shirt. She gifted me a piggy. It's still with me.'[14]

Sindhu loves changing her mobile number. She has an attraction for fancy numbers. Does this have something to do with the fact that she wants her own space far from the crowd?

'No,' is her answer. 'Yes, I keep changing my mobile number. There is no specific reason behind the same,' she says and then breaks into a hearty laugh. 'Why will I have a problem? I will have their numbers. They will not have my number,' the teenager in her comes out. And then she says, 'I like fancy numbers and so I used to change them. *Sab mood par depend hota hai...* I know that even if I keep on changing my number, they will get it. I don't do this any more. I have realized I should have a stable number,' she says. However, old habits die hard. She got her number changed again before the 2019 World Championships.

Whatever may be the mystery behind the changing of numbers, the reality is that her fans cannot have enough of her. Despite this, she often is a loner in the crowd. Like any other girl of her age, she finds herself going through depression, cries and has low moments in her life. How does she cope with this? Does she cry her heart out?

'I don't cry always. But I have cried many a time in my life.

---

[13]P.V. Sindhu said this in an interview with the Youtube channel iDream Sports.
[14]Ibid.

People often ask, "Why are you crying?" The reply is simple. I have lost; what should I do? I do cry when coaches tell me something that is unpleasant to my ears. The tears may not come out every time. But they do fall occasionally,' she says.

'Has Gopichand made you cry in a similar manner ever?'

'He is my coach. On that count, he is strict and tells me about my strengths and weaknesses and what all I need to do. Off the court he's normal and friendly to us. But on it, he's strict, and he should be like that. He's very patient with us as well. If we repeat any mistake, he patiently works on them with us,' she replies.

Are there moments when she feels low on the court?

'There are times when I do go through depression on the court. Suppose I am leading handsomely and then I see the margin getting wiped out. I instantaneously get the feeling, "Oh I am losing". But over the years, I have learnt how to cope with this. My coaches advised me, when confronted with such situations I should ask myself, how do others feel when I snatch matches in similar situations from my opponents? Sports, like life, is all about winning and losing. One loses and learns from the loss to move ahead in life.'

Sindhu is changing with the times and there can be no better tutor and coach to train one than personal experience. 'When I don't get the point I was so close to, I feel bad and depressed. My coach says, "It's over, get ready for the next point". It sometimes takes me two to three points to get over it. Similarly, it does take time to get over losing a match. But I am changing now.' The change is happening for the better. Most already rate her as the best Indian badminton player ever.

Sindhu is now the world champion. When she finishes her career, she might end up becoming the greatest-ever Indian sportsperson. She is humble and down to earth. When one talks to her and her parents she appears to be like any girl next door.

The most important silver lining in her rise is the fact that she is the champion who has come out of the world-class system around her. The athletes before her tried to win despite the system, and in some cases fought the system throughout. The P. Gopichand Academy, its present and former coaches, support staff and her parents—they all have come together to give the country this champion. If we are able to create such ecosystems in different places across the country, they can produce many more champions like her.

TEN

Ashwini Ponnappa:
A Blithe Spirit

ndia is a wonderful, diverse and colourful country. This colourful aspect of the country finds its glorious expression in Indian weddings, which are splashes of many colours—a blur of reds, yellows, greens and dazzling gold. 'Atithi Devo Bhava' i.e. 'guests are like God' is a saying that lies at the core of Indian tradition. Indian marriages are the finest advertisement of Indian hospitality, with guests numbering in the hundreds, and sometimes entire villages treated like God. 'If you want to soak in the different colours of India, take a plunge into the ocean comprising the varied shades of Indian weddings,' my (Abhishek Dubey's) geography teacher used to bore me to death with these words in our school days.

Coorg stands draped in the mountain mist, much like a demure bride. Amongst the diverse bouquet of Indian marriages, Coorgi marriages are special and unique. I realized the significance and deep meaning behind my geography teacher's words when I was invited to attend a traditional Coorgi wedding. The simplicity and uniqueness of the rituals were an eye-opener for me. But the ritual that got etched in my memory was the cutting of banana shoots. This symbolic gesture is the mark of respect to the maternal sides of both families.

The cutting of banana shoots is usually done by the groom, a show of valour to prove himself worthy of one so pretty as the bride in question. There were three sets of such cuttings—the first in honour of the bride's maternal family, the second to respect the maternal families of brides of yesteryears and the third to respect the groom's maternal family. This Coorgi tradition of honouring womenfolk is unique in a conventionally patriarchal Indian society. I was reminded of the Kodava wedding again in the closing months of 2017. This was when the pride and prestige of Coorg, Ashwini Ponnappa, got married to her long-time boyfriend, Karan Medappa, in a traditional ceremony.

Ashwini donned a traditional Kodava saree and Medappa wore a traditional dress, called Kuppasa Datti. Unlike most other Indian weddings, there was no priest presiding over the ceremony. The couple was pronounced married by the parents and the gathering at the wedding bore witness to the happy union. The elders there then proceeded to bless the bride and groom with the Hindu tradition of sprinkling rice over their heads. Substance matters more than superficialities in a Kodava wedding.

The women of the family and society form the fulcrum of many of the rituals related to the weddings in Coorg. The conducive ecosystem for the growth and development of the girl child manifests itself in the personas of the two Ashwinis who hail from this region—Ashwini Nachappa, in the closing decades of twentieth century India, and Ashwini Ponnappa in the opening decades of twenty-first century India.

As Ashwini Nachappa says, 'The name "Ashwini" means "a female horse".' The two mares from Coorg have been brand ambassadors of Indian sports in terms of talent, strength, articulation and finesse. If Ashwini Nachappa galloped to success in athletics, Ashwini Ponnappa has been the stable and consistent force in the Indian badminton story. The two Ashwinis spread across generations give us the trailer of what the daughters of the country can achieve if they get a congenial environment for their growth. We have been through the pages of the sporting journey of India's Florence Griffith Joyner or Flo-Jo, i.e. Ashwini Nachappa. It's the turn of Ashwini Ponnappa now.

Born on 18 September 1989 in Coorg, Karnataka, Ashwini Ponnappa has sports flowing in her genes. 'My dad M.A. Ponnappa was a hockey player. We have uncles who were hockey players and relatives who were into athletics and cricket. So, yes, we do belong to a sporty family. This has helped in my career as well. Dad was pretty fit and helped me with my physical fitness during tournaments, and in the off season when we didn't have any training. Mum helped me with my diet and made sure that I ate right. More importantly, she helped me in keeping calm. The most important aspect is that they were with me always, irrespective of what happened in the match, and encouraged me to follow my dream of playing badminton and doing really well,'[1] says Ashwini. Sports teaches us many things in life. And this is what one expects from parents who understand the meaning of sports.

But did she take up sports as she happened to be from a sports family?

'More than the sports family itself, I was a hyperactive child, and to keep me busy, my parents put me into sports. One thing followed another. Both my parents were working, and to keep me engaged, they put me in badminton. As is common amongst many of the players, I began with enjoying the game and playing with my parents. Thus, it all started as fun with badminton. Then I started attending coaching sessions. Actually, right next to Dad's bank, there was a single badminton court which also had a coach. So it was convenient, as Dad used to drop me off there and then pick me up. After this, as this became part of my routine, Dad and Mom started taking turns to pick me up and drop me off.'

Ashwini takes us down memory lane. This picking up and dropping off continued in the coming years with a new set of challenges. Professional sports demands frequent travel. In the case of a girl child, this becomes critical. For Ashwini Ponnappa, it was more challenging than usual—especially with both of her parents working. Her father used to travel with her for most of the tournaments, as her mother was at home looking after her

---

[1] Ashwini Ponnappa said this in an interview with the authors when they were shooting a documentary series on women achievers in collaboration with the SAI.

younger brother who had asthma.

Among other things, what sports teaches us in life is the ability to take both victory and defeat in stride and move ahead. This lesson of sports, if learnt well, helps the best of the sportspersons not to take or put undue pressure. When a sportsperson is able to reach this zone, they perform their best.

Ashwini Ponnappa says, 'There was no pressure as such from my parents to take up badminton. Most of us start as singles players and it was the same in my case. Gradually, I started moving up through the different age categories. I was runners-up in under-10, but the champion in under-13. Actually, it was from there that things started picking up for me. The state championships was followed by the nationals. I still remember that when I actually beat my partner, there was a change in the way I approached my game.'

Professional sports demand that one peaks as one starts entering the prime of one's youth. This means forgoing many things that look like a sacrifice in the eyes of others. But for those who take up sports as their passion and a way of life, these are not sacrifices, but the means to achieve their end. Ashwini Ponnappa says, 'I saw the best of both the worlds—school life and badminton. I was fortunate to have very good teachers in school. It was in the later stages i.e., when studies started getting serious in class VIII, that I started paying all my attention to badminton. And the fact that I was just an average student and more inclined towards badminton made my decision of taking up sports easier.'

And then she goes on to elaborate this further when she says, 'I do remember my prelims happened when I was busy with my nationals. I fared badly in my prelims, but my teachers were very confident that I would do well in my board exams. They would say, "Don't worry, you will do well." My parents also did not put any pressure on me. It was during this time that I put in a lot of effort in my studies and I felt really happy when I did well.'

Ashwini does understand the significance of easing off the pressure during this crucial phase. She says, 'I had no pressure.

I have seen my peers struggling to get permission to go for tournaments. But contrary to this, I easily used to get my leaves and had the liberty to leave the class early for my training sessions. For instance, my school closed at 3:30 p.m., but I was allowed to leave at 2:30 p.m. so that I could get an hour extra for my practice.'

Sports teaches us to be multitaskers in the formative years of our life. 'At a young age, you learn how to juggle between your studies and sports, and I think this toughens you,' she says.

What was the regimen that gave her the initial rigorous training in multitasking?

'My daily routine then was quite different because I had to manage both, my school, and then my college, along with training. Luckily, I had wonderful principals both in school and college. I was given permission to take off early from college to train. So my daily routine was waking up and starting my day with physical fitness exercises at the ground at around 6 a.m., then rush home to get ready for school which started at 8:30 a.m.

'Then I would leave school at around 2:30 p.m. for practice, even though school got over at 3:30 p.m. I would finish practice and head back home at around 6:30 p.m. So my entire day was filled with training sessions and practice, along with resting and eating,' says Ashwini. If youngsters try multitasking as a routine early in life, it helps them in so many other aspects later on in life. One aspect follows another and eventually a beautifully-crafted success story emerges.

Ashwini Ponnappa says, 'When I was a child, and before the dream to represent India set in, I used to stay busy with the state championships and the nationals. In order to win any national-level tournament, I had to practice and train, and that became the core part of my life, and it still is. I was quite adamant about my training and I loved my sessions in Prakash sir's academy (Prakash Padukone Badminton Academy). The environment there was very good, as all the children who were training there were good. When you see your peers working hard, it makes you work hard as well, so that you do well. You get the feeling that you better train for it and not have regrets later on, for missing out on opportunities.

'I have been playing badminton since I was eight years old, and the All India Tournament since I was twelve, and once you are in the All India Tournament, you realize that everyone is working really hard to do well, everyone is managing their studies along with their games and everyone is travelling. I realized that in order to do well, you have got to work really hard. Apart from that, it was fun too. When I won the Junior under-16 National Championships with Nitya, the top eight of us were from Prakash sir's academy.'

Ashwini gives us an idea of the ecosystem in which she grew up and the environment we need to give to our girl child so that they can make India a truly sporting nation. Apart from multitasking, sports also teaches us that one never gets tired if one puts one's heart and soul into one's passion. Coaches often don't tire of emphasizing on enjoying the game. What is this enjoyment all about?

According to Ashwini Ponnappa, 'The meaning of enjoyment and fun is being on the court, feeling happy about the anticipation of facing the opponents and feeling nice about everything, be it your clothes, your sports equipment, the court, the ambience or anything related to the sport. Once that happens, everything falls into place.'

People like Ashwini Ponnappa, more than the victory and defeat and medal and championship, have made a seminal contribution in bringing about a change in the mindset of the people, in the sporting culture of the country. In a sporting culture which promotes individuality, she has been a stable and consistent women's doubles player. Why and how did she become a doubles player?

One of the best doubles players in Indian badminton, Ashwini Ponnappa started off as a singles player before turning into a doubles player. 'Self-pleasure is the key to success and progress, I believe. In singles there was pressure—whenever I tried to be like any player, I used to mess it up. But whenever I played my own game, I did pretty well. In doubles, the idea was to just go and have a blast, and so, more often than not, I did well. Perhaps this is how I believe I started gravitating towards doubles,' Ashwini says.

Unlike singles, doubles is a team sport. Apart from your own abilities, you need to have trust and confidence in your partner's abilities. The turning point in Ashwini's career came when she got into a partnership with Jwala Gutta.

Ashwini says, 'The turning point for me personally was partnering with Jwala in 2009. I was really lucky to have had her ask me to partner her. It gave me a chance to see what I was capable of.'

After Ashwini started playing with Jwala, gradually she started becoming confident of excelling in the international circuit. The experience, confidence and self-belief of Jwala started rubbing off on her game and personality as well. Gradually, both the partners developed an understanding of each other's game and capabilities. 'It's pretty important in doubles that both partners believe in their partnership and capability,' she says.

How does she rate Jwala as an individual?

Ashwini Ponnappa says, 'Jwala is a great person and a great personality. She is confident, bold and fearless. Actually, the good thing is that she is someone who believes in herself and who wants to do really well. She approaches every game and every event with the mindset that no one is going to stop her and she will go and do well.'

What do they say to each other during the match?

'We constantly say, "Take one match at a time, one point at a time and don't think about the last point and the last match,"' says Ponnappa.

Like every good partnership in life, the Jwala-Ashwini partnership has had its share of ups and downs. But it is the most consistent and effective partnership in the Indian badminton story. Mental toughness is an inseparable part of sports. But there is a human side to every sportsperson that lies hidden behind the cloak of mental toughness. Far beyond the noise of the stadiums and courts, where they do seem ruthless and clinical, they do cry and have their share of insecurities. One of the books which gives us a peak into this aspect of a sportsperson's life is *Rafa*, the autobiography of the reigning tennis legend of our time, Rafael Nadal.

What about Ashwini Ponnappa?

She says, 'When I lose, I get upset. I cry a lot. It's Dad and Mom who console me, and then my partner. They often say, "Don't worry, Ashwini, another tournament is coming up." Gradually, I learnt to take victory and defeat in my stride. My mother helps me in my mental fitness and calmness. She is Internet-savvy; she does a lot of research and provides me with invaluable inputs from time to time. Every athlete has their own approach for dealing with difficult situations. My approach is talking to Mom, reading books and inspirational quotes to keep myself positive and encouraged.'

There are phases in a sportsperson's life when the results don't match the efforts put in. How did Ashwini Ponnappa cope with this?

'Most sportspersons go through that. You train and work really hard and give your best and just do not get the results. I have gone through that a lot of times too, and still go through that sometimes. I used to get exasperated and emotional during the early days, because I used to feel really bad. But I have learnt to cope with such situations with the help of my parents and a really good friend, Ashlesh, whom I first met at the age of twelve. He helped me a lot with my mental training then and showed me how to enjoy the game and made me realize that I played my best when I had fun on the court. I won my first singles state tournament with his help.'

There comes a phase in every sportsperson's life when one leapfrogs from being an unknown person to being a household name. For the Ashwini Ponnappa and Jwala Gutta pair, this moment was the 2010 Delhi Commonwealth Games. Like many in the national media, I too came across her for the first time during the Games. The date was 14 October 2010, and at the Siri Fort Stadium, New Delhi, the final score of the finals of the

CWG Women's Doubles Badminton read: India 2, Singapore 0. Two newbies, the talented Ashwini Ponnappa and Jwala Gutta, representing India, won gold, beating Mulia and Yao Li 21-16, 21-19. Most of the supporters, who were Indians, were cheering and shouting with joy. On the other hand, there were a few Singaporean supporters who were shocked, and in disbelief.

When asked to put into words this beautiful moment in her career, Ashwini says, 'It was something that cannot be put into words, something you cannot explain; it was a feeling that can only be experienced. We were just taking it point by point, and it was only after the crowd's exuberance that we started celebrating. It took us a couple of seconds to realize that we had actually won, and we just jumped for joy.' She further adds, 'When we won, I was over the moon. Since it was in India, the crowd support was really strong, and it did help. Standing on the podium, being awarded the gold medal and singing the national anthem along with thousands of other people...it was simply amazing.'[2]

The pair came to our studio immediately after the event was over. In the interviews, what appealed the most was their sincere and matter-of-fact approach towards the game and their lives. Of course, like on the court, in the television interviews as well, Jwala Gutta looked to be taking the lead. But what helped Ashwini stand out was her innocence, matched by her rational outlook towards her game and life beyond it. Sports comes with another important teaching. When one leapfrogs from being an unknown person to a household name, it's the attitude at that time that defines the altitude of their success in their subsequent professional sporting journeys.

From a girl who fell in love with badminton, as she used to love smashing, to one of India's finest players, did success ever get to her?

---

[2]Ashwini Ponnappa said this in an interview with the authors when they were shooting a documentary series on women achievers in collaboration with the SAI.

'Success never got to me, except perhaps after the Commonwealth Games. My initial feeling was that we have won, it's good and now I will go and celebrate with my family and parents. Moreover, I do remember that I was not keeping well during the games, and wanted to take rest once our campaign was over. But the very next day we were in the studios doing the things we never did. So it was fun in that sense. Overnight we were sought-after persons,' says Ashwini. She may feel so, but the calmness and demeanour of the girl who stepped in and out of the studios gave the indication that she is different and special.

If 2010 is remembered for their victory in front of the home crowd, 2011 was significant for their achievement overseas. Ponnappa and Gutta won a bronze medal at the 2011 World Championships in Copenhagen. The pair defeated twelfth seeds Vita Marissa and Nadya Melati of Indonesia 17-21, 21-10, 21-17 to storm into the women's doubles semi-final. Eventually, they lost in the semis in London to the Chinese fifth seeds, thereby winning a bronze. This was only the second time, after Prakash Padukone (1983), when an Indian stood on the podium at the marquee event. The cameras chased the domineering duo of Indian badminton for the second time. It was at the 2012 London Olympics that we had a chance to observe Ponnappa from close quarters again.

Sports teaches us many things in life. And, to understand some of them, one needs to feel the ambience around the Games Village during the Olympics. One of the beautiful aspects of the Olympic Games is its Games Village. The atmosphere around the village where the masters and geniuses of different sports get to see and interact with each other, is to be experienced to be believed. When one sees the fastest person on the planet walk in and out of the village, the best in the world of tennis interacting with the swimming legend of our times and the best of the judo players sharing their tricks of the trade with the wrestlers, it is simply incredible. No World Cup or professional league could match this ambience. Two days before the London Olympics Opening

Ceremony, we were outside the Games Village along with select Indian journalists and players, soaking in this ambience. We were trying to identify some of the sporting legends and greats whom we have admired and adored over the years.

The Indian sportspersons who were with us included the dynamic duo of Ashwini Ponnappa and Jwala Gutta. Ashwini was taking us through her list of the sporting greats she admired and had come across in the last few hours.

As this process was on, our eyes fell on the great Novak Djokovic who was coming out of the Games Village accompanied by some of the athletes from his country.

The awe and respect with which both Jwala and Ashwini looked at Djokovic as a player and the amount of information they had about his game surprised many of us. We admired their humility and in-depth knowledge about tennis and the know-how of what it takes to be a champion in international sports.

Did she have a role model in her mind when she decided to take up professional sports?

'Not really. As children, we were just asked to sit and watch others and learn from them, but I didn't really enjoy that. Until the under-16 category, I did not have any big dream or ambition; my goals were things such as winning the state championships and getting onto the state team and winning the nationals. I did not have any role model as such, but as I got older, I started enjoying watching other players play, as I could picture myself playing strokes that I liked and tried to implement them in my game. So, ever since, I have loved watching others play, and feel that I can learn from everyone,' says Ashwini. When a fellow journalist complimented her on her looks, Ashwini said, politely but firmly, 'We would love it if people focused on our game and performance per se, and not on our looks.'[3]

At the 2012 London Olympics, Ponnappa and Gutta lost their

---

[3]Mehul Manot, 'Things changed after we won the Commonwealth Games', sportskeeda.com, 3 August 2013

opening women's doubles match against the Japanese duo of Mizuki Fuji and Reika Kakiiwa. They then went on to beat the much higher ranked Wen Hsing Cheng and Yu Chin Chien of Chinese Taipei 25-23, 16-21, 21-18 to register their first win in the group stages. Jwala and Ashwini missed out on a quarter-final berth by a difference of just one point, even though they beat Shinta Mulia Sari and Lei Yao of Singapore 21-16, 21-15 in their last group B match, after tying with Japan and Taipei based on the number of wins.

India lodged a formal complaint with the Games organizers to probe if the women's doubles badminton match involving Japan and Chinese Taipei was played in the right spirit, following the elimination of our medal hopes, Jwala Gutta and Ashwini Ponnappa, but no action was taken. We interviewed them two hours after the complaint was lodged. Jwala was answering most of the questions, but the pain and anger on the innocent face of Ashwini was palpable. After the 2012 London Olympics, Jwala went on a temporary sabbatical from the game.

Ponnappa then partnered Pradnya Gadre for a brief period of time in 2013. The pair of Ponnappa and Jwala reunited later in the year. In June 2015, the Ashwini-Jwala pair won the Canada Open Women's Doubles title. The Indian pair defeated the top-seeded Dutch pair of Eefje Muskens and Selena Piek. It was the pair's first and only title in that year.

2014 turned out to be another fruitful year for the duo. They won the silver medal at the Glasgow Commonwealth Games, and followed that up with bronze medals at the Asian Games in Incheon and the Uber Cup in New Delhi. The country had high hopes from the pair in the 2016 Rio Olympics. Unfortunately, they ended up losing all their matches in the group stage.

When reminded of the Rio performance, Ashwini Ponnappa said to an English daily, 'It wasn't easy. That three-month break after the Olympics was important because physically I was not fit at all. I had dengue just before the Olympics and that shattered my body. Even when I was training again, my body was not responding. In my head I knew I had no injury, but my body did not listen to me. I kept asking myself, "Why am I struggling to play? Why am I struggling to smash?"[4]

What followed was introspection, as Ponnappa spent time on regaining, and more importantly, redefining her physical fitness, along with opening her mind to learning new things about her game. Sports teaches us to redefine ourselves from time to time to stay on top of our game. Gradually, version 2.0 of Ashwini Ponnappa was taking shape.

Physically and mentally, Ashwini finds herself in a good space now. 'Life has changed a lot.' Her words now carry an unmistakable satisfaction—the tone of an athlete who has endured a tough time and managed to break out of it. 'Now I am open to a lot of things that in the past I was closed to. I am open to suggestions that have helped me grow even more than I have grown in the last couple of years. I have accepted that if things don't work out in a particular partnership, it's time to change. I am open to a lot of things now, and am not really narrow-minded in my approach to the game,'[5] she says. While Ponnappa's current doubles partner, N. Sikki Reddy, has been a constant, she has played with three different mixed doubles partners—K. Nandagopal, B. Sumeeth Reddy and Satwiksairaj Rankireddy. Her partnership with Sikki took off gradually.

The pair started playing in November 2016, and in 2017, ranked 110th in the world. Halfway through the season, the duo had reached the top 30. A title has proved elusive, but they came close in the Syed Modi International Grand Prix Gold (GPG), as runners-up. 'Sikki is an excellent mover. I came to realize she is essentially a back court player too, like me. And both of us being good at the back helps us rotate; we can move in, we can mix it up. That has helped a lot. We are finding out areas which are our strong points. With every tournament we are getting more confident with the rotation. That has been important for me; it tells me we are

---

[4]Vinayakk Mohanarangan, 'Life after Jwala: 'Open-minded' Ashwini Ponnappa reaping the benefits of experimentation', Scroll, 14 June 2017
[5]Ibid.

moving in the right direction,'[6] she said in an interview with an English daily when specifically asked about their partnership.

Ponnappa, over the years, had developed the reputation of being the quieter one, with Jwala known to be more vocal. Even their on-court chemistry gave the impression that Jwala was the dominant of the pair, and Ponnappa was a follower. But in the changed scenario, Ponnappa has become the senior-most doubles player in the country and that comes with the responsibility of being a mentor—a role she is enjoying. Ashwini says, 'It is a lot of fun. I just like figuring things out—like how to play an opponent, by watching old match videos. That helps me guide my partners. It doesn't mean I am the senior partner and the other is a junior partner. Once we are on court, we are one unit. My experience does help a bit; I can help them relax and calm their nerves in certain situations.'[7]

Version 2.0 of Ashwini Ponnappa has found a newfound vigour to succeed in mixed doubles. While she played mixed doubles often, she admits that, until now, she never gave it her complete attention. As she started taking mixed doubles more seriously, this helped her to further explore the game. International sports, after all, is a constant learning process. Her agility increased, she started moving on the court with more ease and holding her own at the nets as well. 'With this sort of mindset, I am enjoying doubles, mixed doubles, playing with Sikki, the rotation, the communication and moving to the net. It's just been a whole lot of fun. There is never an end to learning, never an end to growing if you are really excited about the game,'[8] she says further in the interview. This is another important thing that sports teaches us in life.

What has badminton taught her?

'Badminton has made me a better human being—dealing

[6]Vinayakk Mohanarangan, 'Life after Jwala: "Open-minded" Ashwini Ponnappa reaping the benefits of experimentation', Scroll, 14 June 2017

[7]Ibid.

[8]Vinayakk Mohanarangan, 'Life after Jwala: "Open-minded" Ashwini Ponnappa reaping the benefits of experimentation', Scroll, 14 June 2017

with situations I am not comfortable dealing with, like losses; that really makes you go to a different level—it makes you stronger as a person and you understand a lot about yourself as a person in a lot of different ways...about your potential, taking care of your body in a better way and things you want to do in life. Badminton as a sport has taught me lots of things actually.'[9]

What does taking care of the body mean?

'As you start getting older, you need to take better care of yourself. Earlier, when I used to get unwell, it did not affect me, but now it matters a lot,' Ashwini says.

The wheel has turned full circle now. How does she feel now when she is followed by others as an icon?

'You are not taught how to be a sportsperson and a role model and things like that. It remains very important that you stay true to yourself and do what you believe in. That is why people look up to you.'

What is the way ahead for Indian badminton?

Ashwini Ponnappa says, 'Asian countries are good in badminton. Korea, Japan and China, amongst others, are fantastic. They have deep reserve strength. They have four equally good doubles pairs in every category. We need to achieve their level.'

Now that she is a senior sportswoman in India, how does she assess the change in the sporting landscape of the country over the years?

'India has huge potential in sports that is untapped. Things are picking up, and there is more support for the athletes now,' she says.

What is her message to those parents who are hesitant about their daughters taking up sports?

Ashwini comes out with a gem of an answer to this. She says, 'Give it a shot. We can juggle between sports and studies. There is a chance that if we do well in sports, we can make it a serious

---

[9]Ashwini Ponnappa said this in an interview with DD Sports when the documentary on women achievers was being made.

career option. If not, then studies are always there to fall back on.'

In hindsight, after spending years as a serious professional badminton player, Ashwini thinks that she took up the sport as it involves a lot of power. She loves smashing, and thus smashing has been her favourite stroke throughout. Before she learnt how to play badminton, she already loved whacking the shuttlecocks. She simply kept whacking them and other tricks involved in the trade kept on being added to her repertoire. She feels that she is still a work in progress, and that she will continue to be a work in progress even after she decides to hang up her racquet. After all, there is a life beyond the badminton court as well. A flamboyant Kodava girl, Ashwini Nachappa has proven that over the years.

ELEVEN

Sakshi Malik:
It's Not Just a Man's Sport

Kushti, ye aurton ka khel naheen. (Wrestling, this sport is not for women.)

This was the overriding narrative of one of the most popular physical contact sports in India. Then, change started happening. And the change was destined to come from an Indian state that topped the country for its notoriety in terms of patriarchy.

Kushti, hamaaree chhoriyan ab chhoron se kam naheen, aage hain. (Wrestling, our girls are in no way lesser than boys. In fact, they are ahead of them.)

So how did this happen? If change is the only constant in life, this narrative has to be understood to be believed.

There is something in wrestling that has traditionally brought to the forefront the woman rebel with a cause. Hamida Bano, perhaps the first recognized woman wrestler of the country, belonged to a family of wrestlers in Uttar Pradesh. She had defeated quite a few wrestlers during the 1950s. Hamida, belonging to a Muslim family, had declared that she would marry a person who would defeat her in a 'dangal'. It's not clear whether she was married or not, but she was fond of organizing 'dangals' after she retired from wrestling.

As per Tejpal Dalal, a wrestling historian-cum-mathematics teacher and resident of Jhajjar, she had visited Jhajjar town to watch Randhawa, the younger brother of the famed wrestler Dara Singh, wrestle against Kapoor Singh of Mandothi village in 1970. After Hamida, Nanhe Pahalwan from Weir in Bharatpur district in Rajasthan was another prominent woman wrestler in the 1960s.

Barring these aberrations, Indian women lagged behind men in the sport due to social prejudices, as wrestling was considered an exclusive male sport in India.

The man who brought about the transformation in the entire narrative was Master Chandgi Ram. When he introduced two of his daughters to modern wrestling in 1997, he brought about an epochal change in the realm of contact sports. One of his daughters, Sonika Kaliraman, became the first woman Hind Kesari. This set a precedent, which required another change agent outside his family to gather momentum in the years to come.

The distance between Delhi to Rohtak is hardly 80 km, but it took another six years for women's wrestling to traverse the distance. Rohtak is renowned for its akharas and is considered by many as the wrestling epicentre of the country. When the move was initiated in 2002 to let girls train with boys, former wrestlers and coaches questioned the then Haryana sports department coach at the Chotu Ram Stadium, Ishwar Singh Dahiya, on letting 'goats stay among lions.'

If wrestling akharas are the reflection of the oppressed putting up their act of defiance against the oppressor, Indian women wrestlers were all set to challenge the male stereotypes in the supposedly most patriarchal belt of north India. The change agent however came from a further 64 km away from Rohtak, from the Bhiwani district of Haryana.

This is the place where Mahavir Singh Phogat scripted a wrestling revolution. One of the major banes of the country has been the urban elitist mindset of expecting the change agent to be from the neighbour's home and keeping one's home safe and secure. But wrestling by nature is different. The change agent, Mahavir, chose his own family to lead by example.

Mahavir and his wife Daya Kaur have five children: daughters Geeta, Babita, Ritu and Sangita and the youngest being a son, Dushyant. Mahavir's brother Rajpal's daughters Priyanka and Vinesh were brought up by Mahavir after the death of their father. Mahavir was inspired to train his daughters in wrestling when weightlifter Karnam Malleswari became the first Indian woman to win an Olympic medal in 2000.

He was also influenced by his coach, Chandgi Ram, who introduced his own daughters to wrestling several years ago and whose Delhi-based Chandgi Ram Akhara was one of India's first centres to allow women wrestlers.

Mahavir says, 'Masterji opened my eyes; he used to tell me, what you are doing for your girls, you will see one day that it will bring you great happiness. So keep doing it, don't be scared, face your difficulties like you face opponents, and be deaf to the criticism.' Remembering those days, the wife of Mahavir, Daya Shobha Kaur, recollects, 'I told my husband not to push the girls into the sport. I was worried about how they would ever get married as pehelwans wearing shorts and having short hair.' Mahavir Phogat said this to the authors when they were making a documentary on women's wrestling, while they were sports editors with IBN7.

However, Mahavir had made up his mind. He says, 'Everyone was saying that I was bringing shame to our village by training my girls, but I thought, if a woman can be the prime minister of a country, why can't she be a wrestler?'

Mahavir left his job at the Haryana State Electricity Board and began training his daughters. He asked them to start running in the farm every day and made a makeshift akhara next to his house. This was the beginning of the challenge.

When Mahavir found that there were no other girls in the village that the sisters could practise with, he asked Geeta and Babita to start training with boys. The decision led to considerable criticism and ridicule from conservative village elders, but Mahavir held his ground. Deprived of proper facilities in his village, where his daughters wrestled against boys, Mahavir enrolled Geeta and Babita at the SAI centre in Sonepat.

The results started coming. In 2010, the eldest of the Phogat siblings, Geeta, won India's first-ever gold medal in women's wrestling in the 55 kg freestyle category of the Commonwealth

Games. She followed it up with a bronze at the 2012 World Championships, another first for Indian women. She became the first-ever Indian woman to qualify for the Olympics in 2012. The success was emulated by her other sisters, with Babita winning the silver at the 2010 Commonwealth Games and gold in the same competition four years later.

Vinesh won a gold at the 2014 Commonwealth Games and a bronze at the 2015 Asian Wrestling Championships. She, however, had to pull out of the Rio Olympics after suffering a leg injury during the 48 kg quarter-final bout against China's Sun Yanan in 2016. She had to be stretchered off the wrestling arena in 2016, after suffering a horrible knee injury. This was followed by a long and painful period of rehabilitation.

There is something in champion wrestlers that makes them more powerful when they come out of injury. Vinesh rued the missed opportunity but decided not to break down. She started her journey all over again. She bounced back, winning back-to-back gold medals in the Commonwealth Games and Asian Games in 2018. The gold enabled Vinesh to achieve another feat as she became the only woman wrestler to win two medals in back-to-back Asian Games. She also has back-to-back gold medals in the Commonwealth Games—in Glasgow and the Gold Coast.

After the gold medal performance in the Asian Games, she said, 'Injuries are part of an athlete's career. It is difficult both emotionally and physically. But I shrugged off everything to deliver. Someone has said an athlete becomes strong after an injury, and I feel I indeed have become stronger than before. There was pressure, but it was to prove that I was actually stronger than my opponent.'[1]

This shows why the twenty-three-year-old from Haryana is considered one of the most mentally strong wrestlers in India. The mental strength, she says, comes naturally to her.

---

[1]PTI, 'I have become stronger after Rio injury: Vinesh', *Business Standard*, 20 August 2018

'I work on this, but I am like this from childhood. I have always been rough and tough. I take risks in life and they pay off. I have self-belief. I feel there is nothing that I can't do,'[2] said Vinesh.

She is the top contender for the medal in the Tokyo Olympics, about which she says, 'The next major competition is the Olympics, but I will also go for all the competitions that take place in between and give my best there.'

The most talkative and playful amongst the Phogat sisters, Vinesh is now in the ideal physical and mental state to scale new summits.

The Hindi blockbuster film *Dangal* is loosely based on the Phogat family. The development of the film began in early 2013, when the director began writing the screenplay. In 2014, Aamir Khan had invited and interviewed the Phogat sisters on his talk show Satyamev Jayate. Nitesh Tiwari approached him with the script later. From the time the film *Dangal* was conceptualized, to the year it was released, a girl from Rohtak had scripted her own memorable journey from Rohtak to Rio.

The story gave the entire narrative of Indian women in wrestling a decisive push. However, the script differed from real life as it had a huge novelty factor to it.

Sakshi Malik became the first woman wrestler from India to get a medal in the Olympics. Sakshi's rise was not a bolt from the blue. Rather, it was the result of the strong undercurrent at work in the wrestling centre of the country.

By 2014-15, in the Senior National Women's Championships, every fourth medallist was a product of the Rohtak centre. Of the 32 medals, 8 were won by the wrestlers from the centre—Sakshi got gold, Nikki Samra, Ritu Phogat and Suman Kumari got a silver each, and Pinki Jangra, Rekha Kadiyan and Sudesh Kumari got a bronze each. At the 2015 Kerala National Games, half of the Haryana team was from the centre. Sakshi, Suman and Ritu won gold while Nikki won silver. In the international meets in the

---

[2]'I have self-belief. I feel there is nothing that I can't do', rediff.com, 20 August 2018

year leading to the Olympics, girls from the centre, like Sakshi Malik, won bronze in the Senior Asian Championships. Suman was part of the same championship; Nikki was part of the Senior World Championships squad and Pinki part of the Junior Asian Championships squad. How do these undercurrents shape up?

In this, the two coaches, Ishwar Singh Dahiya and Mandeep, played a huge role. Dahiya was the former sports department coach who was instrumental in starting women's wrestling at the Chotu Ram Stadium in Rohtak. In mid-2002, he decided to allow girls to train with the boys. Dahiya says, 'As ours was initially a men's centre, I was reluctant to introduce women's wrestling and delayed their entry by two years. When I finally made up my mind, my colleagues told me that I was creating problems for myself as they could spoil the discipline at the centre. I stayed firm, and the rest is history.'[3] All this started with a wonderful stroke of coincidence.

In June 2002, Kavita and Sunita were allowed to train with the boys. By the end of the year, the number had increased to four. 'Sunita came to me with her elder brother to seek permission to join the centre. She was around fourteen or fifteen and had short hair. I mistook her for a boy and gave her the nod. In the evening when she came with her friend Kavita, I realized she was a girl. As I had already given her permission, there was no question of backtracking. This is how the girls' centre started,' says Dahiya.

The girls finally got an entry. Now the challenge was to get over the hesitation to train with the boys. One of the early birds, Suman Kundu, says, 'In the beginning, we did not wear wrestling costumes during training but track pants and t-shirts. In 2005-06, a competition was held at our centre and we fought in proper gear in front of the boys, and that helped us overcome hesitation.'[4]

[3]Saurabh Duggal, 'Haryana centre puts Indian women's wrestling on world map', *Hindustan Times*, 11 October 2015

[4]Saurabh Duggal, 'Rio 2016: Sakshi Malik is witness to Rohtak's rise as wrestling hub', *Hindustan Times*, 18 August 2016

After Dahiya retired, Mandeep took over. A former trainee of the centre, he completed a diploma course from NIS Patiala in 2010 and took to coaching at the centre. In the beginning, he assisted Dahiya and later on took charge of the centre. With results starting to come in, perception changed and news of the wrestlers' success spread to nearby villages. The biggest break came during the Delhi Commonwealth Games when Suman won bronze in the 63 kg weight category. In the next edition at Glasgow, Sakshi Malik won silver in 58 kg. The stage was thus set for 'the memorable day in Indian women's wrestling'.

Sakshi Malik's living room was the setting for one of the euphoric moments of 2016. It was 16 August 2016 to be precise. It was raksha bandhan—the Indian festival celebrating the unique bond between brother and sister, across the country. The Indian contingent had failed to open its account at the Rio Olympics. India's brightest medal hope in women's wrestling, Vinesh Phogat, Sakshi's wrestling peer in the 48 kg category, was forced to retire hurt early into her semi-final bout after a promising display.

This was the living room that was witness to Malik's mother, Sudesh, jumping with joy in front of hordes of television cameras, as her daughter staged an extraordinary comeback in the dying second of her bronze medal bout in the Rio Olympics. After losing the quarter-final to finalist Koblova Zholobowa, Sakshi Malik went on to win the re-pechage against Mongolia's Orkhon Purevdorj, and then Kyrgyzstan's Aisuluu Tynybekova.

'I was crying,' says Sudesh. 'She told me, "Why are you crying? It's a happy moment."'[5]

After her victory, the entire country, along with Sudesh, saw Malik jogging around the wrestling arena, carrying the Indian flag, before collapsing on the mat as the true realization of her feat started sinking in. 'It's the result of twelve years of wrestling day and night. I never gave up in the bout but gave it my maximum,'

---

[5]Arunabh Saikia, 'The measure of Sakshi Malik's success', *Livemint*, 30 December 2016

she said to the Indian journalists then.

This indeed was a happy moment for the daughters of the country—more for the message than the messenger who brought about the glory.

The parents of Sakshi Malik are from the Mokhra Khas village in Haryana. This is a pehelwan village and every family from here boasts of at least one wrestler son. Ironically, if Malik had lived in her village, her wrestling dreams would have struggled to take off. In spite of its wrestling tradition, women are not allowed to practise in the village's akharas. The fact that she came from a state where she could very well have been killed as a foetus—as thousands routinely are—makes Malik's rise even more remarkable. Sakshi Malik thus not only triumphed over better trained opponents on the mat, but more importantly, against a stubbornly patriarchal society.

Sakshi's is not a rags-to-riches story. She comes from a fairly well-off family which owns several acres of land. Then what is it that motivates her to wake up at the crack of dawn to practise her craft for two hours before going to school? According to her mother, there hasn't been a single day in the last twelve years when she had to wake her up. What is it that stirs her enough to give up on friends, food and fun to be able to pin down opponents? What is it that drives a teenage girl—she was twelve years old when she started—from a semi-urban town to go day after day, year after year, to a stuffy gymnasium, full of seemingly intimidating men and heavy with the smell of piss and sweat?

Sakshi's story is not of parental pressure like the Phogat sisters either. Malik's mother took her to the Sir Chhotu Ram Stadium as 'she was interested in sports'.

'No one instructed that I should become a wrestler. This was my own interest. Sports was my passion right from the beginning. Mummy took me to the stadiums where judo and taekwondo sessions were going on, but they did not interest me. Wrestling instantly interested me. I realized that it's my game and I have to do this,'[6] says Sakshi. Thus, Sakshi's rise doesn't fit into any of the stereotypes. Rather, hers is a unique case.

Sakshi is the one who has always downplayed the protests that she, her family and her coach had to face once she decided to take up wrestling. But the protests were consistent and from too many people. Sudesh Malik says, 'When I used to go to the village, hundreds of questions were asked. I used to say that my son studies and my daughter studies and participates in wrestling. They used to get worked up. "This is a boys' sport, and what is your girl doing in the sport?" was their persistent query. "She has to get married. She has to give birth." They used to say that her ears would get thicker, her way of walking would change and she would get disfigured. I just listened to them.'

Her coach, Ishwar Singh, also had to fend off several questions along similar lines.

'Why are you running an akhara for girls and wasting time, and not one for the boys?' was the standard question asked to him.

Sakshi says, 'My neighbours used to say, "She is a girl—why does she play the sport of the boys?" There were constant taunts amidst my struggle to find my feet in the wrestling arena. I used to get beatings from my teachers in the class as I used to fall asleep after practice sessions. My class friends used to laugh because I carried milk and energy drinks with me.'

Team Sakshi, comprising her family and coach, had dared to venture into an arena that was supposedly a male preserve, that too in one of the most gender-skewed villages of the country. As per the census of 2011, Mokhra village, with a population of 10,780, has a sex ratio of 822.2, low even by Haryana's standards (877).[7]

---

[6]Sakshi Malik said this on the DD Sports show *Hauslon Ki Udaan* anchored by Sangram Singh. Sakshi Malik, her mother and her coach came for the show. The show was conceptualized and directed by author Abhishek Dubey.

[7]Asit Ranjan Mishra, 'Rio Olympics: What Census data tells us about Sakshi Malik's village', *Livemint*, 20 August 2016

How did all this affect Sakshi while she was growing up?

'Yes, people objected initially. They said things, but they came around. It never bothered me,' she says.

Wrestling is high contact sports. Did playing with men bother her?

'No, never. It's a trivial issue.'

For those who manage to trivialize the most difficult issue, the path for them starts getting easier.

Sakshi was a mischievous character as a child. For a while she used to stay with her grandparents in the village. There are stories of Sakshi chasing dogs in the village and getting beaten up by her grandmother for this. There are stories of Sakshi teasing her grandfather by calling him badlu dada (turncoat grandfather). There are many such stories which the people in her village now fondly recollect. Sakshi savours all such fond memories.

'My grandmother is no more, but I was closest to her,' she remembers. When she started living with her parents, her stubborn nature came to the fore innumerable times. When her mother used to leave for work, she used to catch hold of her leg and not leave her till she reached the door.

The tendency continued for a period of time. Once, her father got her long hair cut short. She refused to go to school to appear for her exams. She set a condition. She would go only when her parents would announce in the bus that no one could tease her. Her father left for his work. Her mother had to make the announcement in the bus before Sakshi agreed to go to school to appear for her exam. Against this backdrop, wrestling came to her life, to make her calmer.

'Earlier, my parents used to hear lots of complaints about me in the school. When I took to wrestling, I became calmer. People started wondering how I had become silent, when I used to speak a lot earlier. I didn't pick fights with anyone anymore. This was because I used to focus all my energy on wrestling, and nothing was left after this,' she says.

There comes a time in every sportsperson's life when they find themselves at crossroads—where one has to prioritize between sports and studies. Sakshi also had to face the question early in her life. And, she got the answer. 'Once I got so disturbed trying to find the balance between studies and wrestling that I told my parents, "I can only do either one of them." I thought that they would say wrestling. On the contrary, they asked me to leave wrestling and concentrate on studies. I got the answer,' Sakshi says.

By then, her parents had become convinced that she could not live without wrestling. Wrestling had become her calling in life. But she herself was ignorant about what she wanted to achieve.

'I did not know what the Asian Games, Commonwealth Games and the Olympics were. The people around me used to say that if I did well, I would get to ride a plane. So I started working harder. When Sushil and Yogeshwar pehelwan got the medals for the country, I aspired to reach there. When Geeta didi (Geeta Phogat) qualified for the Olympics in 2012, I had the firm belief that I could also do this.'[8]

The circumstances and conditions were shaping her for the ultimate glory. Step by step, she was getting nearer to it.

'When I used to go to train in the morning, only papa used to be wide awake. Sometimes he used to be awake to get himself ready for his job and sometimes for some other work. Papa used to open the gates and give me his scooty. My standard question before leaving used to be, "Will I qualify?" He used to always say, "Yes, you will." Often I replied, "How can you say this with so much of confidence?"'[9] Sakshi says.

The coach I.S. Dahiya elaborates when he says, 'When Sakshi came to me and I observed her activities, I immediately realized that she has got loads of talent. In 2007 itself, I suggested to the coach of the national team to select her for the national camp. His asked me how he could put someone straight from the sub-junior to the national level. I said that if it could be done with Sachin

[8]Deepa Malik said this on the show *Bitiya Mein Hai Dum* shot in Rohtak University. The show was conceptualized and produced by author Abhishek Dubey.
[9]Ibid.

Tendulkar in cricket, the same applied to her in wrestling. I was convinced that if anyone could win a medal for the country in the Olympics it had to be Sakshi Malik.'[10]

Her date with the 2016 Rio Olympics was finally decided. Sakshi Malik qualified for the 2016 Rio Olympics by defeating China's Zhang Lan in the semi-final of the 58 kg category at the Olympics World Qualifying Tournament in May 2016. Remembering the day, her father Sukhbir Malik says, 'When the qualifier for the Rio Olympics was ongoing and she qualified, I remember that when she returned home, it was late at night. I told her, you have reached a step closer; practise hard, you will get the medal. I don't know, but I already had an intuition that she would get the medal for the country in Rio.'[11] This eventually happened on 16 August 2018.

Rio 2016 has been the most striking destination in her journey till date. But there have been some memorable stops in between. Malik's first success as a professional wrestler in the international arena came in 2010 at the Junior World Championships where she won the bronze medal in the 58 kg freestyle event. At the 2014 Dave Schultz International Tournament, she won gold in the 60 kg category. In the 2014 Glasgow Commonwealth Games, she began her campaign by winning her quarter-final bout against Edwige Ngono Eyie of Cameroon by a 4-0 margin. In the semi-finals she defeated Braxton Stone of Canada 3-1 to assure herself of the medal. She lost the finals to Aminat Adeniyi of Nigeria 4-0 in the closely contested bout and thus got the silver medal. Sakshi, in many of her interviews, calls it the most memorable day before her medal-winning performance in the Rio Olympics. Sakshi faced Anta Sambou of Senegal in the round of sixteen at the 2014 World Championships in Tashkent and won the bout. However, she lost to Petra Oili of Finland in the next round and crashed out of the tournament. At the 2015 Asian Championships

---

[10]Deepa Malik said this on the show *Bitiya Mein Hai Dum* shot in Rohtak University. The show was conceptualized and produced by author Abhishek Dubey.
[11]Ibid.

in Doha, in a total of five rounds in the 60 kg category, she battled through two rounds to finish in the third position and claim a bronze medal. Her passion for wrestling continues. For her, there is no better feeling than pinning her opponents to the mat. There is no sound sweeter than the thud when she throws her opponents on the mat.

'After I won the medal in the Olympics, I could have quit. But I did not and I will not. I will continue to fight, because I love the sport.' She sums it up. She has her eye set on the upcoming Olympics. At the same time, she is not reluctant to discuss the issues that plague athletics and Indian sports.

Every experience of hers has made Sakshi graduate from a good wrestler to a strong woman and sportsperson. She has always stressed on the need for better infrastructure and international exposures in her interviews and discussions.

'The amount of money we get after winning, if we get even a fraction of the same in terms of infrastructure, it will go a long way in India, producing more and more champions,' she says. She believes that there are ample talented sportspersons in wrestling. But what they need is exposure.

'There was the notion created in our minds that the best of the best qualify for the Olympics. If we compete in more and more international competitions, this big-stage fright will go away. From my experience I can say that the ten-day training camp I had in Spain worked wonders for me before the Olympics. The same applies to other aspiring wrestlers.'[12]

Every passing milestone has made Sakshi calmer. 'After Rio, I don't feel any pressure. Friends and well-wishers think that if I lose, the heavens are going to fall. But I practise to win and when one wins under pressure, only then can one be called a true champion. I have some more years of wrestling left. I will take one thing at a time.'

Sakshi's favourite move in wrestling is the double leg attack,

---

[12]Deepa Malik said this in an interview for the show *Hauslon Ki Udaan*.

but she has always believed in wrestling being more a mind game than requiring brute physical power. And it is for this reason that she talks about the importance of academics in a wrestler's life. She says, 'I always tell everyone, to be a good wrestler, it is immensely helpful if one is good in studies. If one is good in studies, one's mind works faster and one is able to focus better.'[13] She says that earlier she was average in studies and used to get 70-80 per cent marks. However, after starting wrestling, she became much more focused. She has completed her master's in physical education.

Sakshi Malik got married to Satyawart Kadiyan. Both of them used to come first in their respective categories. At the junior and sub-junior level, they used to represent the country together.

'Till then, we knew each other as wrestlers. That's it. When we participated in the Commonwealth Games, both of us had our events on the same day. Both of us won silver medals and we became friends,' Sakshi says with a smile on her face. The timing of her marriage was also solely decided by her. 'There were many who were not in favour of me getting married now. My parents were also of the view that as I have a long career ahead of me, this was not an apt time to get married. But whom to marry and when to marry was totally my decision. My husband and father-in-law are both wrestlers and we have an akhara at home. I strongly felt that we would practise together and the marriage was not going to be a barrier in my career.'[14]

The determination and the firmness in her personality clearly come out. Fiercely independent in her thinking, she started handling her accounts even before her marriage. 'Before Rio, my parents used to handle my accounts. But after Rio, I started looking at my finances. This is very critical for any girl, as after marriage, one has to properly handle the finances of the family,'[15] she says. This reveals maturity in her personality far beyond her age.

Sakshi Malik is like the girl next door. This trait of hers is

---

[13]Deepa Malik said this in an interview for the show *Hauslon Ki Udaan*.
[14]Ibid.
[15]Ibid.

hidden behind her image of the one who defeats and puts down her opponent on the mat. She considers her calm behaviour as both her strength and weakness. She still loves soft toys. She still relishes her favourite food 'kadhi chawal'. Inside the wrestling ring, Sushil Kumar is her hero. Outside the ring, she admires Amitabh Bachchan. Her favourite dialogue is the iconic one from the film *Dangal*, '*Hamaare chhoriyan chhoron se kam hai ke*?' (Are our daughters any less than our sons?) She wants a biopic based on her life to be made and Kangana Ranaut to play her role. Sakshi loves to listen to motivational songs before her bouts. If given one chance in life, she would love to change the colour of her medal in Rio 2016. Sakshi Malik may still get an opportunity to change the colour of her medal in Tokyo 2020.

Whether she manages to change the colour or not, she has been able to change the mindsets of so many people in her state and country. As she says, 'The same people who used to talk about my short wrestling signet and abuse me, now desperately want to meet me. Wherever I go, parents come to me and ask whether it's possible to make their daughters like me.'[16] She has put the final nail in the coffin of the notion that wrestling is a sport for men and not meant for women. There are others, from all across the country, who are joining the bandwagon and taking the narrative head on.

---

[16]Deepa Malik said this in an interview for the show *Hauslon Ki Udaan*.

TWELVE

Deepa Malik: Born Again

Joey Reiman, an American businessman and author once said, 'The Olympics is where heroes are made. The Paralympics is where heroes come.'

A gifted swimmer who had promised the South African nation she would make more than a splash in the pool, seventeen-year-old Natalie Du Toit saw her dreams crushed by a speeding car that hit her as she was enroute to school on her scooter, having finished her regular practice at the Newlands municipal swimming school. The majestic Table Mountain bore witness from a distance as the accident crushed her left leg, leaving her with an amputation at the knee and a titanium rod with screws fitted into the femur for stability.

Months later, du Toit would make the world gasp in awe as she not only broke records in the multi-disability swimming events at the 2001 Commonwealth Games, but also swam her way into the final of the 800 m able-bodied freestyle final! How did she do it? Where did she find the strength or resolve? This was an extraordinary feat that made most other sporting achievements pale into insignificance, through its sheer measure of human conquest over disaster. Du Toit would later recollect how she found solace, and the will to firm up, in lines penned down by the poet Benjamin Mays, 'The tragedy of life does not lie in not reaching your goals; it lies in not having goals to reach for.'

Du Toit would go on to make history, winning gold medals in all thirteen Paralympic swimming events she would take part in, through the next decade. 2008 was one of the most glorious chapters in her career as she became the first amputee to qualify for the 2008 Beijing Olympics, a feat yet unmatched. A motivational speaker, du Toit today inspires youngsters to pursue their dreams, however impossible they might seem.

Esther Vergeer was eight when she had to go under the surgeon's knife for a spinal defect and brain haemorrhage. The operation left her paralyzed from waist down, as she revealed in her autobiography, *Fierce and Vulnerable*, bound to a wheelchair for life. The home front, her elementary school and her rehabilitation programme that included sporting involvement, shepherded her along the path of a life that had to be lived accepting her impairment.

Good at playing both wheelchair tennis as well as wheelchair basketball, she chose the former. And ten years on, she was unbeatable in her sport. The Dutch player retired in February 2013 with 8 Paralympic medals to her name. In her incredible journey, she racked up 148 singles and 136 doubles titles. With 42 Grand Slam titles to her credit, she was ranked no. 1 thirteen consecutive times during her tennis career.

American swimmer Trischa Zorn was born in 1964 with a rare, yet cruel anomaly; her eyes had no irises! A congenital condition known as aniridia, it meant she would never be able to see with her eyes. But the feisty Trischa beat the odds, and how, competing in seven Paralympic Games, winning more than 50 medals, with the majority being gold medals. A Paralympic Hall of Famer since 2012, Trischa now practises as an insurance attorney, while also devoting time to coach Paralympic swimmers.

Chantal Petitclerc was thirteen when, in a tragic accident, she lost the use of both her legs. At the age of eighteen, she was introduced to wheelchair athletics by trainer Pierre Pomerleau. She went on to become the greatest wheelchair racer of all time. She has 14 gold, 5 silver and 2 bronze medals to her name. This includes five back-to-back gold medals in both the 2004 and the 2008 Paralympics Games, when she was thirty-four and thirty-eight years old respectively. After her retirement, she coached the British athletics team, prior to the 2012 London Olympic Games.

Yu Chui Yee, popularly known as 'seven-gold princess', has been on a wheelchair since she was eleven. She had lost her left leg to bone cancer. She became a wheelchair fencer and gave a double gold performance at London 2012. She won a medal in each of the nine Paralympic competitions she competed in, 7 of them being gold. In the International Wheelchair and Amputee Sports Wheelchair Fencing World Cup in Warsaw, Poland, she clinched the gold medal. Her romance with milestones and achievements continues.

Sarah Storey was born without a functioning left hand. This did not deter her from becoming one of the most successful British female Paralympians, with 23 medals to her name, 12 of them gold. Besides cycling, she also pursued swimming and became the finalist for the BBC's Sports Personality of the Year Award.

Sports throws up such stories every now and then to showcase the ultimate triumph over adversity, as these inspirational instances have shown to the world. Deepa Malik's story is no different.

Deepa's journey towards being the person she now is began when, as a six-year-old, she had a tumour detected in her spinal cord. The tumour was treated and contained early on, but this taught her important things about the way life is to be lived in the face of adversity. Her recovery took three years, and, in this period, life threatened to be the bully who was hell-bent on taking away everything she valued.

'A tomboy and bully like me, who lived outdoors, who used to climb up trees and steal friends' bikes and ride them into the sunset couldn't be confined to a room and painting. I would not have been able to do that,'[1] says Deepa, remembering those early days. 'When you have mastered the art of gratitude, you have learnt to look at the positives of life. Even on that bed, I decided I had to enrich my mind and prepare for the future, for I knew

---

[1] Binjal Shah, 'She was given seven days to "celebrate" her last moments of walking, here's what she did: Deepa Malik, paraplegic athlete' YourStory, accessed 5 September 2019

life awaited me on the other side.' The tomboy matured into a beautiful young woman who fell in love with the bike and got married in the process.

Bikram Singh, a young army officer with a state-of-the-art Japanese bike, caught her fancy. To the astonishment of the officer, it was not him, but the bike that had the lady ogling. 'Every day I saw this boy going for a run. One day, he came with this gorgeous-looking motorcycle. I wanted to ride it. I went up to the guy and asked him to give me the keys. He asked if I would be able to manage it. I commanded him to hand me the keys then, and he did. I rode the motorcycle and pulled a few stunts and gave it back to him. I told him that I would marry a guy who would not ask me why I needed a motorcycle and would buy me one,'[2] says Deepa Malik. The next day, the young man went to her father and said, 'I will get your daughter a new motorcycle. Can I marry her?' The daughter of veteran, Infantry Colonel B.K. Nagpal, Deepa got married to Colonel Bikram Singh. Remembering those days brings a smile on her face as she says, 'Basically, I was sold off just for a bike.' On a serious note, this was the beginning of the partnership which was all set to achieve far greater glories in life.

Deepa and Bikram started building a wonderful life together. Devika, their first daughter, came into their lives. But history soon repeated itself. Her daughter got hit by a biker when she was barely one. 'There was internal bleeding in her brain, her ventricles got dilated and her left side was paralyzed. We carried her to the Pune command hospital and it was the same ward and same bed as mine, from all those years ago.'[3] She adds, 'I had to fight rumours that I had passed on my disability to my daughter. It was then that I realized the stereotypical image of disability in the eyes of society. I was far away from the venom as a child,

---

[2]Jayati Godhawat, 'Read why Deepa Malik's husband proposed her with a bike and not a ring', IndianWomenBlog, 20 August 2019

[3]Binjal Shah, 'She was given seven days to "celebrate" her last moments of walking, here's what she did: Deepa Malik, paraplegic athlete' YourStory, accessed 5 September 2019

when I was protected, but I could feel it now. But these words of my father have always given me strength—God distributes his challenges wisely. You have been chosen for this one'. She and her husband relentlessly began helping their daughter, day and night, like her parents had helped her. They had another daughter, Ambika, who was a beautiful distraction for the family from their reality. But God hadn't exhausted her share of challenges. In 1999, her husband was summoned to Kargil.

Deepa started facing difficulties again, in walking. She ignored them initially, but when the pain started getting overbearing, she was advised by the doctor to go to Delhi for a thorough check-up. When the doctor saw her medical reports, initially he was reluctant to share the details with her. He insisted on talking to her husband about the same. The daughter of an armyman, Deepa did not want to disturb her husband while he was on duty in Kargil at the India-Pakistan border. 'The doctors gave me seven days to prepare myself before getting admitted for surgery. They had informed me of the consequences; that in most cases, such surgeries resulted in paralysis,'[4] she said. The girl who loved bikes and played many a sport with passion had to suddenly reconcile to the fact that very soon she would not be able to walk again, even if she survived the surgery. Ordinary people would have given up, but she was extraordinary. Rather than surrendering to what was coming, she started preparing herself for the changed circumstances.

Deepa, in the next seven days, organized her house in such a manner that no one would have to face any difficulty even if she was no more; she wrote her will, put all her jewellery in the locker and turned the house into a structure that was totally wheelchair-friendly. She called up her mother to say that she would be sending her daughters to her along with the keys. When the doctors refused to go ahead with the operation

[4]Deepa said this to the authors in an interview during the DD Sports Conclave, 2017. Extracts from the interview have been used in this book.

Deepa Malik: Born Again   215

without the consent form signed either by her husband or by her father, she informed her parents. She handed over a letter to her parents addressed to her husband, where she detailed how to bring up her daughters in case she passed away. When her parents showed their concern about the situation she had been forced to face in life, she replied, saying, 'Yes, things are difficult. But one has to face it.' The family, with a strong defense background and legacy, looked with awe at the most courageous girl they had come across in their lifetime.

On the day of the surgery, the doctors asked her if she wanted to say or do something before going for the operation. Deepa asked for two things. Firstly, aware that perhaps she would be walking on her legs for the last time in her life, she wanted to go to the operation theatre walking, rather than on a wheelchair. Secondly, she wanted to talk to her husband who was fighting the Kargil War.

What followed is something to be noted and recorded by all, to apply when one is about to confront a difficult situation in one's personal or professional life. Deepa was taken to the radio satellite room and the officers got her connected to her husband. Deepa says, 'I said, "I will never be able to walk again after the surgery. Over. I will get paralyzed below the chest after it. Over." And he replied, "I will carry you in my arms my whole life. Over. Just don't die, and wait for me. Over."' As Deepa says, 'There are moments such as these when you realize that the most important thing in the world is to make your family feel that yes, you are there, and are together in anything and everything.'

God had perhaps packaged her challenges well, too. She underwent this predicament while her husband was fighting a war, and casualties and fatalities were coming in every day. The entire hospital had turned into an ICU. 'I was getting operated among the kind of people who had lost their arms, eyes and limbs due to no fault of their own, due to no illness, but out of valour. I had no reasons to complain. My mind was trained to look at things like that,[5] she says. In this situation, the mother in her took over. 'I was emotionally spent and exhausted and this distracted me. I had no idea what my husband's fate would be. I was just adamant to live through this, for my kids. The mother in me subsumed all other emotions,' she says. She was operated upon, followed by severe complications, where her brain tube had leaked. Being taken into her third surgery, she was in a coma for twenty-five days. She fought back in yet another battle of her life. Her doctors were also awestruck by her courage and resilience. Dr V.K. Batish, the neurosurgeon who operated upon her at the Research and Referral Hospital of the armed forces in Delhi, said, 'In the twenty-five years that I have been a neurosurgeon, I have never come across a person like her. Deepa's recovery and her subsequent achievements are amazing. She is the kind who can teach doctors and the society at large.'[6] As she was discharged from the hospital, other far more probing and stiffer challenges awaited her.

Deepa's husband had returned from the war, but the people around started speculating if he would leave her. In the eyes of society, she was a dead body. On the contrary, Deepa had to prove that all the life was left in her. 'I fell prey to a stereotypical targeting all over again—"How will she feed her daughter? She will always need external help." There were similar questions galore,' she says. She overcame all these with the two most lethal weapons in her arsenal, her positive attitude and her sense of humour. She has further built on the same with her experiences. 'I am always on my wheels! Why do you call me wheelchair-bound? I am wheelchair-liberated. The Ashok Chakra has a wheel. I tell everybody like me, you have your inspiration right here, under you!'[7]

---

[5]Binjal Shah, 'She was given seven days to "celebrate" her last moments of walking, here's what she did: Deepa Malik, paraplegic athlete' YourStory, accessed 5 September 2019

[6]Rajni Shaleen Chopra, 'Deepa Malik, turning adversity into success', *Indian Express*, 6 July 2010

[7]Binjal Shah, 'She was given seven days to "celebrate" her last moments of walking,

She started looking after her two daughters again with renewed zeal. It was on one of those days, when she took her daughter Ambika to the swimming pool, that the unthinkable happened. Ambika was reluctant to go to the pool out of fear. Deepa, in her wheelchair, asked her daughter whether she would dive if she did so as well. Her daughter replied in the affirmative and Deepa jumped into the swimming pool. This spurred Deepa to go ahead and take coaching classes in swimming herself. Later on, this played a crucial role in her taking up competitive para sports. Deepa used to browse the Internet and Google late into the night and she got herself acquainted with what disabled people like her had been doing all across the globe. She too went for them. As she was gearing up for fresh challenges, her husband, Bikram Malik, was summoned again when the parliament of the country was attacked. During this period, as the wife of the squadron commander, she started taking care of thirty families, as their husbands had left overnight. In Ahmednagar, Maharashtra, where they stayed, she opened a garden restaurant, Dee's Place, at the corner of her farmhouse, rounding up her domestic staff and some painters who were doing up her room. It turned out to be a widely popular restaurant and a popular hangout for young officers. 'I started feeding around 250 people in the restaurant, plus taking a hundred home delivery orders every day. I also helped the boys whom we employed, to go back to school and take their tenth grade exams. Women had doubts about how well I would feed my own family. Well, now I was feeding theirs,'[8] she says.

After the restaurant business had taken off, one day she saw an army officer, Atul, coming on his new bike. For a moment, she was lost and engrossed, remembering the days when bikes used to be her biggest passion. When Atul told her that she too could ride the bike, she initially gave him a piece of her mind.

here's what she did: Deepa Malik, paraplegic athlete' YourStory, accessed 5 September 2019

[8]Deepa Malik said this on *Stree Shakti*, a talk show aired by DD National.

'I gave him a reality check. Nothing below my chest-level works. My injury is as high as the T1 (thoracic spinal nerve). I have no torso balance, no proper sensation, imperfect lung functioning and no temperature control. My nerve endings are haphazardly cut. I don't even have bladder or bowel control. It's a miracle in itself that I am running a restaurant,'[9] she said. Atul, however, was not willing to give up so easily. He Googled and showed her that customized bikes for people like her could be built and she could again follow up on her passion. He reiterated that it indeed was possible and the very task cut out for a woman of her spirit. This episode was to play an important role in Deepa getting her name etched in the Limca Book of World Records later on in her life. In all her future endeavours, based on her self-belief, she got the total support of her husband, who resigned from his job. He had total confidence in Deepa's confidence.

While Deepa was trying to find her feet in motorsport, she was advised to start exercising fulltime, with particular focus on swimming. Somebody saw her swimming on TV and alerted the sports authorities about an upcoming national tournament. Maharashtra invited her to the nationals. 'I was thirty-six; I thought, "Why not?" 'Opportunities knock on your door and the winner is the one who has the courage to walk through that door. I did, and won many medals. In 2006, I went to Kuala Lumpur and even won a silver medal.'[10] She won a medal in the 2010 Para Asian Games. Tasting success there, Deepa aspired to make a mark at the 2012 London Paralympics. However, she wasn't able to make it, in the absence of a quota, and that only resulted in strengthening her resolve. Rio had to happen. And, in Rio, she fulfilled her ultimate dream. She bagged silver in the women's shot-put event, clinching the medal with a personal best throw of 4.61 m. Fatema Nedham of Bahrain won the gold medal with a throw of 4.76 m. Deepa thus became the first Indian female

---

[9]Deepa Malik said this on *Stree Shakti*, a talk show aired by DD National.
[10]Ibid.

medallist in the history of the Paralympic Games. India, who made its Paralympic Games debut in 1968, has bagged a total of 11 medals, including 3 gold, 4 silver and an equal number of bronze. Deepa, till date, has participated in three Asian Para Games. Earlier, she won a bronze in javelin throw during the 2010 Games in China and a silver medal in javelin throw during the 2014 Games in South Africa. In the Jakarta Games in 2018, she, for the first time, participated in two events—javelin throw and discus. She won the bronze medal for the country in each of the two events. She is the first woman para athlete to win medals at three major tournaments: World Championships, Asian Para Games and Paralympics. In total, she has won 17 international medals and 58 national gold medals in various sports events, setting an example for all physically challenged people around the world. 'There is a legacy which I have set, and I need to maintain that,'[11] she says. Her sporting credentials made her the oldest recipient of the Arjuna Award, at the age of forty-two, in 2012.

Deepa is the first paraplegic woman in the world to drive a quad bike on the highest motorable roads of Leh and Ladakh. Talking about this incredible achievement, she says, 'I started my homework. Being an army wife, my first try was with the army adventure cell. But I soon learnt that only serving army officers' wives were allowed to participate. I kept struggling for three years until I landed at the flag-off of the Desert Storm in Delhi in February 2009. I literally sat there trying to pick up contacts and telling various teams about my wish of doing a rally. Some thought that I was crazy; others felt happy about my courage. But it was the Pune Millennium team who took me seriously and taught me all the skills of navigation. Through them, I learnt what were the qualities required to be on a rally, and that it was going to be a challenge.' Deepa got in touch with the Himalayan Motorsport Association and the Federation of Motor Sports Clubs of India (FMSCI) to accept her as a formal competitor. This was

---

[11]Deepa Malik said this in an interview with Abhishek Dubey for *Organiser Weekly*.

the first time a disabled person had approached them. 'They took their time, but I am happy that they appreciated my love and enthusiasm for motorsport and felt positive; I just held my breath till I saw a ray of hope, when they agreed to take me in. But I had to complete all the required paperwork.'[12] The most difficult task was to get the personal accident insurance on heavy risk basis. But with the proactive cooperation from the varied stakeholders like Maruti Suzuki and three-time Raid-de-Himalaya winner, Rakesh Diwan, her dream came true. Her husband joined her as an attendant. 'After a long struggle for permissions, sponsorships, a rally vehicle, a professional team partner and procurement of snow clothing, I found myself in Shimla. Initially, people thought I was there to cheer a friend, but the moment I got the name sticker on my car and competitor's license and an identity card on my back, everyone took me seriously.' Her dream had finally turned into reality and she was able to send across the thumping message to the world, 'Disability is a state of mind and not of the body.'[13]

The rally that was flagged off on the morning of 7 October was harsh: a nine-day, 1700-km drive in below freezing temperature. 'Even at an altitude of 18,000 ft, with oxygen shortage, I was able to sustain it. It was tiring, but the adrenalin rush was so high that I never felt tired.'[14] Deepa was awarded the True Grit Trophy for outstanding courage. 'More than the trophy, what made me happy was the declaration that henceforth disabled persons would also be eligible to compete in the rally. I was thrilled that my efforts opened doors for people with disabilities to the world of motorsport.' During the journey of nine days, she covered nine high altitude passes while going through extreme conditions. For this feat, she entered the Limca Book of Records.

In fact, Deepa Malik has featured in the Limca Book of Records

---

[12]'My 'Raid de Himalaya' experience: Deepa Malik', Disability News and Information Service, 15 January 2010

[13]Deepa Malik, jatLand.com

[14]'My 'Raid de Himalaya' experience: Deepa Malik', Disability News and Information Service, 15 January 2010

for a record four times. First, as illustrated above, in 2011, she became the first paraplegic women to drive to Khardung La pass, the highest motorable pass in the world. Second, she completed the longest drive in India (3,278 km, from Chennai to Delhi) in 2013. Third, she rode a special bike for 58 km in 2009. Fourth, in 2008, she crossed a 1 km stretch of the Yamuna river against the current.

'Biking and sports had become a good way to break the stereotypical images of people on wheelchairs. To be heard, you have to be an achiever. If you have to find your voice, you have to do something crazy,'[15] says Deepa. It is this mantra that has led to her exploring and conquering new things in life.

Today, Deepa Malik is the role model in her family. Speaking at an event at Rashtrapati Bhavan, she once famously said, 'There was a time when I was emotionally distressed and confused as to how and what I would be able to give my daughters. Initially, there were a lot of social stigma and taboos and stereotypes that surrounded my physical condition. I am happy that my motherhood and womanhood became my strength to recover and reclaim my life as an abled person with a lot of passion. My determination paid off, and I was able to bring home the first ever female Paralympic medal for my country in 2016.'[16]

Her elder daughter Devika says, 'People read books, watch movies and hear speeches to be inspired and achieve something in life. I need not go beyond my home. I look up to my mother. Everywhere we go, people are in awe of her. It's nothing short of an adventure, being her daughter.'

While awards and recognition have kept coming ever since, Deepa knocked off another milestone, becoming the first Indian woman para athlete, and of course, the oldest athlete

---

[15]Binjal Shah, 'She was given seven days to "celebrate" her last moments of walking, here's what she did: Deepa Malik, paraplegic athlete' YourStory, accessed 5 September 2019

[16]'I discovered my abilities beyond my disabilities: Para-athlete Deepa Malik', *Outlook*, 21 January 2018

at forty-nine, to win the prestigious Rajiv Gandhi Khel Ratna award, India's highest sporting honour, in 2019. Deepa isn't just an extraordinarily brave and gifted sportswoman, she is also a shining example for all who care about sports. She is the best story of grit and determination that we can possibly have, and is proof that never was it about facilities and infrastructure as it is often made out to be. It was always about the will and determination to succeed.

It was about the fire in the belly and the conviction to make a mark at the biggest platform of them all. It was about the burning desire to make the country proud. Her life comes across as a strong message to everyone. Deepa was not born disabled, but she became so later on in life. Her life is a strong message for all those people who think it's all over—nothing is ever over. The challenge is to reinvent oneself to gear up for new situations. She reinvented herself by getting much more focused in life. 'The things I had taken for granted when I was not disabled now seemed like big hurdles. A step just six inches high could actually restrict my accessibility, the same step that I possibly never ever noticed before! My life used to be all about fashionable clothes and gossiping. But disability brought my life into focus. I started a restaurant, supporting the education of a few children, and set out on a mission to motivate people like myself with the help of my activities. In short, I learnt to give back to society and realized the true sense of living.'[17]

Deepa, like others, could have easily fallen prey to stereotypes. Rather, she fought against the stereotypes and has emerged triumphant. 'The first natural reaction of any paraplegic is to stay indoors. Instead, they should realize that they are alive and like any other people on the planet, they have the right to live their lives to the fullest. There may be barriers and issues related to their normal routine and movement, but then there are means of managing them and moving ahead. The world is there for you,

---

[17]"Disability brought my life into focus," Deepa Malik, DNIS, 15 December 2009

provided you are there for the world,' she says. 'People said I was going to die in a room—here I was, with two full passports, travelling the world. Riding alongside John Abraham one day, or cradling the Arjuna Award in my hand on another,'[18] she adds. Deepa is the super-abled who has got a firm message for all the so-called abled persons like us. We got the message when she came for the Doordarshan Sports conclave. She called upon four handsome men to pick her up from the wheelchair and put her on stage. And then she said, 'Many of you might feel that four people normally shoulder a dead body like this. But for me it is like four handsome men picking up the palanquin of a queen. It all depends on the way you look at life.'

---

[18]Deepa said this in an interview with the authors during the Doordarshan Sports Conclave in Chandigarh.

THIRTEEN

Santhi Soundarajan and Dutee Chand: 'I Am A Woman'

At the 2016 Rio Olympics, there was not much to crow about in terms of the medals tally of the Indian contingent. But the road to Rio will remain unforgettable for three brave women athletes. These three women athletes were born to run to win. But they had to fight to run.

Just a day before the Rio Olympics began, a campaign in the media caught the nation's attention. Thappad, the Facebook community, released a video of the forgotten story of Santhi Soundarajan. 'Santhi's story is important now because we are all cheering for the true spirit of sports at the Olympics, all the while discriminating against our sportspersons. The time is right to visit her case,'[1] the video's producer Sandesh B. Suvama said.

The video was made in direct collaboration with Tamil and Telugu actor and director Dheepa Ramanujam and activist Gopichand Shankar Madurai. The video was part of an online campaign asking for Soundarajan's name to be included in the official records again. Importantly, the campaign demanded that the government should give her a permanent job to rebuild her life. 'I dream of a future where no one goes through what I went through,' she says at the end of the video.

Just before the 2016 Rio Olympics, the concluding chapter of Pinki Pramanik's athletics career was being played out. At the same Olympics trial race, where Dutee Chand first broke the

---

[1]'Why we should join the campaign seeking justice for runner Santhi Soundarajan,' *Huffington Post*, 9 August 2016

100 m national record and earned herself the reputation of being the country's fastest woman, Pinki was the one who brought up the rear. She was in her thirties then. Her appearance, in a way, was an assertion that the track from where she had been barred for the best years of her professional life was where she belonged.

Pinki was impressed by the refreshing change she had noticed. 'The biggest difference I found during my attempted comeback was the respect and love shown towards me by the other athletes. Dutee Chand, Srabani Nanda, Himashree Roy and many others approached me and told me how I had been an inspiration for them. Whereas, in my prime, my competitors saw me as just someone who needed to be beaten,' says Pinki.[2]

In the years leading up to the 2016 Rio Olympics, there came several moments in Dutee Chand's life when it looked like everything was over. In those testing moments, her coach used to console Dutee by saying that even Lord Rama, whose coronation was almost certain, had to live in exile. He tried to make sure that she remained hopeful that good days would eventually arrive.

The day indeed arrived at the Rio Olympics, when she ran for the country in the 100 m race. More important than running itself, she had to prove her identity and eligibility for running, which was significant. In 2014, people started asking, '*Dutee ladki nahi hai, ladka hai. Tu* real *main kya hai*?' (Dutee is not a girl, but a boy; what are you actually?) By Rio 2016, all of them had got the answer.

The three Indian bravehearts fighting for themselves, with Rio 2016 as the signature tune, had a South African athlete to look up to. Caster Semenya won a gold medal in the 800 m race in the Olympics. In Caster Semenya's case it was about sports, sex, gender, ethics, politics, culture and science—all rolled into one. The experts are divided in their opinion about her, the arguments

---

[2]Dipankar Lahiri, 'Hounded out of track, golden girl Pinki Pramanik now a face in the crowd', *The Bridge*, 19 July 2018

are going back and forth, and everyone has been trying to find the black and white in all the shades of grey. As things stand today, Semenya should now take a cue from India's Dutee Chand who fought in order to run.

The Indian story on the fight to run starts from Santhi Soundarajan. The middle distance runner, her quick rise and fall, had rocked the athletics world twelve years ago. She was born in Kathakuruchi village in Pudukkottai district of Tamil Nadu to Dalit parents who were engaged in daily labour at a brick kiln. Her mother and father had to go to another town to work in the brickyard. She had to overcome malnutrition as a child. She grew up in a 20/5 ft hut across the road from the home she lives in now. The home had no bathroom or outhouse, running water or electricity.

Amidst all this, Soundarajan's taking up running seems to have been destined. It so happened that while the parents were gone, Soundarajan, the eldest, was in charge of taking care of her four siblings. There were times when her grandfather, an accomplished runner, helped while her parents were away.

When she was thirteen, he taught her to run on an open stretch of dirt outside the hut. He also bought her a pair of shoes. 'I come from a rural background where very few games like kho kho and kabaddi are played. These are the games which don't require expensive equipment or facilities. Running was my natural strength. My grandfather was an athlete who provided me with the drive to develop my skills. Moreover, I saw athletics as a sport that gives an opportunity to the economically underprivileged to make their mark, more than in any other sport,' she says.

When we try to unravel her entire journey, it's difficult to point out the reason that kept her going, irrespective of the setbacks she faced in her life. If her grandfather was her mentor, her mother was her pillar of strength. 'My mother, Manimegalai, is my pillar of support. I am able to overcome the challenges faced every day only because of her. As every other child would, I want to keep my mother happy too. Every time I think of giving up, I think of her and the many struggles she has faced. It fuels me to keep "running" in life,' she says.

The girl started winning prizes at school sports events. At her first competition, in the eighth grade, Soundarajan won a tin trophy. 'Nothing great, tumblers, glasses and things like that,' she says, laughing. But more than anything else, they worked as an incentive for her to work hard. The sports coach at a nearby high school took note of her performance and recruited her. The school paid her tuition fees and provided her with a uniform and lunches.

In this manner, Soundarajan started taking three daily meals for the first-ever time in her life. After high school, she got a scholarship from an arts college in Pudukkottai, the nearest town. In the following year, she got transferred to a college in Chennai, which was seven hours away from her home. The medals followed her as she graduated from one level to another.

Soundarajan won 11 international medals for India. This includes the 800 m silver at the Asian Athletics Championships in South Korea in 2005 and the 1500 m gold at the South Asian Games in Colombo in August 2006. She was declared the best athlete at the National Open Championships in New Delhi in September 2006. However, the 2006 Asian Games in Doha was the big chance that she had been waiting for.

The twenty-five-year-old Soundarajan ran the 800 m as if her life depended on it. She fell flat on the track and looked up at the sky. After this, she looked at the cameras in utter disbelief. She won a silver medal in the women's 800 m race at the 2006 Asian Games, clocking 2 min 3.16 sec.

She lost the medal in two days. From the news on television she got to know that she had failed the 'gender test'. Till then, she had no inkling as to what the test was all about.

Dr Arun Kumar Mendiratta, the chairman of the Athletics Federation of India (AFI) Medical Commission, brought her in for the gender tests but did not tell her the reason. This was a day after her victory. The report sent to the Indian Olympic Association said, 'Soundarajan does not possess the sexual characteristics of a woman.'[3] Lalit Bhanot, the then secretary of AFI, conveyed to her on the phone that she had to stop competing.

Soundarajan says, 'The officials made me sign some papers in English, a language I have trouble reading and speaking in. I was stripped of my Asian Games silver medal and didn't get the prize money.'[4]

As the loss of the medal started sinking in, her life changed. She had to return to her village. She had to face humiliation at every stage. Probing looks and nasty comments about her gender identity made her vulnerable. She went into depression and attempted to kill herself by ingesting a type of poison used by vegetarians. A friend found her vomiting uncontrollably and took her to the hospital.

'I was shattered by the failed test. The AFI did not support me, did not fight my cause. I was hoping they would. I was depressed. I felt like I had lost everything. It still hurts. I loved the sport so much. My dream broken, I attempted suicide,' she says in chaste Tamil.

Soundarajan invested some of the ₹15 lakh the state government had given her as a prize to start a running academy. She had to shut it down soon after the money ran out. Her job as an athletics coach with the Sports Development Authority (SDA) of Tamil Nadu did not last long either, as the temporary nature of her job and meagre salary of five thousand per month did not provide her any financial security. In a way, life turned back to square one. She went back to her village and set up a brick kiln of her own and worked eighteen hours a day.

After years of struggle, and with the help of gender rights activists, she was accepted into the SAI's diploma in sports coaching programme in 2013. She completed the course in 2014. She still did not get a permanent job. She was almost forgotten by

---

[3]Monica Jha, 'Are you ready to give me my medal back?', Fountain Ink
[4]Ibid.

the sporting fraternity. There were rare ones like Olympic shooter Anjali Bhagwat, who termed the incident as 'shameful', and said 'the athlete should be given at least a central or state government job for her financial stability in lieu of what she has done for the country.'[5]

On 29 July 2015, the Madras High Court directed the state government to consider her plea for relaxation in educational qualification and help her become a coach at the SDA of Tamil Nadu. As per the notification issued by the Youth Welfare and Sports Development Department in April 2015, an applicant contesting for the post of coach should have an educational qualification of a bachelor's degree, and Soundarajan did not have one.

Social media also joined her cause on the eve of the 2016 Rio Olympics. Finally, on 16 October 2016, Soundarajan was informed that the state government had decided to appoint her as a permanent athletics coach under SDAT. She received her appointment order on 20 December 2016. More than the economic support, this has given her a new lease of life in terms of fulfilling her incomplete dreams. As one enters her bare house, with almost no furniture and a lot of natural light, one can feel the vibrations of her dreams all around.

Santhi's words are spirited and jovial. Her wide, bright smile conceals the loss and pain of a decade. She has cropped her once long hair, and switched from wearing a saree, bindi and jasmine flowers to a shirt and trousers. This change in dressing came when people started hounding her by calling her a man. The makeover was also intended as a disguise.

When some of her students started doing well at state-level competitions, people in the small town of Mayiladuthurai started recognizing her—this time as a hardworking and inspiring coach.

As she starts opening up, so does her wounds.

---

[5]PTI, 'Santhi Soundarajan incident shameful: Anjali Bhagwat', *The Times of India*, 25 July 2012

'I looked up to P.T. Usha when I began my career. However, as time went by, I realized that there were so many athletes whose achievements went way beyond Indian sportsmen. That ignited me to become one who represented India at an international level and make a statement to the world that Indians are no less capable of making a name in sports.'[6]

What next?

'My legacy will remain not with my medals but with the determination and hope to overcome my past torment and my present struggles. I want to live my dream through my students,'[7] she says with a wry smile on her face.

As our television crew starts packing up and we leave her village, one of her statements starts resonating in our ears. 'Poverty is never an obstacle to an aspiring champion, as success comes to those who truly work hard, not to those who have money. If not an athlete, I would have been just an ordinary person working in a brickyard in a village that many would not have heard of,'[8] she said.

One gets a stronger feel of this as one touches tiny Gopalpur, a village located on the banks of the Brahmani river in Odisha's Jajpur district—about 80 km from Bhubaneswar. The protagonist this time is Dutee Chand.

Dutee was born to Chakradhar and Akhuji, a weaver couple who could barely sustain their family of six daughters and a son on a daily income of a hundred rupees. This too was not assured. Their day started with worries about rice for the next meal. The children of the family were used to waiting for their father to bring groceries at night and staying up late in the process. In fact, as the priority was the customers who used to pay, the turn of Dutee's father in the grocery shop used to come at the end. Almost every

[6]Akshaya Raju, 'The living phoenix speaks—an exclusive interview with Santhi Soundararajan', *Guindy Times*, 7 April 2017

[7]Susan Ninan, 'Poll ticket, crowd-funded academy on Santhi's agenda', *The Times of India*, 20 March 2016

[8]Ibid.

day, he had to wait in the shop between 7:00 p.m. and 11:00 p.m. Once the father returned, the children waited in the dim light of the bulb as the mother prepared the meal. By the time the family managed to have their dinner, more often than not, it used to be past midnight.

Another thing that Dutee and her sister Saraswati remember about those days is the fact that the family was never invited to weddings or birthdays. The neighbours sent leftovers the next morning. The children, especially the elder one, Saraswati, used to feel angry and bitter about this as they grew up, but such was the impact of hunger and poverty in the house that they used to eat the leftovers grudgingly. Dutee's elder sister, Saraswati, soon realized that the answer to the family's problems lay in athletics. 'We figured on the BPL (Below Poverty List). Bagging a government job through the sports quota seemed like the only logical option,' Saraswati said in an interview with the local daily.

Saraswati was a kabaddi player, but switched to running because the state police had running competitions as qualifying events. Dutee, who was three years old then, accompanied her to the practice sessions.

One fine morning, Dutee got bored sitting by the Brahmani river in their village, while her sister practised. 'I started running, loved it and started doing this every day,' says Dutee.

However, there was resistance to this in the village. The parents had to hear complaints about the girls running along the river wearing tiny shorts and vests. Despite this, Chakradhar never stopped Saraswati and her sisters from practising, even though the villagers were not happy about it.

As a child, Dutee tried to replicate the character from a Tamil film, where the protagonist chucks her shoes in the middle of the run and wins the race barefoot. However, whereas in reel life, the protagonist's father got her dry fruits and cans of energy drink, in real life Dutee was not lucky enough.

'This did not happen with me,' she laughs.

By 2004, Saraswati was a police constable and encouraged her sister to run, as she was a natural. 'While didi took care of some of the expenses, we were still struggling,' Dutee says.

The family narrates an event in Dutee's life, which sounds filmy. The aspiring runner was accused of running away from home. When she was around eight years old, she left home to see her sister in Cuttack, 60 km from the village, all by herself. The driver thought that she was running away from home and so refused to let her board. One of the passengers, who happened to be from her village, finally had to convince the driver. And this was the first of many times when she travelled unaccompanied.

Dutee was soon selected for the state sports programme in Bhubaneswar. She had to stay away from her home and family. But she was getting to run in shoes. She had a coach. She also got eggs, chicken and milk—all these things were a rarity for her at home. The seniors and the coach talked about sports offering opportunities for foreign travel. More importantly, there was the chance of her getting a job like her sister—which was a necessity for her family.

She decided to stay in the hostel and live her dream. Her friends there remember her as extremely focused on running and regular with her hectic training schedule before and after school. She kept to herself but was ever willing to help even all those who were not nice to her. One of her friends from the hostel days stood by her even when she was banned from running, later in her life.

By 2007, the eleven-year-old Chand was participating in the 400 m and 800 m races at the junior level, winning medals and setting national records. In 2009, a new sprint coach joined. This was going to be another major turning point in her career. The coach immediately noticed that though she lacked endurance, she had tremendous speed. After his counselling she decided to focus on the 100 m and 200 m races. Nagapuri Ramesh, a coach, who was working with SAI, had spotted the young Dutee Chand in Kochi in 2008. In 2011, at the national camp in Patiala, Ramesh ran into Saraswati and enquired about Dutee. Saraswati said that she had returned from the hostel after matriculation and was training by herself in the village.

Ramesh, in an interview with the local daily, says, 'When I asked as to whether Dutee could come to Patiala, Saraswati was worried about the cost but I offered to pay. Chand arrived in Patiala on the next train. Arrangements were made for her stay a little way from the city. It cost ₹3,000 a month, an investment that was worth it.'[9] In March 2012, she became a resident athlete at the Netaji Subhas National Institute of Sports, Patiala. 'I thought she could do well enough to get a job under the sports quota and help her family. It's only when I started coaching her that I realized her immense talent. She has got this strong, never-give-up attitude. She is all fired up when she is on the track. She doesn't care if the girl running next to her is a world champion,' says Ramesh.

In 2012, Dutee Chand became a national champion in the under-18 category, when she clocked 11.8 sec in the 100 m event. She won the bronze in the women's 200 m event at the 2013 Asian Athletics Championships at Pune, clocking 23.811 seconds. That year also saw her become the first Indian to reach the final of a global athletics 100 m final, when she reached the final of the 2013 World Youth Championships.

She was just eighteen then and India's best bet for an Olympic medal in 100 m. In the same year she became the national champion in 100 m and 200 m events, clocking 11.73 sec in the final in 100 m and a career-best 23.73 seconds in 200 m at the National Senior Athletics Championships at Ranchi. But then came the major turning point in her career.

In July 2014, Dutee was at the SAI training camp in Bengaluru. She was preparing for the IAAF World Junior Championships at Eugene, USA. Her focus was on improving her timing and maintaining proper form leading up to the tournament. She was also informed about her selection for the Commonwealth Games in Glasgow. It was during one of those days that Dutee was called for a medical examination by the SAI. This was unlike the routine

---

[9]Monica Jha, 'Dutee Chand: Born to run', Fountain Ink, 17 August 2016

dope test she had gone through many a time in her career. Later, in her testimony to the Court of Arbitration for Sports (CAS), she described the test as a 'humiliating examination by a male doctor, who asked intrusive questions about body hair, menstrual cycle, surgical history and hobbies.' A team of doctors conducted physical examinations, including in the genital area. The athlete felt vulnerable, but she had no choice. She smelled something odious, but she was forced into it. The bombshell was dropped when nine days were left for the US event and ten days for the Commonwealth Games.

The SAI'S scientific officer of sports medicine said that she would no longer be able to compete because her 'male hormones' were too high. Male hormones? Was I tested for male hormones and why was I tested for the male hormones? These were the immediate questions that haunted her. The rules require that athletes be informed about the nature of medical tests they undergo as well as the reason for the same.

But the examination was carried out without her written consent or even basic information about the test. Her disqualification was announced on 15 July, and two days after it, the director general of SAI, Jiji Thomson, issued a statement saying a gender test was conducted on a woman athlete in Bengaluru and her name would be deleted from the Commonwealth Games list. Calling it a gender test itself was a huge blunder.

The Director General of SAI, and SAI as an institution soon realized that they had committed a huge blunder by calling the medical exams 'gender tests.' Over the next two days, SAI issued two press releases, clarifying that 'the test does not determine the athlete's gender', and they were conducted to 'find out if the athlete has excess androgen in her body.'[10]

The SAI statement also said she would be eligible to compete in the female category 'if she took proper medical help and lowered her androgen level to the specified range.' It was too late

---

[10]Monica Jha, 'Dutee Chand: Born to run', Fountain Ink, 17 August 2016

and too little. The media had extensively covered by then that Dutee had failed a gender test. Her identity was leaked and her privacy was compromised.

But what is 'proper medical help' in this specific case? It implies the measures to bring down natural testosterone levels by hormone suppression therapies or genital surgery. This discourse may be a part of the valid academic debate in sports universities and governing bodies of world federations. But they were nowhere in the realms of the female athlete who was facing the worst existential crisis in her journey as a sportsperson just when her career was in the 'take off' stage.

Why was the gender test done? How could I fail them? Am I wrongly implicated in the doping test? Am I to blame for the food supplements that I had taken, the reason for failing the dope test? These were the immediate questions plaguing her mind.

'I heard people say I was a boy and not a girl. And that I could not compete any more. The only two things I identified with—being a girl and being an international athlete—were being questioned,' she says about those days. And she could find no answer in the system that thrives on sporting ignorance and bureaucratic rigmaroles and the tendency wherein sporting celebrities are treated as demigods and discarded the moment they face rough weather.

Whereas the overwhelming voices around her were suggesting that she quit, the rebel in her, who had got emboldened by the conditions she faced in life, challenged her. She had been living away from home since she was ten years old. She had no opportunity in life to develop closeness with her siblings and parents. Sports, in a sense, was not just the important thing, but the only thing in her life while she was growing up. 'I only know to run. I have spent all my life doing this. How could I quit sports?'

Moreover, if she quit, she would have to fight the battle of her life in the village she was born, but with which she could not relate anymore. Further elaborating on this disconnect she says, 'I had gone back home after a long while. I saw my friend, ran and hugged her. She told me the gesture was foreign and asked me not to do it. *Log kya kahenge?* (What will people say?) On the contrary I had often seen friends hug each other in cities.'

In the village where public hugging is frowned upon, the news of Dutee Chand failing a gender test reached before her. An official suggested Dutee leave Bengaluru with the story that her mother had fallen ill. Dutee could not digest this idea. Saraswati, her sister, told her not to leave unless they gave an official explanation or the authorities themselves sent her home. Dutee found this idea to be the better one. Though the news had spread by then, the government of Odisha was formally notified of Chand's ineligibility.

The government sent two female coaches from the state to escort her home. They took an afternoon flight to Bhubaneswar. As they travelled to Chaka Gopalpur in a government car, the director of the sports and youth services department joined them. The drive along the NH-16, the Chennai-Kolkata highway, took ninety minutes. Perhaps these were the most difficult ninety minutes in her life.

As the car entered the service road and turned into the village, going past the huts and the handful of brick houses in the weavers' colony, it was dark. Dutee emerged last from the car and climbed the ramp quickly, as she wanted to avoid the neighbours. Her parents too were relieved that it was dark, for her neighbours would not be able to see her.

But cars were unusual in that part of the world and whispers grew louder. Her mother, who was standing at the entrance said, 'Dutee'. Tears rolled down the cheeks of the daughter and mother, something which they desperately wanted to control to remain strong to fight the remaining battles in their lives. The days following that night were horrible for the entire family.

She would sit for hours without speaking. She stopped eating. After the long silence, sometimes anger would overwhelm her and she would throw things around. Her parents became concerned that she may end her life. She would sit, hugging her spikes and tracksuits and cry endlessly. On television, she would watch athletes competing, in tears. Her mother also was inconsolable after some neighbours told her that Dutee was a boy and that was the reason she was not allowed to compete.

As her sister Saraswati says, 'My mother told me once, I gave birth to a girl. She has lived and competed as a girl. Why are they now saying she is not a girl?'[11] They were worried that it would be hard for Dutee and her four sisters to get married. The financial troubles started staring at the family again. Dutee had lost her income from sports and there was the fear that she would lose her job with the railways too. But gradually, she and her family reconciled to the fact that there was no option other than to fight. As Dutee made up her mind, others started joining in the cause. Gradually, a cohesive team was formed.

Around 600 km away from her home, in faraway Kolkata, Dr Payoshini Mitra, a researcher and activist in the area of gender and sports, read the news. Mitra had consulted the union ministry of sports and youth affairs on the standard operating procedure in female hyperandrogenism cases earlier.

She was not satisfied by the final version of the document she had received. She then fought for the SOP to be withdrawn. She had worked with other athletes including Pinki Pramanik and seen the impact the suspicion of gender can have on an athlete. Mitra reached out to Dutee. To begin with, Dutee was hostile. Mitra explained to her sister, Saraswati, that she could help Dutee if she accompanied her to meet SAI's chief, Jiji Thomson. The fact that the expense of the trip to Delhi, where she met the sports minister and DG, SAI, was met by the SAI, helped to convince her to take the road ahead.

Meanwhile, Dutee, by then, was tiptoeing around the idea of hormone suppression therapy—assuming that she would need to take tablets and injections. She desperately wanted to go back to sports. However, after consulting a doctor whom the Odisha

---

[11]Saraswati said this in an interview with Doordarshan.

government persuaded to come from London to meet Dutee at Cuttack Medical College, the sprinter changed her decision. She decided against any change in her body and said no to corrections.

She requested Payoshini Mitra to find an alternate option for her. Mitra said that she could appeal against her suspension. She got the idea from Professor Bruce Kidd, the world's leading activist for equality in sports and a former Canadian Olympian. Bruce Kidd came out in Dutee's support. 'I am who I am. I want to remain who I am and compete again,' she said. She had decided to appeal in the Court of Arbitration for Sport (CAS). More than the letters, the spirit of the statement counted. It was Dr Katria Karkazis from the Center for Biomedical Ethics at Stanford University who brought Mitra and Kidd together on Chand's issue. Even those who had harmed her case in the beginning started to make amends.

Jiji Thomson, the SAI head, by then seemed more than eager to make up for the mishandling of Chand's case. Thomson took an unexpected approach in the Indian sports bureaucracy, when he nominated Mitra, instead of an official, to act as mediator and consultant for Dutee. This was a critical break—as the SAI officials had never before ceded their space like this. Thomson agreed when Dutee, advised by Mitra, decided to appeal to the CAS, aware of the massive expenditure the government would have to incur.

This was unprecedented. Santhi Soundarajan and Pinki Pramanik were left to either quit sports or fight for themselves with no help from sports officials. No Indian athlete had received such support.

Caster Semenya had been a catalytic agent in this. The entire world watched in awe at the way Athletics South Africa and the country rallied behind the middle distance runner, to the point of allegedly bullying the IAAF to let Semenya retain her world championship and prize money.

Mokgadi Caster Semenya was born on 7 January 1991 to Dorus and Jacob Semenya. She was born in Ga-Masehlong, a village near

Polokwane. As a child, Semenya went to live with her grandfather, Maputhi Sekgala in a nearby village. She played soccer at school. She trained every day after school, often running from village to village.

She attended Nthema Secondary School. Later on, she went to study sports science at the University of North West. Her career took off in the year 2009, when in the African Junior Championships Semenya won both the 800 m and 1500 m races with the time of 1:56:72 and 4:08:01 respectively, simultaneously breaking the 800 m senior South African records held by Zelda Pretorius at 1:58:85 and Zola Budd at 2:00:90. In August of the same year, when Semenya was only eighteen years old, she won gold in the 800 m World Championships with a time of 1:55:45 in the final, setting the fastest time of the year. She was voted Track and Field News' top women's 800 m runner of 2009. However, as so often happens in life, controversy started dominating her achievements in life. There were controversies about her sexual identity and she was forced to being the centre of a public debate about hyperandrogeny or high levels of testosterone in female athletes in women's sports. With her also came to the fore the entire gender debate in sports.

Historically, after World War II, the International Olympic Committee (IOC) had put in place requirements that each nation certify that its female Olympic athletes were actually female. A short-lived and controversial policy was implemented, whereby a visual inspection of genitalia of female Olympians by a panel of physicians took place. Infamously, it was called the 'nude parade'. In 1966 the IAAF instituted a chromosome-based test, called the Barr-body test, in which a cheek swab was used to detect the presence of a Y chromosome and any female athlete who failed this test was required to leave the sporting world.

The IAAF, and subsequently, IOC, then abandoned chromosome-based gender testing and replaced it with a less invasive method. This method was brought to international scrutiny after Semenya rocked the sports world by winning the 2009 IAAF

World Championship 800 m race by 2.5 sec. The intense focus on Semenya also brought issues of racism to the fore. Previous women's world championships competitors of Caucasian descent and with similar masculine characteristics had not brought on such widespread scrutiny, and led directly to policy change.

Ironically, though India's Dutee Chand's decision to go for an appeal was inspired by Caster Semenya acting as the catalytic agent, it was the first of its kind. Even Semenya by then had not challenged IAAF, but negotiated the terms of her return to the competition. Before approaching the CAS, formalities in terms of official communication on Chand's medical examination and her ineligibility to compete had to be completed.

On 14 August 2014, Jiji Thomson invited Chand, Mitra and AFI's C.K. Valson to his office in Delhi, where he gave Chand's test reports to Valson. At this meeting it was decided that AFI would officially notify Chand about her disqualification. Thomson, on 22 August 2014, wrote to the AFI president saying that Chand's hyperandrogenism test was positive and she had been informed of SAI's recommendations of 'exclusion from participation in women's events till her androgen level was brought down to permissible levels'. It also asked the AFI to formally notify her 'immediately so that she could make an appeal against the decision.'[12]

The letter asked SAI to address three issues. Firstly, the specific detail of her alleged violation of the policy along with a copy of the policy. Secondly, a deep regret about the fact that Dutee Chand was not clearly told about the test beforehand and information was not kept confidential. Thirdly, an outline of appeal processes available, with relevant documents and a letter stating that with mutual consent AFI and SAI would support her appeal to the CAS.

In response, AFI drafted a 'Decision Letter' dated 29 August 2014, addressed to Chand. The letter said that she was 'provisionally

---

[12]CAS 2014/A/3759 Dutee Chand Vs. Athletics Federation of India (AFI) & The International Association of Athletics Federations (IAAF), Interim Arbitral Award delivered by the Court of Arbitration for Sport, 24 July 2015

stopped from participation in any competition in athletics with immediate effect' based on her medical reports from SAI. Valson handed the 'Decision Letter' to Chand in person at the Railway Athletics Meet in Chennai. She was not allowed to compete at the Chennai Meet. Her suspension now was official.

On 18 September 2014, Dutee sent a letter to Valson requesting AFI to reconsider its decision. She wrote that her high androgen levels were natural and she did not dope or cheat. She asked AFI not to share her records and reports without her consent. Most importantly, the letter specifically emphasized that she felt perfectly healthy and that medical intervention to reduce the androgen level would be invasive, irreversible and harm her health.

The letter urged AFI to support her appeal to the CAS and let her make use of the IAAF policy that said they could make her provisionally eligible while she contested her case. On the same day, Thomson wrote to AFI again asking it to reconsider its decision to disqualify Chand or support her appeal to CAS, informing that SAI intended to support her. Under the prevailing guidelines, SAI was authorized to conduct tests and analyze the result of hyperandrogenism.

Thomson, at this time, called the IAAF policy 'unscientific, unfair and unethical' and recognized any medical intervention as 'invasive, irreversible and harmful.'[13] He appreciated Chand's courage to appeal the decision. Dutee needed to file an appeal within thirty days of suspension and she appealed just four days short of the deadline, on 26 September 2014. Her legal representatives asked for arbitration proceedings to be public except for her personal medical records, which she wished should remain private, as the case raised important issues of public interest and general application.

The days during which her appeal went on, tested her to the hilt. Dutee worked as the junior ticket collector in Bhusaval,

---

[13]Monica Jha, 'Dutee Chand: Born to run', Fountain Ink, 17 August 2016

Maharashtra. She had chosen to challenge her suspension but still was not allowed to compete. There was advice from certain quarters that she was wasting her time and should go for medical intervention. An athlete's life has got a shelf life, and these were, after all, the prime years of her life. When it seemed that she was on the verge of giving up, Mitra made an attempt to convince the CAS to allow her to compete provisionally, while the proceedings were going on.

The request stated that she was under significant pressure to undergo medical intervention from her major sponsor. After IAAF's consent, she was first allowed to participate in a national level competition and then in the Asian Athletics Championships in June 2015. But like all other athletes in similar situations, getting back to the track was not easy. Her speed had decreased drastically and her mind used to waver. The challenge was to get back on the track with renewed focus and purpose.

Ramesh, her coach, asked Dutee to move to Hyderabad to train with him. She didn't want to stay at the SAI facility. Ramesh asked his good friend Pullela Gopichand and explained the case to him. Later on, in an interview with Fountain Ink, Ramesh said, 'If I would write to some organization or other authorities, by that time she would disappear. So, I only had one option—of asking Gopichand. He understood the pain of the player and readily accepted her. So she was given the best stay, best food and everything fell in line.'

Remembering those days, Dutee, in an interview with Doordarshan, says, 'When I went there, the players thought that I was a coach. Sindhu met me very respectfully till I told her I was a sprinter and my name was Dutee Chand. Now she is a great friend and Gopi Bhaiyya is my pillar of strength.'

The countdown for the day of reckoning in her career had started. For Chand to compete again, she needed to prove that Hyperandrogenism Regulations (HA) did not hold for her. The Canadian team that had fought pro bono had adopted a broader strategy—HA regulations were invalid not just in her case, but for all athletes. The next eleven months saw a case involving complex legal, factual and ethical issues unfolding, drawing upon a diverse range of expert scientific evidence, accounts of the evolution of HA regulations and the experiences of female athletes subjected to earlier policies of sex verification and philosophical arguments about the meaning of fairness in sports. After submission of the written statements by experts and witnesses, a hearing was held at the CAS Court office in Lausanne, Switzerland from 23-26 March 2015. This was followed by several rounds of discussions and arguments between both the sides. The matter was unique and many existing rules and regulations on the subject were put to test. Finally, the most important day in the entire matter arrived.

There were arguments from both sides and the date of judgement was set for 24 July 2015.

On this day, after the normal training, Dutee went back to her room at the Gopichand Academy. Mitra remembers Dutee telling her, 'Don't worry, madam. Our efforts will pay off. Everything will be fine. It surely will be.'

There was one strong basis for this self-belief. During the hearing in Lausanne in March, Justice Annabelle Claire Bennett AO (Officer of the Order of Australia), Federal Court of Australia, Sydney, asked her what she wanted.

Dutee said, 'Madam, I don't know if you are going to change the rules. All I know is that I want to compete again. If you give me a chance to run again, I will be extremely happy. When a child fails in an exam, he is given another chance. If you deny him the chance, his life will be ruined. Sport is all I have known and done since I was little. If you stop me here, I would not know what else to do. Please let me run again.'[14]

The judge asked her to focus on her training. Finally, at 7 p.m. on 27 July, Dutee Chand was called by her lawyer, Jim Bunting, on Skype. Bunting's broad smile was reassuring. He spoke in English and Mitra translated. Dutee Chand had won the right to compete,

---

[14]Monica Jha, 'Dutee Chand: Born to run', Fountain Ink, 17 August 2016

and HA regulations were suspended for two years.

Dutee says, 'My first feeling was like I was coming back to the track. As it started sinking in, I realized what the judgement had done, beyond me. I was happy that I got to be the reason for bringing an end, even if temporarily, to a rule that had caused pain and humiliation to so many athletes. Nobody would stop me now.'

The panel also gave IAAF until July 2017 to submit evidence to support HA regulations. If evidence was not provided, the HA regulations would be automatically revoked. In case IAAF submitted such evidence, team Chand would have the right of counter-argument.

Dutee Chand resumed her international career in a stunning fashion. She set a national record in the 60 m heats at the Asian Indoor Athletics Championships in Doha and became the first Indian woman to make it to the World Indoor Meet in Portland. She was included in the Target Olympic Podium Scheme (TOPS), after she broke the 100 m national record. She declined the offer as only three months were left for the Olympics and she did not want to waste time travelling and settling down in a new environment with a new coach and a new training regime. On 25 June 2016, when there were only sixteen days left for the Olympics qualification, Dutee was in Almaty, Kazakhastan for the 26th Kosanov Memorial Meet.

In the Almaty heats, Dutee shot off the block like a bullet, with Zyabkina close behind. She maintained the lead till the finish line. Dutee was through in 11.30 sec, smashing her own national record by 0.03 sec and qualifying for Rio. After qualifying time was introduced for the Olympics in 2000, she became the first Indian woman to make it. The last had been P.T. Usha, thirty-six years ago, in the Moscow Games of 1980. Dutee also became only the fifth Indian woman to compete in the Olympics sprint, the other being Mary D' Souza (1952), Nilima Ghosh (1952) and Usha (1980).

Dutee could not make it to the semi-finals, but she ran the 100 m race for the country in the 2018 Rio Olympics. This was vindication that the girl from India had won her right to run. As she was born to run, the medals also have started following her. After the Rio Olympics, Dutee clinched two bronze medals at the 2017 Asian Athletics Championships—one in the women's 100 m and another in the 4x100 m relay.

In the span of four days, Dutee found space on the podium twice in the Asian Games in 2018, winning silver medals in the 100 m and 200 m events, joining an exclusive list of Indian athletes who have won two individual medals at the Asian Games.

Her eyes are now set on Tokyo 2020 and beyond. While she cautiously gallops her way to her goal, Caster Semenya finds hurdles in her way. This time, Dutee's fight could be the model for Semenya to emulate. When asked about this, she smiles and says, 'I met Caster Semenya during the Rio Olympics. I took her number and e-mail id. When I read about the new rule which bars her from participating in her preferred event, I wrote to her about my legal team. I told her she can take their help. She replied that her advisors will get in touch.'

For a change, Semenya, an international star, may have to take a detour to Delhi, if she wants to land from Rio 2016 to Tokyo 2020 and make a lasting impact.

FOURTEEN

Dipa Karmakar and Deepika Kumari: Pivot Point

Sports transcends victory and defeat, medals, rewards and accolades. The real romance of sports lies in challenging stereotypes. When a sportsperson rises, all artificial barriers in the name of society, economy, gender and class are thrown out of the door. Rather than being deterrents, they become the catalytic agents. When athletes burst onto the scene from nowhere and cross the finishing line, glass ceilings are broken, narratives redrawn and scripts rewritten.

There are two states in India which are least discussed, if not least known in the country. We are talking about Tripura and Jharkhand. The mainstream media largely ignores them. And if at all these two manage to find the headlines, it's for extremism and Naxal violence. From these two states came up two sportswomen, who made their name in the most unconventional of sports.

Dipa Karmakar, the gymnast from Tripura, says, 'Initially when people used to ask me about the place and the state I belong to, and I used to say Agartala and Tripura, some of them used to wonder whether it's in Bangladesh.'

Deepika Kumari, an archer from Jharkhand, says, 'I am happy that people now recognize there are sportspersons other than Mahendra Singh Dhoni, who have emerged from Jharkhand. I take pride when they say that I am a daughter of Jharkhand.'

The respective sports which these two girls are passionate about are not just atypical, but the least popular too.

Dipa Karmakar says, 'When they asked about my game and I

said gymnastics, many of them would confuse it with circus. And those who understood used to say Indian girls could not have a future in a sport monopolized by the US, Russia, China and other bigger countries.' It may seem ironical, for gymnastics is known as the mother of all sports.

Deepika Kumari says, 'Our country needs to pay more attention to archery. Nobody knows the sport well enough, and even after we win medals, nobody makes an effort to learn about the sport or its rules. For people, it is boring to watch, so they don't. It's important for the country to understand the sport. It's not just about shooting arrows, which is a notion people generally have about the sport.' This, too, is full of irony. Archery finds a prominent place in Indian classical literature, particularly the epics and religious texts.

Despite their humble origins, if their talent does not translate into medals, the media turns merciless. When a famed cricketer or a tennis player refuses to appear for an interview, it is by and large ignored by the mainstream media, the common refrain being they are busy superstars. But when players like Dipa and Deepika express their inability to appear for an interview, it's attributed to the fact that stardom has gotten into their heads and that they are losing their way. Deepika faced the heat when she refused an exclusive interview to a television channel. When asked about her relationship with the press, she says, 'To be honest, I am not comfortable handling the media. It's not that I don't like to talk to the media, but it is just that I am not at ease with the press.'

Dipa Karmakar once refused to go for an exclusive television programme based on her. Her objection was that her coach was not accorded proper treatment by that television network. Only after her coach was given due respect did she relent. When asked about this, she says, 'My coach is like God to me. Whatever I am, I am because of him. You may insult me, but not my coach.'

When the mainstream media fails to understand them, the ignorance all around is not surprising.

The much coveted Olympic medal eludes both these girls. Dipa finished fourth in the Rio Olympics in 2016. The nation rightly rejoiced, but she was gutted after the fourth-place finish. Speaking to a reporter after her fourth-place finish, she said, '*Dada, eta ki bhabe hoye gelo, eto* practice *korechilam, tobou* fourth. (Brother, how did this happen, I practised so hard but still finished fourth.) Promise *korchi* next time medal *ashbei ashbe, tumi aamar dik theke* India *ke* sorry *bole dio.*' (I promise that I will win a medal in Tokyo, please tell the country on my behalf that I am sorry.)

Deepika faced even worse. The archer was billed as a strong medal contender in the London Olympics 2012. In the 2016 Rio Olympics, the nation counted on her as well. Both times, she failed to live up to the expectations. She says, 'Indian archers have been consistently winning medals in World Championships. But we need an Olympic medal. If we can achieve that, the sport will be more respected here in India, and many more kids will pursue archery.'

Dipa and Deepika have not won Olympic medals yet. But both, from humble backgrounds, have contributed significantly to bring their respective sport back in the reckoning. The girls from Tripura and Jharkhand have forced the international fraternity to take India more seriously. They are classic sports stories to be understood more for what they would have achieved than what they have achieved.

For the four years leading up to the 2016 Rio Olympics, the Gymnastics Federation of India had been divided into two factions, affecting the growth of the sport adversely. With petty internal rivalry among administrators, Indian gymnasts were not even exposed to the infrastructure required. Lack of proper coaching camps and negligible international exposure was surely going to take its toll. It is against this backdrop that Dipa's performance in Rio 2016 needs to be understood and appreciated. As Federation of International Gymnastics (FIG) president Bruno Grandi said, 'Gymnastics needed Dipa more than she needed gymnastics. The sport, for the longest time, has been restricted to the major high-performance countries such as US and China. But for Dipa to come and consistently perform at this level was simply amazing.[1]

Everyone from the fraternity was just hoping that she would finish third; after all, it would be great for the sport. However, what made her Olympic journey really special was the callousness of the association to overcome petty politics and help the sport. She did it without anyone's help, apart from her coach, and that's what makes it special. She got noticed outside. For a change, her performance received appreciation in India as well. In fact, her performance was lauded as much in the country as that of the two Indian girls who stood on the medal podium in Rio. Why? We need to understand the journey more than the destination to fully appreciate this.

Pejorative remarks that gymnastics was akin to circus tricks to entertain the masses were passed for a long time in India. And Dipa, despite her tears and hurt, persevered. Even those who understood the sport disparagingly told her that women had no future in it. And that gymnastics in India was a male bastion. She silently worked hard. There were many who were almost convinced that hers was an exercise in futility. Though a reluctant starter when she took up the sport, she had since transformed into a spirited competitor, unwilling to give up. The same Dipa Karmakar made sure that 14 August 2016 would become a memorable date in the history of Indian sports. If Nadia Comaneci had made gymnastics a sport to marvel at in India, Dipa Karmakar turned it into a new sporting aspiration for the nation. Her journey from Agartala to Rio needs to be unravelled for us to understand her.

Dipa's early childhood was like that of any other kid in Agartala. She loved to jump. She loved to climb trees. She loved playing and fighting with her favourite Puja *didi* (elder sister).

'My sister was my best friend. I used to fight with her for just about anything. I used to snatch things from her and run

---

[1]Soumitro Basu, 'A teary-eyed Dipa Karmakar: "I'm sorry for letting you down India, will win a medal in 2020—promise!"', Sportskeeda, 15 August 2016

away. She used to get all the beating from our parents every time, because she stood there while I ran away,' says Dipa, the impish joy still visible in her eyes. Coming back to the present, she says, 'Not much has changed since. *Didi* is married and has kids now. But I still beat her and fight with her.'

Her mother Gauri Devi adds, 'She was a mischief maker then. Even now, when she comes home, everyone immediately comes to know that Dipa is here.'

Her *pishi* (paternal aunt) adds, 'She used to eat my *jarda paan* (tobacco and betel leaf). She was hard to control. However, later on, she changed, focusing all her energy into sports. I always pray to God that she does well for the country,' her voice choking with emotion.

Dipa says, '*Pishi* was my saviour when *maa* (mom) and *baba* (dad) used to beat me. She is a very emotional person. Even today she gets sentimental and starts crying.'

As we go through her surroundings, we get to understand why ordinary people with a simple approach to life are the ones who do extraordinary things in life. Her mother says, 'Like any other mother, I just tried to provide her with everything that was possible. I used to pray for her. The only thing I used to tell her was always to give her best to make the country proud.'

But Dipa knows her contribution goes far beyond this. 'My mother never dissuaded me. When I was a child of eight years, I broke my hand, my legs were fractured, and I went through surgery, but she never discouraged me from taking part in sports,' she says. The role of her father was equally important in her life. The little girl, on most days, would ride on the back of her *baba*'s Vespa scooter to the gymnasium.

Dulal Chand Karmakar, her father, was a national weightlifting champion and worked with the SAI. Though Dipa belonged to a simple family, she was privileged in the sense that she imbibed a thriving sports culture at home from childhood.

'I have been in this sport since I was five. At that time there was not much knowledge about other sports. The state that I come from didn't have any popular sport that I could have thought of joining. We didn't even have the Internet that we could research which sport would be good for my future. Papa introduced me to gymnastics and I continued doing it,' says Dipa.

But what did he see in Dipa that he introduced her to gymnastics?

'I have two daughters. My wife and I decided that we should put at least one child into sports. The elder one, who is married, was not a sports enthusiast, but Dipa was very energetic. She was restless and wouldn't settle down in the house even after school. Her height and figure were good for gymnastics. There was not much interest in other sports like table tennis and basketball, so I introduced her to gymnastics,' says Dulal.

So was this his gut feeling?

'Perhaps, yes,' he says. The gut feeling of his was to decisively change the course of gymnastics in the country.

'Three other girls started training in the sport with me. But they left after a point of time and are well settled today. I could reach so far because there was a congenial atmosphere for sports at my home from the very beginning.

My father used to say that you may or may not go to school to attend classes, but never ever miss out on your practice sessions,' Dipa says. The decision to send their daughter for gymnastics was helped by the fact that Tripura had a strong legacy in the sport. Nonetheless, it was a daring one.

As per the Bleacher Report published in 2011, gymnastics is counted amongst the ten toughest sports in the world. 'There may not be big hits and hard tackles, but these guys and girls put their bodies through a lot more than that in search of perfection. Just one day of training with this lot would break most people, and they do it every day. Parallel bars, beams, floor routines, vaults and a whole lot more mean these athletes are incredibly skilled, have unbelievable agility and have strength to match,' the report says.[2] Dipa did not take to gymnastics easily. She was so scared of falling that she wouldn't even step on the beams. 'I used to throw tantrums and complained a lot. But *baba* was confident that a day would come when I would get over the fear. He was soon proved right,' Dipa says.

The little girl started cartwheeling, and sailing through the air. This taught her the first major invaluable lesson in life. 'Nothing is possible in life without courage. Gymnastics is the sport that is based on courage. And Produnova, which I do, needs courage,' Dipa says with her trademark chuckle.

The term Produnova, once an alien term, became known to the entire country after 14 August 2016. It had, however, become common parlance in the gymnastics world by then. Before Rio 2016, forty-one-year-old Uzbek gymnast Oksana Chusovitina had made headlines even before she competed in the women's vault competition. She created history by qualifying for her seventh Olympics in Rio, a staggering achievement in itself, in the process becoming the oldest ever to compete in women's gymnastics. But Chusovitina wasn't done just yet. In an attempt to upstage competition and challenge American champion Simone Biles (who was just two years older than Chusovitina's seventeen-year-old son), Chusovitina attempted the Produnova.

Many deemed it as 'the vault of death'. Biles eventually won the gold with her flawless execution, but Chusovitina and Dipa somewhat stole her thunder as they executed the scary Produnova routine, with millions watching, spellbound, on the telly.

Introduced in 1999 by the legendary Russian gymnast Yelena Produnova, the rare vault involves a front-handspring entry with a double somersault off the table, and its official highest D-score (for difficulty) rating is seven in the women's vault. Only four gymnasts, Produnova herself, Chusovitina, Dipa and Dominican Republic's Yamilet Pena, have successfully pulled it off.

---

[2]Chris Siddell, 'What Is the Toughest Sport in the World?' Bleacher Report, 14 September 2011

Things did not go as per the plan for Chusovitina, who had first competed in the Olympics at the 1992 Barcelona Games, and was once part of the erstwhile USSR gymnastics team. The double somersault duly executed, Chusovitina lurched forward on landing, with her head perilously close to the landing mat, as everyone watching feared a fatal injury. Luckily the trained Uzbek was able to wriggle out safely. Perhaps a grim reminder of the narrowest of margins that lay between supreme athletic skill and a serious injury in the Produnova. And Dipa, who had endured a stumble in the qualifiers, would she fare any better? Past the stroke of the midnight hour on India's Independence Day, Dipa launched herself, her swinging legs going into two rotations mid-air for the twin somersaults, and then landed, feet first, in a somewhat low squat. Body touched mat, but the shy, reticent kid from Tripura stayed in position, thus pulling off her signature vault. Dipa's attempt at the vault was cleaner than Chusovitina's and it helped her move into second place behind eventual bronze medal winner Giulia Steinbruger of Switzerland. Dipa would follow it up with a D-score of 6 in the Zamolodchikova (stretched double twist routine), but ultimately it wasn't enough for the much-coveted podium finish. But India won't forget her fearless, supremely confident vaulting that was now on par with the best in the world. Rio 2016 had bestowed upon India a new flaming torch, a new story of Indian sportswomen standing shoulder to shoulder with the best in the business, daring newer generations back home to reassess and reimagine their latent potential.

As in her fearless run to the vault, with nothing held back, Dipa's elemental attribute comes shining through when confronted with the dangers of the Produnova. Speaking to *The Wall Street Journal* following her Rio performance, Dipa had said, 'Whenever someone tells me this vault is very dangerous, I say, "Thank you, I like risk."' Two years on, when reminded of it again, she would say, 'There is no such thing like the vault of death. It's a name given by the media. Moreover, my coach Nandi sir has made me practise it so many times that it does not look risky at all now.' Dipa's father Dulal jokingly says Produnova Karmakar had become Dipa's new name for millions of Indians after 14 August 2016. 'That is the day I will never forget in my life. She may have lost the medal by a whisker but she made the country, state, myself and everyone feel proud. To get into the top 8 in a competitive sport like gymnastics at the world level is simply great.' After Dipa's electrifying performance, suddenly India was talking about the Produnova. However, he adds, 'I would be lying if I say that I don't rue the fact that she missed the medal by a score of 0.15.'

The naughtiness in Dipa comes to the fore again when she says, 'My parents hardly knew what Produnova is or what the finer points of gymnastics are, but now they do understand and talk about the various intricacies of the sport like an expert. I often tell them, as if training sessions were not enough, you continue to goad me at home too! Honestly, I could not thank them enough for the things that they have done for me in my life.'

Dipa, under the supervision of her coach Suma Nandi, started practising hard and late. When Dipa turned nine, she participated in the 2002 Northeastern Games. She won the gold medal. Suma recognized that Dipa was special, as she turned from being the reluctant pupil to a willing student who needed to be shepherded carefully. 'The position she has reached today is a matter of pride for all of us. This is more so, considering the fact that she used to practise at the place that had literally no facilities,' says Suma.

Old mattresses and outdated equipment, this was all Vivekananda Byamagar on Gangail Road in Agartala had in the name of a gymnasium.

'The secretary of the Tripura Sports Council called me to his office and said that Dipa had talent, and considering the fact that she was deprived of facilities here, she should be handed over to NRCC,' says Suma, reminiscing Dipa's formative years. 'After a moment's contemplation, I replied that I was willing, but only if she was handed over to a good coach. The moment he mentioned the name of Bisheshwar Nandi, I immediately agreed. Had I not agreed then, she would not have reached so far in her life,' Suma recollects, taking pride in the small but vital role she played in the budding gymnast's career back then.

Dipa puts the entire thing in perspective when she says, 'Madam (Suma) is the wife of my present coach Bisheshwar Nandi sir. Even today, I am scared of facing her. I would not have been here without here. She never used to beat me, but her firm and strong words more than often conveyed the message. They were worth more than hundreds of slaps for me.' Interestingly, just as Dipa was initially reluctant about taking up gymnastics, equally reluctant was Bisheshwar Nandi about coaching girls.

There is far more to Nandi's profile than just being the coach of Dipa Karmakar. 'I was a good gymnast too. I participated in eight to ten internationals in gymnastics. I was the captain of the Indian team that participated in the 1982 Asian Games in Delhi. One of my proudest moments was the day when in the same hall where I represented the country in 1982, my *shishya* (disciple) Dipa was to perform her routine in the finals of the 2010 Commonwealth Games,' Nandi says.

He further adds, 'My aim was to become a world-class gymnast, good enough for the Olympics. Though I could not accomplish this goal in my career, I wanted one of my students to achieve that goal, and it is this desire that brought me to coaching. I used to train boys in gymnastics. One day I was called by the secretary of sports, government of Tripura, to his office. He asked me to take up the coaching of women's gymnastics because girls were lagging behind in the sport. I told him that I didn't know much about women's gymnastics and would rather concentrate on boys.

'But he reminded me I had been a good gymnast, and since the grammar of the sport was the same, I would be able to work wonders with the girls' team as well. "They need someone like you," he said. I didn't commit to him and left his office thinking that the matter would subside,' he says.

But that was not to be.

'Soon I received a letter designating me as in-charge of the girls' gymnastics team. I was not enthused since I had the feeling that girls pick up things later than boys, and girls' gymnastics has got many complications as well,' Nandi adds.

Perhaps Dipa and Nandi were destined to forge an impactful partnership. And, like any good long-term partnership, it took its time to flourish.

'I still distinctly remember the day when she came with her father in 2002. Her father told me how she was bustling with energy all the time, as to how she picked fights with her sister and thus the need of her being handled delicately. Very soon I realized that she was too demanding. Whenever I used to focus on senior players, she used to ask me why she was not being given proper attention. She used to complain about this and become more exacting as a pupil. She said that she was the daughter of a weightlifting coach and so was used to rigour. She used to insist that her diet at home consisted mainly of milk and *ghee*, and that's why she was strong.

'She wanted to train hard and beat her seniors as soon as possible. I used to tell her that she was in the sub-junior level, and being a coach myself, I knew how much load I should give her. Eventually, I had to prepare a schedule for her, along with that of three other girls. I had by then decided that out of the four, I would ensure that at least two of them participated in the upcoming 2010 Delhi Commonwealth Games,' Nandi says. However, as the coach was planning to put her schedule to action, he found out she was flat-footed.

The SAI refused to take her as a trainee because of her flat feet. Flat feet are an issue in gymnastics because they reduce the springiness in the feet and affect the take-off. 'When a sports doctor from the SAI saw the girls who were training under me, he said that except Dipa, the rest of them might become gymnasts. For Dipa, it was impossible because she was flat-footed,' Nandi says. 'Fortunately, being a gymnast myself, I had a fair understanding of the subject. I researched a bit and suggested certain exercises to her to enhance her capacity. These exercises had to be done at home, for she had to pick up things quickly. Some of the exercises were strenuous. One of them was standing with the foot bent, to create arches in her feet. Such was her dedication that she kept rehearsing the exercises even while eating, as her father told me one day. She picked up fast and did not look back from there,' Nandi adds.

In 2008, she won the junior nationals in Jalpaiguri. Her performance there convinced Nandi that she had special talent. As Dipa graduated to the senior group, Nandi discovered that during a performance she used to become tense and come under pressure because of him. She used to get worried that her coach might get angry if she performed badly.

'Once I became aware of this, I only reprimanded her during practice sessions. Gradually, this too started becoming lesser and lesser,' Nandi says, looking at Dipa.

There is one specific trait that defines their partnership. The determination to not let the lack of resources hinder them from realizing their goals was deeply engrained in both of them.

When the world saw Dipa Karmakar fly, spin and somersault through the air at the Rio Olympics, very few were aware that the foundation of the skill was based on a 'Do-It-Yourself apparatus' cobbled together from second-hand parts of a discarded scooter. Nandi says, 'Initially we had no apparatus and had to use our imagination to improvise. Eight to ten crash mats were stacked on top of each other to make a vaulting platform and an assortment of used spares from old scooters like springs and shock absorbers handed over to the local carpenter to forge a springboard. So when Dipa first started to vault, she used to jump from a rudimentary springboard onto a pile of mats.'

With this, the girl from Tripura mastered something as difficult as the Produnova.

Dipa says, 'Nandi sir was scared when I first started doing the vault because he thought I might break my neck or end up dead, especially when I wanted to push the boundaries. However, both of us were aware that we had to take calculated risks if we intended to compete with the best.'

Nandi adds to this and says, 'At times my heart was in my mouth when she took off for the vault. I was so scared, but she was fearless. Such has been her dedication in perfecting the skill that we decided to note down her attempts for one week, in a diary she keeps. The final tally was 127 vaults.'

In comparison, Simone Biles normally attempts about 15 to 20 complete vaults a week. The difference is understandable. The very infrastructure that has been missing in Indian sports, more so in gymnastics, was something Biles had access to when she began, and did not have to overcome the challenges faced by Karmakar.

'I don't think my rivals know what obstacles and hardships I have had to face to get myself to Rio. There were barely any world-class gymnastics facilities in the whole of India. In a small city like Agartala there was practically nothing. To have started off with nothing and having got to the level I have today proves that Indian gymnasts have the kind of talent people see in someone like Simone Biles,' she says passionately. Her struggle for proper facilities continued despite her initial success.

'Dipa faced gender bias because whenever we went to the national camp, the officials invariably made it a point to hype up the achievements of the male gymnasts only. Ashish Kumar got so much of recognition for the silver and bronze medals he won at the 2010 Commonwealth Games. I was really disappointed that women's gymnastics was not getting the same recognition or investment. I always had big dreams for Dipa. But I remained confident she was going to make a name for herself, no matter what the obstacles were,' Nandi gets emotional saying this.

With next to no funding, Dipa, for a major part of her career, had to make do with practising her skills with out-of-date apparatus. After Delhi hosted the 2010 Commonwealth Games, manufacturer Gymnova gave her the cast-offs from that competition. By the time she started practising with the equipment, the world of gymnastics had moved on to more high-tech gear. The funding started coming in properly only after she qualified for the Rio Olympics. By the time she was preparing to leave for Rio, her list of 'firsts' was a long one.

The Produnova for instance. Live TV missed Dipa's sensational feat as she rolled out the high-risk manoeuvre at Glasgow's Hydro Stadium, enroute to winning India's first women's gymnastics medal, a bronze, at the Commonwealth Games in 2014. Just months after she and Nandi had decided to train for it!

She subsequently won a bronze in the Asian Gymnastics Championships and finished fifth at the 2015 World Artistic Gymnastics Championships, both firsts for India. In April, she managed to grab a berth at the Olympics with a score of 52,698 points.

Since 1947, only eleven Indian male gymnasts have made the mark—and Karmakar was the first Indian woman to do so. With 77 medals—67 of them gold—under her belt, the Bengali girl from Tripura had finally arrived. But as the Indian contingent was leaving for Rio, one after another, Dipa Karmakar had few takers. There were no second glances, no whispers or requests for selfies, not even an interview. When asked about this, her standard reply used to be, 'It doesn't really matter. But slowly people are getting acquainted with gymnastics.'[3]

With gymnastics beginning to get recognized as a full-fledged sport, a change appeared on the horizon. One that would alter mindsets. So sudden would it be that even Dipa could not anticipate the turnaround one performance would do to her life.

'That was the moment of pride for me. On a stage like the Olympics, I had reached the finals. I was mentally totally free and was not putting any unnecessary burden on myself that I had to get medals or anything. My only focus was on giving my best. In the practice sessions my biggest fear had been my coach. I had always feared that he would be angry if I failed. But that day my coach came to me and said, "Today is your day and you do what you want to do. Even if you perform badly you will not fall below

---

[3]'No mean feet', *The Telegraph*, 1 May 2016

no. 8, so give it your best."

'I was so happy that finally I was standing on the vaulting table of the Olympics. Not even for a fraction of a second did I think of medals. Rather, I was only thinking about giving my best,' she says, often struggling to put words to her emotions. And then she adds again, 'I did not know what was happening back in my country. I did not have a phone, and the SIM was taken away by my coach so that I could concentrate on the job at hand. It was my birthday week too. I just called home once or twice. When everything got over, I was telling my coach that we would take a taxi and head straight for home. It was then that my sir told me that I didn't even know what had happened in the last seven days. "The entire country has been praying for you. You are the new star." It was then that I realized that the entire country had been watching me on television that day.' This started getting clearer with each passing hour.

She adds further, 'When I came out of the flight I saw the SAI project officer and the SAI coach waiting for us. They had all come to receive me. One after another everyone was saying that I may not have won a medal but my performance was worth a thousand medals. Suddenly I could see a sea of humanity following us along with camera crew all around. I was happy that gymnastics as a sport was at last recognized throughout India. They would not call gymnastics part of a circus now. For them gymnastics would not be only boys' sport.

'They would now be able to easily locate Tripura on the map of India,' she sums up the rare moment in the country's sporting history with these words.

The change was discernible in the body language of Agartala as well.

As we headed towards the main city from the airport, which is about 25 km away, we could only see Durga Puja pandals, and billboards and posters of the coach-pupil duo—a testament to what Dipa had done for Tripura, the 'gymnastics hub' of the country.

Till the late 1980s, the state dominated gymnastics in the national competitions. Over a span of two decades, twenty-four gymnasts from Tripura went on to win sixty national championship medals. But soon there emerged a dearth of gymnasts, particularly in the 1990s, and Tripura did not get much recognition. To change that required special talent, and Dipa broke the drought, winning a bronze medal in the 2014 Commonwealth Games.

Tripura's decades-long romance with gymnastics was born primarily through the efforts of an army man-cum-gymnast from Haryana, Dalip Singh. In 1964, Singh was sent from the National Institute of Sport (NIS) Patiala to see what Tripura could offer in terms of talent. While it is not known as to why Tripura was specifically chosen, or what it could offer to the sport, Singh, now fondly remembered as the father of gymnastics, turned things around like a miracle.

He began where everyone else does too, even now, the same Vivekananda *byamagar* (gymnasium), where even Dipa and her coach Bisheshwar had started off. By the time he was done with his assignment, Tripura had held absolute sway over Indian gymnastics for two decades, while Singh himself, adopted by the state, had married a local, and had become one of Tripura's own.

Chuffed with Dalip Singh's efforts, SAI even brought in a world-class team of Soviet gymnasts in 1968, to compete with the locals. The entire landscape was changed, as Tripura boasted of champions who would draw the multitudes.

Mantu Debnath, India's first Arjuna awardee in gymnastics, Bharat Kishore Deb Barman, who won Tripura's first national gold medal, five-time national champion Bisheshwar Nandi, the super talented Kalpana Debnath who was India's best 'All Round Woman Gymnast' a record nine times, they were all finished products of the Dalip Singh school of gymnastics.

Dipa reignited the potential of the legacy. She is facing challenges galore to live up to the promise. Dipa injured her right knee while preparing for the Asian Asiatic Gymnastics in 2017. Most of the year was spent in recuperation. After a difficult

2017, Dipa made a golden comeback at the FIG Gymnastic World Challenge Cup at Mersin, Turkey. She won the gold in the vault event, the first Indian gymnast to achieve the feat.

Dipa says, 'For a gymnast to come back after surgery, it is very very tough. Some said I was finished since it was two years after the Olympics. But I was ready to go through the surgery after I knew I had an ACL (anterior cruciate ligament) injury. There are other sportspersons who have made a successful comeback. I tried to take it positively and due to the support of my coach, family, physio, SAI and the sports ministry, I succeeded.'

She needs one major breakthrough in terms of form, fitness and qualification to live up to her promise of the medal at the Tokyo Olympics in 2020. Whereas the country waits for what the feisty gymnast has up her sleeve, she has managed to bring gymnastics back to centre stage through the sheer weight of her performance. In Dipa, future gymnasts have got their role model and an inspiration to unleash their potential.

For aspiring Dipas, her simple message is, 'Follow your parents and teachers and work with discipline and sincerity. You will become better than Dipa Karmakar.' She further adds, 'Work hard, results will follow. Look, I did not get an Olympic medal; still the government gave me all the recognition that was given to the medal winners. The proudest day of my life was when I got the Rajiv Gandhi Khel Ratna award along with the other medal winners and my coach got the Arjuna Award.'

What is the one thing she would like to change in her life, if given a chance? She jumps in even before the question ends. 'I would like to be standing on the podium and improve from fourth to third, second or even the first position,' she says with innocence writ all over her face.

Gymnastics aside, a fan of Hrithik Roshan, the Bollywood actor, Dipa wouldn't mind if a biopic was made based on her life. Who would be her favourite actor to play her role? Her answer stuns everyone present there. 'The decision will be of the director's, but ideally she should be able to do the Produnova,' she says and starts laughing heartily.

Whereas the girl from Tripura is open to the idea of a biopic based on her life, Deepika Kumari, from Jharkhand, has already had an offer to act in a film. The poster girl of Indian archery was all set to star in a Hindi movie, *Bisahi*.

She was to play the lead in a story revolving around the evil practice of witch-hunting. 'Initially, I was very excited to star in the movie. I was struggling with my form and I wanted to give acting a try. The shooting was being planned in the month of March 2018, but then I realized if I plunged into the world of celluloid, I would lose focus on archery. It was an important year and I desperately wanted to turn around my fortunes in the sport. So, I finally rejected the offer.'

She did, indeed, reject the offer, but what were the circumstances that prompted one of the most talented Indian archers to think of something other than her sport, one she had given herself to?

'When you are not winning for a long time, negativity creeps in and you are shrouded in self-doubt,' Deepika Kumari says.

Hers is the case of a much too talented sportswoman not living up to the high standards that her peers and sports lovers had set for her. It was very different, though, at the time she started off in 2006, checking into the Tata Archery Academy in Jamshedpur.

It was here that Deepika got access to proper archery equipment and uniforms for the first time in her life, along with a monthly stipend, of ₹500. Proper regimen, better diet, and superior infrastructure at the academy meant that soon enough, Deepika would be making waves in the archery circuit.

First came the Cadet World Archery Championships title in 2009, when Deepika became only the second Indian archer to achieve the feat.

Was it just a coincidence or did the state of Jharkhand have something to do with the fact that Paltan Hansda, an eighteen-year-old kid from Kharsawan, a city just an hour's drive from Jamshedpur, had become the junior world champion at the Ninth

Junior and Third Cadet World Archery Championships in Mexico, in 2006, thirty-six months before Deepika's title?

For Deepika, it was just the start. At just fifteen, she won the 11th Youth World Archery Championships in Ogden City, Utah, US, in 2009. And a year later, two gold medals at the Commonwealth Games in New Delhi, one in the women's individual recurve event, and the other in the women's recurve team event with Dola Banerjee and Bombayla Devi Laishram, firmly put her in the mindspace of fans and sports aficionados alike, as she emerged from being just the 'next big thing' in archery.

And when she struck the bullseye for her first Archery World Cup gold medal in individual recurve at Antalya, Turkey, the expectations of a medal-thirsty nation came tumbling out as all and sundry declared her to be a sure-shot medal contender at the 2012 London Olympics.

Ranked world no. 1 in the lead-up to the London Olympics in 2012, Deepika crashed out in the first round, beaten by Amy Oliver of Great Britain. Unable to best the windy conditions and her fever that she carried into her match, Deepika would face many disparaging reports in the Indian media that trashed her abilities altogether.

Stringing together some good as well as disappointing performances over the next three years, Deepika again became the centre of attention as in April 2016, she equalled the world record in the women's recurve event. And the Rio Olympics later that year started well too, as she eased through the first two rounds. But a poor show in the round of 16 against Chinese Taipei's Tan Ya-ting meant she would exit another Olympics empty-handed. And it would be a lonely road back home, as the disparaging media, the federation officials, and everyone who mattered deserted the lonely archer as she sought to reflect on what had gone wrong.

In those six years since the Antalya high, through many World Cup stages, World Cup finals, the two summer Olympics, one Commonwealth and one Asian Games, the gold medal continued to elude her. The six-year-long drought finally ended when she clinched gold in the recurve event at the World Cup at Salt Lake City in the US in June 2018.

What had gone wrong in the past?

'Maybe I could not cope up with the pressure and made mistakes at crucial junctures of the competition, allowing the momentum to shift. Mental strength will be my main focus for the rest of my career,' says Deepika.

Former international archer Dola Banerjee who participated with Deepika also agrees on this. 'She is a very hard worker with great technique. But the new scoring system puts a lot of emphasis on the mental strength of an archer, and that is where many of our Indian archers like Deepika are losing out,' she says. The earlier scoring system during head-to-head match-ups included twelve arrows being shot by each of the two participants and the top scorer going on to win the match. This has been replaced by matches of five sets.

Each set consists of three arrows and the winner of the set gets two points. Each of the archers gets one point apiece for a drawn set.

'The fact that you are starting a new set after every three shots means the opponent can make comebacks at any time, and one has to be very strong mentally,' says Dola. There are two things in international sports. The first thing is having the talent and the second thing is honing the talent. The second aspect becomes more important if athletes come up from challenging and underprivileged conditions. Deepika's life is one such story.

Born to Shivnath Mahto, an autorickshaw driver, and Geeta Mahto, who worked as a nurse at Ranchi Medical College, Kumari grew up under a thatched hut in her village of Ram Chatti, about 15 km from Ranchi. There was never enough food on the table, not to mention discord within the family. Hers had become a life filled with the inevitable struggle. Starving, and with the noble intention of lessening the burden on her parents, a twelve-year-old Deepika left her village. On a cousin's recommendation, she joined an archery academy.

'I got interested in archery in the year 2007 at the age of thirteen. I had gone to the training centre in Seraikela, Kharsawan, which is just outside Jamshedpur. Initially, I was not that interested in the sport, and in fact my cousin used to practise archery there. I had just heard of the sport. I used to watch the sport, and through that, and while staying at my cousin's place, slowly my interest piqued and I started practising archery.'

Her only experience in the sport at this point was with homemade bamboo bows and arrows. More than the sport per se, a roof over her head and three meals a day were something she couldn't turn away from.

'After I trained in Saraikela, for a year, I got selected to join the JRD Tata Sports Complex, where I train now. I have two coaches, Dharmendra Tewari and Purnima Mahato. They have been my coaches since I joined the JRD Tata Sports Complex. My coaches not only trained me in archery but have also trained me to handle life. For example, when they teach us about confidence in archery, it applies to my life as well. It was that confidence which helped me perform in front of a crowd or talk to people I didn't know. All the principles I acquire as a sportsperson automatically apply to my personal life as well,' she says.

Deepika is the classic case of how sports brings about change in one's personal life. Hers is also the example of how someone from humble origins can develop the requisite skill, through ardour and tenacity and compete at the international stage.

'As such, difficulty in playing and performance does not occur. But there are times when I am not able to perform well. That affects the way people perceive me. They either get negative or stop talking to me. They question my work; complain that I am not working hard enough, that I do not have enough focus. They say I don't concentrate, and that's why my performance is dipping. They start questioning and doubting whether I will win medals again. What they don't realize is that this is a sport and no one person can win every single time or perform the same always,' Deepika says, further elaborating on this.

The rise from humble origins, the mindset attuned where failure is not an option, playing the sport about which there is ignorance all around, lack of a setup where her skills could be honed and weaknesses worked out—all these combined together to get her into a situation where she thought of quitting.

'In the last few months, I have been working with the mental conditioning coach Mugdha Bavare and she played a key role in helping me to get out of the rut. The thought of giving it all up crossed my mind, but the love of archery, the determination to fight back kept me going in spite of these difficult times.'

What is the difference in the way she tackled her problems then and now? 'Now from my side I just let it be, because I do not know those people. Explaining my stance is not an option because it is incorrectly perceived as excuses. I have learnt to make peace with the talk and just focus on improving my skill. I work harder and try to answer such doubts through my work. I do not let this negativity affect my work,' she says.

While most in and around the Indian Olympic contingent deserted her at the moment she lost in Rio, Deepika found some solace in the company of the documentary film unit that had been filming her story for a while.

Her trials and tribulations, her compelling story, from being born in abject poverty, to battling hunger, and thereon chancing upon archery, thus becoming the best archer in the world, are all depicted in *Ladies First*, a riveting thirty-nine-minute documentary directed by Uraaz Bahl and Shaana Levy-Bahl. The film would go on to win a bunch of international awards, be screened at film festivals, after having found a producer in two-time Academy Award winner Sharmeen Obaid Chinoy. And even though most in and around the sporting fraternity in India were ready to consign Deepika to their own list of 'has-beens', her story was picked up by Netflix, allowing the the rest of the world to know her story. Deepika's story. India's Deepika.

'The one thing that I would like to say is that focus on one thing and don't be too scattered with your interests. Be disciplined in whatever you do, along with, of course, dedication and hard work. Just follow this simple rule and you are bound to do well.' Deepika finally seems to be at peace with herself. The medals will follow.

Dipa Karmakar and Deepika Kumari have nothing in common, except that both faced extreme hardships—from equipment failure to the lack of it, thereof, to acquire their skills and hone their talent. While they have yet to reach the pinnacle of success, let's doff our hats to Dipa and Deepika.

The message they seem to convey to us all is, *Zid karo, haath-pair patak ke mana lo, but give up mat karo.* (Create a fuss, throw your arms and feet about, and try to change mindsets, but never give up.)

FIFTEEN

The Show Must Go On: The Promise of Eternal Sunshine

n Dhing, a town in Assam, there is a small village, Kandhulimari. This village is roughly 23 km away from central Assam's Nagaon district headquarters. This story is about a girl child born in the village where roughly a hundred families live. She is one of five siblings. Her parents, Jonali Das and Ranjit Das, are rice farmers and they belong to the indigenous Kaibarta community. As far as the parents' memories go, the girl loved playing every kind of sport as a child. She just wanted to go outside and express herself through sports. The passion followed her when she started going to Dhing Public High School. She played every game in the school and clinched gold and silver medals in them. But of all the games she played, she had a soft spot for football. She could often be seen playing football in different grounds, whenever and wherever she got the opportunity. Then one fine day, everything changed.

Shamshul Sheikh, the physical education teacher of Jawahar Navodaya Vidyalaya, gave the most valuable tip to the girl. Impressed with her incredible speed while playing football, he advised her to leave her first love, football, and instead focus on sprinting. For a better future in athletics, Sheikh advised the girl and her father to get in touch with Gauri Shankar Roy, a sports teacher in Nagaon. When they went to meet Gauri Shankar Roy, he asked the girl to run. She got selected for the district meet. Her father gave her company while she practised early in the morning. Both of them used to wake up at 4:00 a.m. every day and go for long runs. After two weeks of running, she started waking up her father earlier, to run even longer distances. Meanwhile, her love for football continued. While she participated in the athletics meet, she continued playing football with the local boys.

Once, a women's football tournament was held in Dhing. She wanted to participate in the tournament and her father met the coach, making the request. The coach agreed. She played for one of the teams in the second half and scored a goal within a few minutes. She became so popular after this that different teams started hiring her whenever there was a football match in the area. She used to get ₹400-500 for every match that she played. She ran hard on those muddy football grounds to train herself for the athletics competitions as well. There was no professional track near her home where she could practise.

Along with running, she used to help her father in the paddy fields whenever required. She ploughed and flattened the field when her father needed rest. She used to carry the produce weighing around three quintals, home on a bicycle. She could not bear to see her father struggling.

Gradually, the girl started dreaming of wearing the Indian jersey. She realized that her dream would remain unfulfilled if she didn't focus solely on athletics. The resilient sprinter scalped a bronze medal in the state meet. And then the nationals, and finally the big day came.

12 June 2018.

In the 400 m final in the IAAF World U20 Championships at Tampere, Finland, she clocked 51.46 sec to reach the finishing point. She started slowly in the first half, but accelerated in the last 100 m. She overtook three competitors to reach her goal. She became the first Indian sprinter to win a gold medal at an international track event.

She dared.

She is Hima Das. The entire country now knows her as the Dhing Express.

Hima Das has been improving with every event. However,

she is still a work in progress. She has to go a long way to reach the podium at the Olympics. However, off the field, some of her statements of intent reveal her inner self and her true character. The determination of Hima Das represents the mindsets of the emerging athletes of new India. When her home state of Assam was in the throes of one of the worst spells of flooding in recent years, she was participating in training camps and athletic meets in Europe. However, Hima Das came out in support of the flood victims. She donated half her month's salary, which she gets as an HR officer of Indian Oil Corporation. More importantly, in her tweets which followed, she appealed to corporates and individuals to come forward with assistance.[1]

Before this, she had already taken the lead in the village's fight against country liquor vending. When Hima came to know about a few members of the village selling country liquor, she took with herself a team of women from the village and demolished the liquor shops.

In 2013, Hima Das formed a social help group 'Mon jai', an Assamese phrase meaning 'I want to' or 'I feel like', with the support of six local friends. This group is engaged in social work and this includes helping the lesser privileged sections of society. Sportspersons of previous generations used to think of philanthropy on retirement. But Hima Das represents the generation of Naya Bharat athletes who are conscious of their responsibilities towards their society, state and country even while they play.

There is a uniqueness in Hima Das's narrative. The north-eastern states of India continue to surprise us with similar stories. Though the legend of Mary Kom has forever etched the name of Manipur as the major sports pilgrimage centre of the country, another young woman from there is making rapid strides.

Born in Nongpok Kakching, she was raised in Manipur's

---

[1]Hima Das, 'Flood situation in our state Assam is very critical, 30 out of 33 districts are currently affected. So, I would like to request big corporates and individuals to kindly come forward and help our state in this difficult situation', 16 July 2019, 12:31 a.m.

capital, Imphal. Right from her childhood, she was a tomboy in the hearts of her neighbours. She had many male friends in her school and she loved playing outdoor sports with them. Her first love was archery. However, when she saw the exploits of Kunjarani Devi, she decided to become a weightlifter. Interestingly, weight training for her began while she accompanied her elder brother to collect firewood. The road ahead was bumpy. The resources required to get her going in weightlifting were almost non-existent. There was no weightlifting centre in her village. Daily, she cycled 60 km both ways, for training. For the first six months of her training, she only lifted bamboo canes, before switching to the iron bar. The sport requires a nutritious diet with different proteins, vitamins and supplements. Born in a poor family, what she could afford at best was chicken and eggs two to three times a week. She then made a deal with her parents. She would quit sports if she failed to qualify for the Olympics.

She dared. She is Saikhom Mirabai Chanu.

When she was eleven, she won gold at the sub-junior level. In 2011, she again won gold in the junior nationals. This was followed by medals in the Commonwealth Games. After she got the silver medal in the women's 48 kg weight category, she travelled to Rio for the 2016 Olympics as India's medal hope. She put in lots of hard work to prepare for the big event. However, her nerves got the better of her in the high pressure situation and she got disqualified. People thought she was finished. But like a true Manipuri, she bounced back.

In 2017, she won gold at the World Weightlifting Championships in Anaheim, US. After the iron lady of Indian sports, Karnam Malleswari, she became the second Indian to achieve this feat. The diminutive Manipuri now has her sights set on the 2019 World Championships followed by the 2020 Tokyo Olympics. The entire country has started seeing her as the Olympic medal hope. Fighting injury, both physical and mental, and adjusting from the 48 kg to the 49 kg weight category will be her biggest challenge. The state of Haryana may be separated by hundreds of kilometres from the north-eastern states of the country, but they share one common narrative in India's growth story in sports. If India aspires to be a strong sporting nation, Haryana, along with the north-eastern states, has to be the engine of this growth story.

Haryana has contributed the lion's share of medals at different international competitions, but the state has immense potential to fuel further growth. In the district of Kurukshetra, a girl was born in a family with a humble background. Her father used to work as a cart driver with a meagre income of ₹100 per day. The entire family, comprising her parents, two brothers and their wives, along with her, used to live in a shanty. The girl had only one wish—to somehow pull the family out of poverty. She tried to convince her parents to let her pursue hockey. The family got worried that she would bring a bad name to them, if she went to play outside regularly. Her challenges ranged from financial crisis to social stigma—but she overcame them all.

She dared. She is Rani Rampal.

When one dares to try and achieve something big in life, one often meets someone who helps them make the first major move. This has been the case with the captain of the Indian women's hockey team, Rani Rampal, as well. In Shahabad Hockey Academy, she met someone who changed her life. Whenever she thought of quitting hockey because of poverty, the Dronacharya Award winner, coach Baldev Singh, supported her in every possible manner. As she dared to move ahead with his support, her time had no other option but to change for the better. Baldev Singh taught her the importance of time early in her life. One day, she turned up late for her practice. Baldev fined her ₹200 for this.

How will I pay the money? From where will I get the money? How will I go for practice tomorrow? As she pondered over these questions, she cried the whole day. Somehow, she managed to secure ₹100, which was her father's income for a day when he got work. She gave the money to Baldev Singh. The coach returned the money to her, along with an additional note of ₹100 in the evening. She was so touched by the gesture that she was never

ever late for her practice sessions again.

Rani's mother used to wake up early so that the girl could reach her practice sessions every day at 5 a.m. Her mother could never sleep properly, as the family didn't even have a watch, and she was afraid of oversleeping.

Once, there was a handwriting competition in her school. Her handwriting was not good. But she practised hard and won a clock for her mother. Once the clock came to her house, her mother started sleeping peacefully. It was this concern for her family that pushed the girl to work hard in her field.

Rani took part in the Champions Challenge Tournament in Russia in 2009. She was adjudged the best player and awarded the Player of the Tournament award. In the 2009 Asia Cup, she was part of the team that won the silver medal. In the 2010 World Cup, when she was barely fifteen years of age, she won the Best Young Player of the Tournament award. In the process, she became the youngest player in the national team to participate in the World Cup. She scored seven goals in the tournament. In the 2013 Junior World Cup, she was again the player of the tournament. In 2017, she was part of the champions' team of the Asia Cup held in Japan. In 2018, the team won silver in the Asian Games.

Brick by brick, Rani Rampal, the striker, has built her reputation based on her stellar stick work and electric speed. She is the best woman hockey player of India. She is amongst the top players in the world. Under the guidance of coaches like Glenn Turner, Harendra Singh and Sjoerd Marijne, the Indian women's hockey team has gone from strength to strength in the last few years. The Indian women's hockey team is now known for mental toughness and self-belief. They reached the quarter-finals of the Women's Hockey World Cup in London in 2018. Leading the upsurge of the team is Rani Rampal, 'Captain Cool' of the women's hockey team. The team is no longer treated as underdogs in international competitions, but as a formidable side capable of beating the best.

From living in a shanty to building her dream house for her family, Rani Rampal has come of age. Like most girls of her age, she loves listening to music and shopping. Dhanraj Pillay is her all-time favourite hockey player. Apart from hockey, she follows badminton and tennis. Saina Nehwal is her favourite player in badminton. One of the proudest moments in her life was when she became the flag bearer of the Indian contingent in the closing ceremony of the Asian Games in 2018. At a very young age, she has become an inspiration and a beacon of hope for all those girls who face obstacles in their way and still dare to dream big. From conventional sports like wrestling and hockey, the girls of Haryana have now started aiming high in sports like shooting as well.

Universal Senior Secondary School in Goria village in Haryana's Jhajjar district has, over the last couple of years, become the nerve centre of many young dreams. The school, located 125 km from Delhi, came into the limelight when sixteen-year-old Manu Bhaker won two gold medals for India in the International Shooting Sport Federation (ISSF) World Cup in Guadalajara, Mexico. The school has fast emerged as a cradle for shooting talent, with students winning medals at the state and district levels regularly since 2013. The school is being run by Manu Bhaker's family. Her mother, Sumedha, is the principal of the school, which was started by her uncle. The school offers shooting as a sport option for all students above Class V.

The infrastructure of the school, when compared to international standard schools, is far from the level of being called state-of-the-art. The school uses a manual machine costing around ₹25,000 as opposed to the automatic machines costing around ₹3,00,000, used in the international competitive arena. The school provides dummy guns and pistols, and consumables like the pellets and targets which cost around ₹1,500 per month are borne by the students. But all these deficiencies are more than compensated by the fact that one of the former students who trained there has become a world champion. Stories of Manu's hard work are routinely shared among classmates there. One such story is the fact that nothing, not even sickness, bad weather or any temptation could stop her from going to practice regularly, on time.

Haryana is a state steeped in patriarchy. But we have many many catalytic agents spread across the state who are coming forward to break the glass ceiling and salvage the state's reputation. The Phogat sisters, Sakshi Malik and now the Bhaker family are such catalytic agents.

Right from Manu Bhaker's childhood, her father, Ramkishan Bhaker, encouraged her to be adventurous. Her mother wanted her daughter to be fearless. A yoga enthusiast herself, Sumedha gave Manu and her brother lessons when they were toddlers. She was keen that Manu learn martial arts as well. This environment at home, coupled with the talent that she possessed, meant that the little girl started excelling in every sport she played. She won competitions in racing, boxing and martial arts like judo and thang ta. She was also a state-level skating champion. In 2016, she injured her eyes during boxing practice. This led to her total focus shifting from boxing to shooting. In December 2017, Manu was busy with the nationals, where she won 15 medals. During the 61st National Shooting Championships in Kerala, she broke Heena Sidhu's long-standing record of 240.8, with 242.3 in the finals. She could focus on her Class X studies only two months before her final exams. In 2017, she also won a silver medal in the Asian Junior Championships. In 2018, she won two gold medals at the ISSF World Cup in Mexico, making her India's youngest shooter to win the World Cup gold. Inspiring the girls of Haryana to take up guns, Manu Bhaker has brought shooting to the mainstream of the medal heartland of the country.

After Rajyavardhan Singh Rathore won a silver medal at the 2004 Athens Olympics, shooters have consistently delivered for the country. Though the 2016 Rio Olympics was an aberration, the 2020 Olympics is expected to follow the trend. One girl who could follow in the medal-winning footsteps of Rajyavardhan Singh Rathore is from his state, Apurvi Chandela. Apurvi, along with Anjum Moudgil, are in stellar form and they are the first two

Indians to have earned Olympic berths in September 2018. Both of them complement each other well. Leaving the disappointment of Rio 2016 behind, Apurvi has moved ahead in life and has put her entire focus on Tokyo 2020. In Anjum, she has got someone constantly pushing her to improve.

Apurvi was born in Jaipur, to Kuldeep Singh Chandela, a hotelier, and Bindu Rathore, a homemaker. Right from her childhood, she had a keen interest in sports. She was good in academics, and becoming a professional sportsperson was not even on her mind. Instead, she wanted to become a sports journalist. One golden letter day in the history of Indian sports changed it all for her. Abhinav Bindra created history on 11 August 2008, as he became India's first participant to win an Olympic gold medal in an individual sport. This incredible achievement of an Indian shooter in the Beijing Shooting Range Hall inspired fifteen-year-old Apurvi Chandela to become a professional shooter herself. She scored a perfect ten in one of her first tries with the rifle at a local shooting range. Enthused by her performance, her family backed her to the hilt. Her father gifted her a new rifle and her uncle built a shooting range in her backyard for her practice. Practising hard in her backyard for months, she maintained a fine balance between her passion for shooting and academics, even as she moved to Delhi to pursue her bachelor's degree in sociology.

Apurvi won the gold medal for the 10 m rifle event in the 2012 National Shooting Championships. In the 2014 Intershoot International Championships in Netherlands, she won 4 medals. Just a few weeks before the Commonwealth Games in the same year, she got injured. But this could not deter her from winning a gold medal for the country. Like most of the Indian shooters, the 2016 Rio Olympics turned out to be a major setback for her. She bounced back in the Commonwealth Games and Asian Games in 2018, winning a bronze medal each in both the events. In the ISSF World Championships in September 2018, she finished fourth, and along with Anjum Moudgil, qualified for the 2020 Tokyo Olympics. 2019 has turned out to be the defining year for

Apurvi. She bagged gold at the ISSF World Cup in New Delhi and followed this up by bagging the fourth place in Beijing. This catapulted her to the first place in the world ranking in her discipline. She firmed up her grip on the top rank with gold at the Munich World Cup.

Shooting and painting are poles apart, but a young woman from Punjab and colleague of Apurvi Chandela who has been pushing her hard, Anjum Moudgil, has been trying to paint the portrait of a shooter.

'Portrait of a painter as a shooter' is how Anjum Moudgil is increasingly being recognized in the shooting fraternity. Along with Apurvi, her eyes are now set on the 2020 Tokyo Olympics, but she has got her plans ready for when she quits competitive sports. Anjum faces a pleasant challenge whenever she packs her bags when she goes to participate in shooting events. The silver medal winner in the Shooting World Cup has to devotedly find space to squeeze in a set of paint brushes and coffee decoction in her bulky bag stuffed with shooting gear. The twenty-four-year-old from Chandigarh also had to squeeze in time from her congested training and competition calendar to brush up her world of colours and canvas.

Buddha is the theme that appears in most of her work. And her paintings are in great demand amongst those from her fraternity. Some of them are also displayed in one of the popular shooters' clubs in Chandigarh.

Painting, for Anjum, is a stress-buster and favourite pastime. This helps her to prepare for the sport that requires Zen-like concentration. The fact that she has done her masters in sports psychology further helps her to reflect on her sport. She has made a name for herself in shooting and is destined to enrich Indian sports, but it's her life outside the shooting range that could inspire the future generation equally well. Anjum represents the athletes of Naya Bharat who can strike a balance between two worlds with ease and shine in different walks of life.

One girl of this generation from Delhi, Manika Batra, has been getting modelling offers. Instead, she wants to do in her sport what Saina and Sindhu have done in badminton.

There is something unique about racquet sports for any aspiring Indian athlete. In sports like badminton and table tennis, if one is able to break the Asian barrier, progression towards becoming a world champion gets easier. Saina Nehwal and P.V. Sindhu have shown the way in badminton. They scaled the Great Wall of China to be the badminton champions of the world. Manika Batra wants to break through the hurdles of the Asian giants in table tennis to be the best in the world. Her star performance at the 2018 Gold Coast Commonwealth Games was just a glimpse of her potential. Her incredible display in high pressure encounters against higher-ranked opposition is the silver lining for the country. Manika aspires to be the best in ping-pong. The twenty-four-year-old won as many as 4 medals at the Commonwealth Games, including a gold. She and veteran Sharath Kamal almost did the unthinkable at the Asian Games, by clinching a mixed doubles bronze, ending India's sixty-year-long wait for a medal in the sport. When specifically asked about her chances in the 2020 Tokyo Olympics, Manika says, 'All the paddlers are working hard for the Olympics and if we play our best and are lucky, we will win a medal. But I don't want to put pressure on myself for 2020. I am aiming for a singles medal in the 2024 Games.'[2]

Manika Batra symbolizes the refreshing change that has taken place in Indian sports in recent years. The approach to winning at sporting competitions including the Olympics has changed drastically. In terms of planning and preparations, today India is not only thinking of shaping up well for the Olympics ahead, but also for the next two editions. There is Navneet Kaur Dhillon, a discus thrower from Hoshiarpur in Punjab, who, at the age of seventeen, won a bronze medal at the IAAF Junior World

[2]PTI, 'Don't Want to Put Pressure on Myself for 2020: Manika Batra Aims for Singles Medal in 2024 Olympics', News18, 26 July 2019

Championships in Eugene, USA. Navneet's family, mentors and coaches stand rock solid behind her as she aspires to conquer new frontiers.

Deborah Herold, born in the Andaman and Nicobar Islands, is a tsunami survivor. She is India's biggest hope in cycling. In 2013, she won two gold medals at the Women's Junior Individual Sprint at the Asian Cycling Confederation track Asia Cup in Thailand. The list is increasing in number every year and with each tournament. From Gopichand's Academy in Hyderabad to the Prakash Padukone Academy in Bangalore, the Mary Kom Academy in Manipur to the Wrestling Hall in Rohtak, young girls across the country are diligently practising their craft every day.

As Shivangi Gupta, the youngest Indian to climb Mount Everest at the age of sixteen tells us, 'I went to the Everest to fulfil my childhood dream. I have only one mission, to conquer every mountain on this beautiful planet.'

All these dreams may not come true, but when the girls of India dream collectively, India will be the sporting nation to reckon with, especially on the Olympics stage.

Acknowledgements

My dear Manvi and Kabir, my loving daughter and son. I wrote this book for you and your cousin Aadhya. And through you, for the millions of daughters and sons of 'Naya India', who will be inspired and fired up by the sheer achievements and unforgettable journeys of these incredible women of substance. Whenever you meet obstacles and challenges in life, I hope this book serves as the rearview mirror, helping you to navigate your way ahead. I dedicate this book to my *maa* (Chameli Devi) and *maiya* (Seedha Devi), my grandmothers. People say that they have passed away. But they are with me, always. I would like to thank my loving mother (Mridula Dubey), for being the most amazing mother in this beautiful planet. To your lovely mother (Tripti Pandey) for caring, guiding and mentoring your lives. Words are not enough to express my gratitude to the two lifelines of my life—my father (Umakant Dubey) and my brother and his wife (Anubhav and Rajni Dubey). The book highlights the significant roles of the gurus or coaches in shaping the lives of these legends, and we get a glimpse here of our age-old Guru-Shishya parampara. I would like to bow my head to the gurus of my life, Nanaji (Late Harendra Prasad Dubey), Chachaji (Muchkund Dubey) and Mamaji (P.K. Dubey) for being my gurus and giving my life a sense of direction. This book has come up in the testing phase of my life. Thank you my Mausis (Nirala, Manjula & Baby) and my Chachi (Basanti) for always being there for me. Thank you Amit Tripathy and Samarendra Singh—my friends and my truest critics.

The writing of the book entailed travelling extensively to various parts of our beautiful country. This includes M.C. Mary Kom's village, IMA Keithal and the SAI centre in Manipur, Vivekananda Byayamgar and Netaji Shubhash Coaching Centre in Agartala, Tripura, the SAI regional centre in Guwahati, Rajiv Gandhi Stadium, Mualpui and Hawla Indoor Stadium in Aizawal, Mizoram, Rattu Chatti Village and Birsa Munda Academy at Silli in Ranchi and JRD Tata Archery Academy in Jamshedpur, Pullela Gopichand Badminton Academy and SAI centre in Hyderabad, SAI regional centre in Bangalore, High Altitude Athletics training centre at Ooty, Usha School of Athletics in Kinalur, Kerala, NIS Patiala and Wrestling Hall in Rohtak, Haryana. These are some of the emerging sports pilgrimage centres of the country where the characters of these legends were formed. I would like to thank the administrators and management of these centres for giving us access to these places, lining up the interviews and providing all logistics and support.

The book gave us an opportunity to interact with the family members and coaches of these living legends of our time. In this regard I would like to specifically thank Ashwini Nachappa, Anju Bobby George, M.C. Mary Kom, Karnam Malleswari, P.V. Sindhu, P.T. Usha, Dipa Karmakar and Saina Nehwal and their families for giving us time, at very short notice. This book would not have been possible without the contributions of the libraries of the organizations where I worked, NDTV, Network18 and Doordarshan. I would like to thank the officials of Jawaharlal Nehru Stadium, National Stadium, Delhi University Library and my friends in the print media for providing all the material for research. In this regard, I would like to especially thank Pravin Sinha and Amitesh Shrivastava. I would like to express my sincere gratitude to all the regional centers of AIR and Doordarshan and colleagues at DD Sports for being supportive in the venture throughout. The role of the organizers of the indigenous games festival in the north-east, the organizers of Asian Athletics Champions and Sports Federations was crucial in the shaping of the book.

I will remember this book as the melting pot of the three musketeers—ex-Network18 employees, Rudra, Sanjeeb and myself. My fights with Sanjeeb will resume after this book. My earnest acknowledgement to the publisher, Rupa, and its thoroughly professional staff.

The journeys of these women have given us the message—if they can, so can we...

Jai Baba Baidyanath!

—Abhishek Dubey

My deepest love and gratitude to my late father, who would have been very happy to see this work, my mother (a promising sprinter in school) who still keeps me on my toes enquiring about work and health, and Sandeep, Simana and their son Sreyaansh for their love and support; Manoj for the endless cups of tea and the trusty editors at Rupa who helped me and Abhishek through this. A big thank you to Seshadri SUKUMAR, one of India's best sports photographers, and Debashish Datta, for the photographs, without which this book would have been incomplete. A big shout out to GoSports Foundation, JSW Sports and Olympic Gold Quest (OGQ) to name a few organisations that are quietly working behind the scenes to realise India's sporting dream. Finally, a big thank you to a friend who once gifted me *The Promise of Endless Summers*, egging me to start writing someday.

—Sanjeeb Mukherjea